LOCALLY
GROWN

LOCALLY GROWN

The Art of Sustainable Government

JIM FINI

ISBN 978-1-7340773-0-8

Singing Buffalo Press
PO Box 64361
Vero Beach, FL 32964-3601
www.singingbuffalopress.com

Quantity sales. Special discounts are available on quantity purchases by corporations, associations, U.S. trade bookstores and wholesalers. Please email inquiries to sales@singingbuffalopress.com.

Edited by Edward Levy and David Aretha
Designed by AuthorSupport.com
Publishing Consultant: Martha Bullen, Bullen Publishing Services

First Printing October 2019
Printed in the United States of America

To Kati, who is my true north.

*Government outlives
the conditions that brought it
into existence.*

Haiku adapted from *The Sovereign Individual* by
James Dale Davidson and William Rees-Mogg

*"Eventually, social democracies all arrive
at the same tipping point: where half the
country depends on the other half."*

From *The Mandibles: A Family,
2029-2047* by Lionel Shriver

*"Collapse is a sudden, involuntary and
chaotic form of simplification."*

From *Currency Wars* by James Rickards

Table of Contents

ACKNOWLEDGMENTS

I am grateful to the many people who helped shape who I am including my parents, siblings, grandparents, teachers, friends, bosses, and work colleagues. I'm especially thankful to my wife, Kati, and teenage kids, Marcus and Emma, who have inspired me to be a better husband and father. I am also grateful to the bad bosses, bad relationships, and bad business deals I've been involved with because those also taught me important lessons and revealed personal flaws that I needed to change. I still have my share of flaws, but I think I've made progress at least.

I am also grateful to a group of politically diverse buddies who have sometimes changed my thinking on weighty matters, an occurrence that is critical to the continuous improvement model. They are a strange coalition of guys from different backgrounds equally split between liberal and conservative. I appreciate them all for different reasons, but the common thread is they are all smart and funny as hell. When we've been fortunate enough to get together over the years, it's usually a "pee your pants funny" party involving lots of outdoor activities, followed by sitting around a late-night fire in animated political discussion. I remember one such gathering shortly after September 11, 2001, and the discussion was predictably immersed in the horror we had all witnessed. That might have been the last time America really came together and agreed on and acted on something big.

Shortly thereafter, I started an email blog with these pals. I called it "Passionate Pragmatics" to reflect my desire to find middle ground that could be acted upon politically. I believe we reasonably represent the American political spectrum throughout the thousands of posts on every topic imaginable. The name reflects the principles of good-faith, passionate, funny, and mostly civil discourse we engage in to find solutions in order to govern more effectively. Each side gets some things they want but not everything. That's the most important feature of effective negotiation, one of my Locally Grown principles.

This 18-year digital conversation with friends has certainly shaped some of my thinking. Sometimes, the civil part of the discussion devolves into what we call "the rock fight," which can be a little mean with people defending their worldviews at all costs. However, we are friends first and try to not let political differences divide us. Still, "the rock fight" is generally entertaining and instructive in trying to understand our current political culture.

One final thing. As a "serial simplifier," I am always looking for the shortest distance between two points. I'm not sure if I learned this in my career trying to solve tough business problems or reading Cliff Notes as a substitute for books I was supposed to read in school. Either way, I have always been drawn to communication that is only as long as it needs to be to make its point. I love writers who can sum up big, hairy, complicated concepts into pithy, entertaining quotes. Several years ago, I was returning from a West Coast trip with my family, and my daughter was learning haiku poetry in school. After helping with her homework, I went back to reading my *Harvard Business Review*. With the 5-7-5 three-line syllable format rolling around in my head, I started summarizing the main point of each business article I was reading into haiku. I managed to get decent three-line haikus for every single article. I then grabbed every magazine I could find and continued my haiku distillation process for the rest of the flight. It's now become a bit of an obsession as I have written hundreds of haiku on every topic imaginable. So, in homage to this incredible ancient and useful Japanese artform, I have included a haiku at the start of each chapter in this book. Maybe you can just read that as Cliff Notes? In any case, I hope you find some useful thoughts in this book.

INTRODUCTION

America has become top-heavy and is starting to display stress fractures along familiar ancient lines. Unsustainable social programs, income inequality exacerbated by rapid technological change, and the pressures of being the global policeman are creating deep ideological divisions in our nation. Citizens are losing faith in institutions once considered unassailable strengths of our republic. Civil political dialogue has been replaced by shrill emotional attacks against those with differing opinions. Agreement on the common good, our historical binding force, is no longer agreed upon. Lots of folks see the problems, but their solutions seem limited to either more government control or tearing down the government. As always, the solutions lie somewhere in the middle.

Locally Grown: The Art of Sustainable Government invites readers to join in the important American civil debate to re-establish the middle ground we seem to have lost. The book introduces the concept of "sustainability" as the guiding principle for determining the size and scope of government. Our bottom-up constitutional architecture is aligned with "self-evident" natural laws that can sustainably balance local, state and federal government and the competing forces of individual freedom and the common good. Locally Grown Government explores how our twenty thousand state and municipal laboratories are positioned to handle many difficult problems better than a leviathan federal government led by a few bureaucrats. This crowdsourcing of problem solving has been the bedrock of science for centuries, so we know it works.

Locally Grown Government is not a new idea. James Madison and Thomas Jefferson, the chief architects and salesmen of the Constitution, weighted the balance of power clearly in favor of state and local government with the construct of "limited enumerated powers" at the federal level. They were witnesses of how a tyrannical central government trampled on the rights of the governed. Opposing their limited government view was Alexander Hamilton, our first Treasury secretary and also a founder who attended the first Constitutional Convention. He saw a much larger role for federal government justified by the "general welfare" clause in the constitutional preamble. Hamilton and Madison debated the role of federal government in public through the Federalist Papers which acts as a lens through which our judicial system has interpreted the Constitution. These opposing views of the role of federal government have been at odds with one another since our founding just as they are today. However, the brilliance of our national architecture is that it forces compromise and balance. I try to make the case that the United States has become significantly out of balance and we need *more* Thomas Jefferson and James Madison, and *less* Alexander Hamilton to restore that balance.

Centralized decision making just doesn't make sense if we are interested in solving hard problems, but it makes perfect sense if you are a politician looking to increase your power and wealth. The same dynamic that creates corporate monopolies also insulates government elites from the consequences of their decisions, which invariably leads to mismanagement and corruption. As it begins to take on a life of its own, the interests of government and citizens begins to diverge and "OUR government" becomes "THE government."

Imagine your town or county having much more funding for

things like education, healthcare, infrastructure, and elder care with just a modest increase in your taxes? By agreeing to pay a little more in federal taxes, along with a modest reduction in the federal budget and transferring more money and autonomy to the state and local level to implement social programs, the US can run surpluses instead of deficits as far as the eye can see. States and municipalities will have more money and freedom to craft efficient government solutions that fit their geography and demography so there can be accountable and responsive government we can all trust. Instead of partisan bickering in Congress, citizens will see results. With less money and influence at the federal level, less attention will be paid to Washington D.C. and instead, to where it matters most: where we live. Local media will matter again as it covers the economic and social renaissance happening on main street.

Locally Grown Government focuses solutions on where life is actually lived. Where we work, shop, and go to school. It celebrates that life is richer and healthier when lived more locally. For example, local production of food is more transparent and accountable because we can visit the local farms and see how the food is produced. More localized government can similarly provide better quality, transparency and accountability than a distant central government because public servants are more accountable to the citizens they see every day. Locally Grown is a way of performing government functions that respects diversity and freedom while acting as a natural immune system against the ideological diseases that plague our federal system and the media. Restoring the proper balance between our three levels of government is like the Marshall Plan and New Deal combined. There will be plenty of challenges. But getting it right will usher in a new era of American prosperity that is more sustainably distributed.

CHAPTER 1

The American Experiment

*A government big
enough to give everything
can take everything.*
– Adapted from Thomas Jefferson

A merica came of age during the great Enlightenment period (1685-1815) that challenged the philosophical, scientific, and political traditions of Europe and spawned the idea of classical liberalism. Our founding fathers were keen students of history and were certainly familiar with the work of heavyweight minds like Thomas Hobbes (1588-1679), who saw the natural state of humanity as "solitary, poor, nasty, brutish, and short" without an absolute monarch to protect them from chaos. Eighteenth century Americans seemed to be doing just fine as colonies under the British monarchy, but they became increasingly suspicious of the benefit of living under a monarchy that compelled increasing taxation flowing to a government from which they saw diminishing benefit. The seeds of the American revolution were sown in the churches and public houses of Massachusetts, and it spawned the slogan "No taxation without representation."

In contrast to the earlier ideas of Hobbes, English physician and philosopher John Locke (1632-1704) believed that natural law emanated from a divine creator. In Locke's view, natural laws govern the material world as well as the spiritual world. He founded the concept of "Empiricism," a theory that believed knowledge comes mainly from sensory experience or what can be observed in the physical world. It emphasizes the role of empirical evidence in the formation of ideas rather than innate ideas and traditions. However, he also argued that traditions come from common experiences of large groups of people over time and are critical in establishing the firm ground from which new ideas could be tested and deployed. Locke reasoned that the individual was the primary source of power in society with natural inalienable rights of "life, liberty and property" that cannot be taken away. This is the inherent power of the individual that cannot be usurped by any institution including the church or the state. Locke rejected the divine right of kings because he saw government as a delegate of the people and could only be created by the will of the people. Locke also believed that individuals had a responsibility in society to provide for the common good. He believed there should be a contract or constitution between government and the people defining the role of government in providing for the common good while protecting their inalienable rights and inherent power.

Thus, America began as an experiment that implemented the ideas of Locke and others to form the first nation based on the inherent power of its citizens rather than a central authority. In his final speech before the Constitutional Convention, Benjamin Franklin gave his thoughts on what they had accomplished:

"...when you assemble a number of men to have the advantage of their joint wisdom, you inevitably assemble with those men, all their prejudices, their passions, their errors of opinion, their local interests, and their selfish views."

Franklin believed it was not realistic to expect a "perfect production" from our constitutional republic but that, "with all its faults," it was better than any other solution that would have been acceptable. When asked by an observer what kind of government they had just created, Franklin famously said "a republic, if you can keep it." He was aware of the natural tendency of centralized power to become corrupt over time as it begins to serve itself at the expense of the people.

His compatriot Thomas Jefferson also knew the risks, as the haiku opening this chapter indicates. In the early days, there were many competing factions among the colonies, not the least of which, were the southern colonies whose economies were largely agricultural and supported by slavery. It's not as if there weren't plenty of people in colonial America who abhorred slavery and fought actively against it, but unfortunately keeping it intact was an unsavory compromise required to get a constitution that everyone could live with. It took another 75 years and a brutal Civil War for America to correct that terrible defect by abolishing slavery with the 13th Amendment to the Constitution. It took another hundred years for America to fully implement gender and racial equality with respect to participation in the most important expression of inherent power: the right to vote. There have been other "if you can keep it" moments in our history, and some would say we are in the middle of one right now.

Hamilton vs. Madison

At certain points in my book research, I found myself unconsciously engaged in those foundational public debates between Madison and Hamilton in the Federalist Papers. As I write, I find myself weighing the relative merits of both sides of the debate to challenge my own views. I can definitely see how their different personalities influenced how the Federalist Papers writings were perceived by the public. Madison is hailed as the "Father of the Constitution" for his critical role in drafting and promoting the Constitution and Bill of Rights. To me, it is self-evident that his view of the limited government won the day at the Convention and ended up the foundation of the grand document. Being born into an agricultural Virginian family, his sensibilities reflected rural America, which is where 95 percent of the population lived in 1790. He identified with John Locke's image of the self-reliant free man that didn't need a government to regulate his affairs.

Contrast this to Alexander Hamilton, who was born an orphan in what is now St. Kitts and raised by a wealthy merchant who sent him to New York to be educated. He was a Revolutionary War foot soldier who quickly rose to become a senior aide to George Washington. After the war, he briefly served as an elected representative to the "Congress of the Confederation," after which, he became a lawyer and founder of the Bank of New York. He shared the same love for his country as Madison, was brilliant, ambitious, and, in contrast to Madison, very much a self-made man. Oh, and he didn't own slaves like Madison. However, like so many powerful men, he became a victim of his own vanity when a salacious extramarital affair destroyed his political career. Sound familiar?

Against this backdrop of characters, how is it that the constitutional interpretations of Hamilton, whose views were so soundly rejected in the actual Constitution, most influenced the Supreme Court? After all, we have the actual text of the Constitution, which represented the views of the Founders. I think part of the reason is that Hamilton was a more compelling personality than Madison and a brilliant orator with a grand benevolent vision of larger government. He was aspirational and passionate. In contrast, Madison was an analytical and thoughtful introvert who preferred to work informally with others. With America obviously on the rise after having defeated the greatest world power at the time, there were lots of optimistic people who rightfully saw a bright future. It's easy to see how they would be more attracted to Hamilton's vision and confidence than Madison's stodgy, limited government self-reliance.

Digging deeper, I found an irony that is fascinating. It turns out that the most cited of the Federalist Papers by the Supreme Court is No. 78, where Hamilton describes judicial powers in detail. As is the case with all of the three federal branches, he believed representatives should be of an elite, educated class. The president would be elected for life and would appoint a Supreme Court that would also serve for life, with the caveat that both demonstrate "good behavior," whatever that means. The Supreme Court lifetime appointments made it into the Constitution despite the wariness of Madison-led Democratic Republicans of unaccountable power. Hamilton countered those concerns by describing the Supreme Court as the "weakest branch" of government that possessed neither "the power of the purse nor the power of the sword." Judicial power would be limited to determining the constitutionality of the acts of a potentially "capricious" Congress, and well-educated, non-political men and women of good character would surely make the right decisions.

I believe Hamilton's grand vision of federal government as a "force for good" is the kind of positive vision that rightfully attracts nearly all people. Who doesn't want a better world where all pain and suffering are removed, leaders are smart and benevolent, and everyone plays by the rules? Sign me up because I'll take optimism over pessimism any day. But this "benevolent vision" requires that citizens trust their government to always act in their best interest in exchange for giving up some of their rights. I believe the historical evidence shows that, as government takes more power for itself, it comes at great expense to its citizens. The original concept of the benevolent government working for citizens to protect their rights, transforms into a government that seeks to preserve itself. "My government" turns into "THE GOVERNMENT."

The Catholic Church unconsciously followed this script as it grew from a worldwide religion based on Jesus' radical message of "love thy neighbor as yourself" into a powerful pseudo-political organization of men that transformed the world in good ways and not so good ways. The Church hierarchy justified its bouts of bad behavior by quietly insisting that God looks the other way because "the cause is righteous." Like Christianity, communism is also oriented around that original message of "love thy neighbor as yourself" and similarly invoked "the cause is righteous" clause to justify unimaginable atrocities. I forgive Hamilton for not being able to see far enough over the horizon of unintended negative consequences of that "weak little" Supreme Court power of interpreting the Constitution. It's no surprise then that our federal government often behaves the same way as any powerful organization despite its original limited power architecture. It's no surprise that the US Supreme Court has been biased in favor of greater government power, and that it would justify that bias by citing the Federalist Papers as it interpretive lens. The same Federalist Papers dominated by a man whose ideas were rejected in our Constitution.

Now lest you think that I am dissing the Supreme Court and ignoring the important benefits of Hamilton's views, I am not. The Supreme Court is an essential component of our government. We would have torn ourselves apart without it. The Federalist Papers are also a worthy and important part of our founding architecture. In Federalist 41, Hamilton states that no constitutional amendment was needed to justify federal spending beyond the enumerated powers as long as the money went to the general welfare of the people, and not to the particular interests of a state or local area. For the first 147 years of our republic, the federal government held to that Hamiltonian "general welfare" limitation as it expanded its territory, strengthened its military, abolished slavery, established universal voting rights, and built infrastructure to facilitate interstate commerce. All these federal actions can be credibly tied to either enumerated powers or defense of individual rights. For its part, the Supreme Court mostly upheld any challenges to those powers.

Then in 1936 things changed. In the landmark case *United States v. Butler, 297 U.S. 1 (1936)*, the Court held that the US Congress's power to tax isn't constrained by needing to be tied to the enumerated powers in Article I of the US Constitution. Rather, it is a broad authority to tax and spend for the "general welfare" of the United States. In the following year, the Court reinforced this new view that federal power was mostly unlimited in *Helvering v. Davis, 301 U.S. 619 (1937)*. The Court decided that Social Security was a constitutional federal power to spend for the general welfare, thus upholding the Social Security Act of 1935. These key decisions occurred during the presidency of Franklin Roosevelt, the most passionate advocate of expansive federal power in our history to sit in the White House. Roosevelt, a Democrat, went so far as to attempt to "pack the court" by adding new members that he would appoint, thus marginalizing any opposition to his New Deal policies of broad government expansion. Although he was unsuccessful in his attempt, two justices, Hughes and Roberts, switched their opposition to support for New Deal initiatives, which paved the way for the "great expansion." Roosevelt then cemented the legacy of an expansionist Supreme Court by appointing nine new members during his unprecedented three-term presidential tenure. The nation followed by electing Democrats to control at least the House of Representatives for all but four years between 1933 and 1995. In fact, Republicans only controlled four years of both House and Senate during that tenure. The role of federal government increased dramatically during this 62-year period in which our nation grew into the preeminent global superpower while simultaneously planting the seeds of its potential demise with the creation of the modern entitlement state.

Franklin Roosevelt as well as Abraham Lincoln before him and Hamilton before him were visionary advocates of strong federal power who were able to sell that vision to an aspirational nation. Yes, this helped make America the indispensable country, but no more so than our Constitution's defense of personal liberty. This tension between the actual words of our founding document and the interpretation of those words has existed from the beginning. There can be no doubt that, by any measure, the United States has become biased towards more federal power than less. Left unchecked, this view of a preeminent federal government is unsustainable as it takes more power for itself at the expense of individual freedom. Don't take my word for it. Just look at our $23 trillion federal debt and tell me honestly that this resulted from a limited government worldview.

The problem with visionaries is they can see past some horizons but not all of them. Eventually, a new horizon emerges where the ship is no longer equipped to handle uncharted waters. The big ship that was built for open oceans becomes a liability when the rocks emerge. Smaller, more nimble ships are what you want. Hamilton's vision was brilliant and appropriate for a great country on the rise where there were few challengers. His vision was perfect for the open ocean that has been the last 220 years. But things have changed. The United States now is a raucous, diverse, and polarized nation of 327 million that is creaking under the weight of an expansive Hamiltonian government that makes nearly limitless promises in exchange for nearly limitless power.

Building from the Bottom up

You don't build a house from the top down. It defies the natural physical laws of our reality. But it is certainly possible that, even with a solid foundation, it is possible to build a house so large and heavy that eventually the foundation crumbles and the house collapses. So, it's no surprise that our Founders would build the architecture of the nation in a bottom-up fashion. It is consistent with the primacy of the inherent power of the individual that the Founders believed in so strongly. They also understood there were important things a federal government could do better than the states individually. Things like a system of justice, common defense and common currency were obvious functions better performed by a federal government. Collectively, these and a few other enumerated powers form the basis of our concept of "the common good" at the federal level. But the key control mechanism for federal authority is that *any powers not specifically granted to the federal automatically inured to the states.* This is a critical underpinning for the principle of consent of the governed.

When French historian Alexis de Tocqueville came to America in 1831, he found amazing and appalling things. He was aghast at the institution of slavery that powered a healthy portion of the economy.

There was already an active abolition movement in France in 1831, and slavery was abolished there in 1848. He also found a thriving republic built from the bottom up where, in his words, "government was more or less invisible." Problems were solved at the local level by an interwoven network of community government, churches, and volunteer organizations.

When people are unshackled from the constraints of a powerful centralized state, they become free to make all kinds of choices. The phenomenon of millions of individuals acting in their own best interests is called "the free market." Scottish philosopher and economist Adam Smith (1723-1790) codified this collective behavior in his seminal book *The Wealth of Nations*. Smith's main observation was that a byproduct of all this self-interested productivity also benefitted society at large. Individuals don't necessarily intend to promote the common good, but it happens anyway. When this behavior is transposed over large populations, it's like an "invisible hand" guiding the market to make beneficial allocations of the means of production of land, labor, and capital. It allows for discovery of the right price for a product where demand equals supply. Smith saw capitalism as empirically true by observing the great mercantile powers like Britain, and Rome before it. Encouraging the relatively free flow of trade between people created great wealth for a much larger group of people than the rulers and their cronies. Bottom-up government combined with the common good of free-flowing goods and labor was the invisible government de Tocqueville had witnessed.

By 1905, the United States was among the richest nations on the planet. It contained five percent of the world's land area and 6 percent of its population but accounted for nearly 50 percent of global Gross Domestic Product (GDP). More importantly, immigrants from around the world were streaming into the United States to take advantage of its freedom and seemingly boundless opportunity. To be sure, the rise of America also included some difficult times including wars, racial injustice, and multiple financial crises. However, overall the trajectory has been strongly up and to the right for the vast majority of its citizens. Table 1 depicts the structure of government at our earlier history, with the power at the bottom of the pyramid in the hands of individuals and their families:

Table 1 – Power Pyramid in 1900

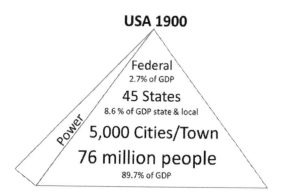

Using GDP and population as general measures of growth, you can see that federal government spending represented only 2.7 percent of the overall GDP of the country in 1900. Most government services were performed and paid for by state and local taxes except during major wars. It seems de Tocqueville's "invisible government" was really the bottom-up model we see from the above graphic.

Things began to change in the early twentieth century. As a response to several severe financial panics in the prior century, the federal government contemplated different ways to reduce the severity of the boom and bust cycles that characterized a rapidly growing country. As a result, the Federal Reserve (the Fed) was created in 1913 as the federal government relinquished its constitutional authority to create money. "The Fed" was a private consortium of the largest banks that was charged with maintaining a safer, more flexible, and more stable monetary and financial system. In 1913, Congress ratified the 16th Amendment authorizing a federal income tax, which was consistent with the theme of the emergence of strong central governments that characterized previous centuries. Since 1913, the top-down government model seems to have become predominant. More power is now concentrated with government instead of the individual and the family. Many believe this growth in federal power was a necessary evolution of the American nation-state and was contemplated by the Founders in their statement in the Constitutional Preamble:

> "We the People of the United States, in Order to form a more perfect Union, establish Justice, insure domestic Tranquility, provide for the common defense, promote the general Welfare, and secure the Blessings of Liberty to ourselves and our Posterity, do ordain and establish this Constitution for the United States of America."

The "in order to form a more perfect union" clause suggests a constant evolution to ensure the country accounts for a growing, more complex nation while remaining sustainable. Here the Founders added a brilliant mechanism to provision for a future they could not imagine. The core principals of life, liberty, the pursuit of happiness, and attending to the common good were aligned with natural law but couldn't be achieved without the ability to "amend the Constitution" for unforeseen circumstances. The original document provided for an amendment process whereby either 2/3 majorities of both houses of Congress, or 2/3 of state legislatures, can call a constitutional convention to vote on an amendment proposal. Since 1789, there have been 11,539 congressional proposals to amend the Constitution with all but 27 failing. The 27 ratified amendments mostly codified more individual rights, but a few expanded the role of the federal government. Landmark changes were made based on better data: separation of church and state, right to bear arms, unreasonable search and seizures, abolishing slavery, and universal voting rights. This is our brilliant system at work. We fix mistakes and have had an orderly transition of power without bloodshed since the Civil War. No document has ever expressed more beautifully and succinctly the competing forces of freedom and the common good.

The Constitution provides Congress with all the tools it needs to define the common good. This has included caring for the poor, keeping citizens safe from foreign and domestic invaders, building major infrastructure, providing healthcare, and retirement income. However, over the years and many Supreme Court battles upholding federal power, we may have also planted the seeds of our own demise. At what point does the cost of an ever-expanding federal government become counter-productive and unsustainable? Are there really any limits to its expansion? To answer these questions, we need to understand the costs that drive our federal budget. By any measure at the local, state, and federal levels it is social spending and interest on our debt that drive two-thirds of our budget and therefore deficit and then national debt. Some would also add defense to this list. However, this function is an enumerated power of the federal government and part of the discretionary portion of the budget, so this doesn't qualify as an equally major offender. That said, there is plenty we can do to streamline national defense and reduce cost.

How did Social Security, a program for widows and orphans, turn into a retirement program for everyone? Healthcare for aged, wars on poverty, real wars. It has all added up. The common good calls for some modest amount of redistribution because we can't have a few people get all the benefits of capitalism. This is a noble goal because compassion is both morally and rationally correct. Franklin Roosevelt's "New Deal" ushered in a needed public safety net amidst the ravages of the Great Depression. However, it was also a massive increase in the power and breadth of the federal government. With one political party controlling all branches of government and a supportive Supreme Court for more than a decade, we the people cemented the 1930s New Deal initiative as common good obligations that persist to this day.

Near the end of WWII, it was clear America was the most powerful nation on earth. As if to signal that fact, the Bretton Woods Conference of 1944 was convened with 44 nations to establish a new global trade and monetary system with the US at the center of it. All nations would conduct international business in US dollars, and in exchange, the US Navy would guarantee free and open sea lanes for all nations. These new responsibilities of being a world policeman were examples of the "foreign entanglements" our Founders warned us about. But were we simply going to sit idly by while Hitler decimated Europe and committed horrific genocide? My reading of history shows that evil left unchecked will not stop. Eliminating the empire building of Germany and Japan were in our national interests. At the time, there were plenty of citizens against US involvement in WWII, but I just cannot imagine a world if we had not stepped in.

This new global responsibility for America was further complicated by an aggressive ideological adversary that also happened to be part of our WWII strange coalition. The bloody Communist Revolution of 1917 created a formidable military power that helped us defeat Germany. They too had visions of empire building and saw the US as their primary ideological competitor. The post-1945 Cold War was an expensive war to wage. President Truman's intense animus for the Soviet Union also ushered in a US policy that enlisted some pretty bad actors as allies in the new bipolar world. Still, the centrally planned economy and authoritarian rule of the Soviet Union were no match for American principles of capitalism and freedom. Seventy-four years after its founding, the communist dictatorship collapsed under the weight of its own top-down control over the Soviet economy. I remember vividly President Reagan shouting "tear down this wall" in 1987 Berlin, memorializing that collapse. Despite our massive structural advantages, prevailing over a failed ideological adversary with nukes was expensive, and the trajectory of American federal government spending was never to return to the modest levels of its past.

Table 2 illustrates the 2018 version of our power pyramid showing that the size of our government has more than tripled since 1900, with the majority of that growth coming from the federal government. When we modify the shape of our power pyramid to reflect the size of the economy represented by the public and private sector GDP, it becomes a trapezoid rather than a pyramid. Making matters worse, there is a huge weight on top of that less stable shape. It is the public debt load, which is more than 1.7 times our entire GDP. That's like balancing another person on your shoulders using only one foot instead of two.

Table 2 – Power Pyramid in 2018

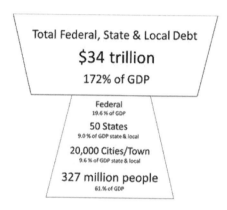

Of course, the money for this increased government spending comes from somewhere. The answer is that it comes from we citizens. We are productive and pay a portion of the fruits of our labor for the common good. Whether it's our directly paid tax dollars or the government issuing debts and other future obligations, the citizens are responsible. If a family or business has income that is less than its expenses, that shortfall must be financed. For one-time events like an illness, buying a house, or sending kids to college, debt is a perfectly appropriate tool if you can afford to pay it. There are supposed to be consequences if you cannot repay your debts so, theoretically, there is a lot of incentive for people to be careful.

This isn't how it works for the US Federal Government. The US dollar has the "exorbitant privilege" of being the world's reserve currency. As economist Barry Eichengreen summarized: "It costs only a few cents for the Bureau of Engraving and Printing to produce a $100 bill, but other countries have to pony up $100 of actual goods in order to obtain one." [1] One of the important ways that other countries "pony up" is by buying our debt. And the world has ponied up to the tune of over $22 trillion in outstanding federal government debt as of end of 2018.[2]

This represents 106 percent of our entire GDP and growing. This is the fourth highest debt-to-GDP ratio within the Top 20 industrialized nations. When you add the state debt of $1.18 trillion and local debt of $1.87 trillion, the ratio is even higher. Take a look at the shape of our federal debt growth since our founding in Table 3.

Table 3 – Accumulated Federal Debt

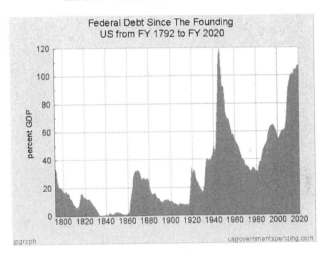

You can see the massive spike in the 1940s, which was needed to finance WWII. In fact, most of the spikes went to finance wars including the Revolutionary War, War of 1812, Spanish American War, WWI, and the Gulf Wars. The 1920s spike in federal debt was New Deal expansion. In each instance, a debt spike was followed by a fall where great economic activity swelled the tax coffers and we reduced debt. Now we are very close to the same debt-GDP level of the 1940s, but the military conflicts we are engaged in now are nothing compared to WWII. In fact, at 3.1 percent of GDP (and six percent of the total federal budget), defense spending is the lowest in decades. So, what is driving the debt? The answer is entitlement spending.

And this debt keeps growing if we do nothing to fix the structural imbalances in our fiscal policy. Our government deficit has grown from one percent of GDP 10 years after WWII to nearly five percent at the end of 2018. Many will say there were good reasons to deficit spend, including to finance wars and infrastructure, but we cannot remain structurally negative forever. Expenditures are mandatory if they are required by law and discretionary if renewed annually as part of the government budget process. The mandatory expenses include healthcare (Medicare and Medicaid), Social Security, and interest on the national debt. They will continue to crowd out other government spending to the point that somewhere between 2030 and 2040, mandatory spending will exceed all federal government revenue. Let that sink in. As Table 4 shows, the shape of this economic curve will soon be exponential (not in a good way) if no action is taken.

Table 4 – All Tax Revenue Spent on Entitlements

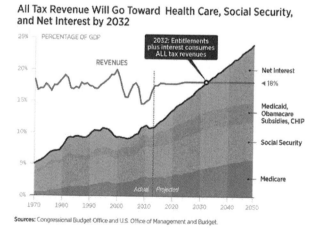

All Tax Revenue Will Go Toward Health Care, Social Security, and Net Interest by 2032

Sources: Congressional Budget Office and U.S. Office of Management and Budget.

From now until 2030, about 10,000 American Baby Boomers per day (74 million total) start collecting Social Security and Medicare as they retire.[3] Despite being told for decades by politicians that Social Security funds are sequestered in a special "trust fund," all that spending comes from general government funds. There's no magic pot of money. Social Security looked healthy and fine in 1950, when five workers supported each retiree and the average life expectancy was 68. By contrast, there are 2.6 workers supporting each retiree who are living to until 78, on average. By 2035, there will no longer be sufficient revenue to pay 100 percent of the benefits. Then comes the benefit cuts.[4]

Compounding this problem is that fewer able-bodied people are working. Over the past 20 years, the labor force participation rate has been steadily declining, as Table 5 shows. The working-age population is the number of people between 16 and 64 years old considered able to work. It is an estimate of the total number of potential workers in our economy. The labor force participation rate divides the total number of employed people plus those looking for work into the working-age population. This declining rate is the result of some major forces: automation of jobs, global trade, and the rapid increase of government benefits like disability insurance, which becomes an unfortunate substitute for work.

Table 5 — Declining Labor Force Participation

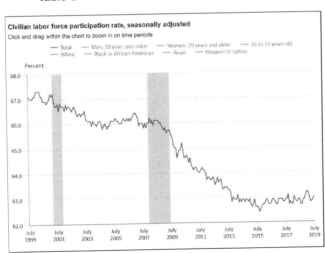

Piling on to this horror show is an American fertility rate of 1.8 percent, which creates a demographic catastrophe steaming down the track. The tax rate required to pay for this will be incredible and will hit every income level. These taxes will put further strain on young workers and make having a family even more out of reach and further exacerbate the demographic problem. One can see how things could quickly spiral out of control if they remain as they are. According to former Clinton chief of staff Erskine Bowles and former senator Alan Simpson (R-WY), co-chairs of the presidential commission on deficit reduction, this upside-down math is "the most predictable economic crisis in history."

I'm in the camp that believes immigration can help forestall this crisis. We have always welcomed new immigrants eager to work, pay taxes, and pursue their dreams in freedom. However, our immigration must be legal and controlled by the federal government, just like the Constitution says. We have a right to sovereign borders and to control our immigration in a way that meets the needs of the country. However, our immigration laws, and the way they are enforced, are a complete mess and there seems to be no collective political will to solve the problem. It's difficult to see how 140,000 mostly low skilled immigrants streaming illegally across our southern border every month is going to help our government budget implosion.

Every year the US Treasury publishes its "Financial Report of the United States Government."[5]

In the management summary of the most recent 2018 report, our own federal government starkly states the challenge in front of us:

"An important purpose of the Financial Report is to help citizens understand current fiscal policy and the importance and magnitude of policy reforms necessary to make it sustainable. The past nine years saw the national debt nearly double as a share of GDP, bringing it to a level not seen since World War II. A sustainable fiscal policy is one where the debt-to-GDP ratio is stable or declining over the long term. If current policy is left unchanged, the debt-to-GDP ratio, currently 108 percent, is projected to rise to 297 percent in 2092 and continuously thereafter. While this estimate of the '75-year fiscal gap' is not certain, it is nevertheless certain that current fiscal policies cannot be sustained indefinitely. Delaying fiscal adjustments (combination of tax increases and expense reduction) for too long raises the risk that growing federal debt will increase interest rates, which will, in turn, reduce investment and ultimately economic growth."

Politicians mislead citizens with promises that taxing wealthy people will close the gap. In reality, according to the Congressional Budget Office (CBO), increasing the top 37 percent federal income tax bracket to 74 percent would close just 20 percent of the long-term Social Security and Medicare shortfall.[6] When state and payroll taxes are included, it's laughable to assume that most people would keep working when 90 percent of what they earn are confiscated by taxes. When these tax rates on the wealthy are combined with slashing defense spending to European levels, only 34 percent of the gap would be closed. And this nightmare applies for current levels of spending, never mind the trillions more in spending being promised by many of the 2020 presidential candidates.

Some might argue that the top personal tax rate in the 1950s was 91 percent and our economy was booming. The reality is that in the 1950s the top one percent of households paid an effective tax rate of 42 percent with all the loopholes in the tax code, according to a September 2017 paper, Distributional National Accounts: Methods and Estimates for the United States, by economist Thomas Piketty, Emmanuel Saez, and Gabriel Zucman. [7] According to the IRS, as of 2016, the top 10 percent of US households earned 46 percent of national income and paid 70 percent of the federal income taxes, and half of the country paid no federal income taxes.

Table 6 reveals the lie that taxing the rich is the solution to all our government problems as we are told by many politicians. I developed the table using data from the CBO, the IRS, and the Federal Reserve combined with findings from a 2007 study, *The Macroeconomic Effects of Tax Changes: Estimates Based on a New Measure of Fiscal*

Shocks,[8] by President Obama's top economic advisor Christina Romer. Her study showed a strong statistical *inverse* relationship between taxes and economic health. Ms. Romer found that each one percent increase in taxes as a percentage of GDP lowers real GDP by about three percent after two years.

Table 6 – Inverse Relationship between Taxation and Economic Health

Real GDP	$ 20,500	$ 21,136	$ 21,770	$ 21,770	$ 20,265	$ 18,865	$ 18,865	$ 18,865	$ 18,865	$ 18,865	<<
GDP growth	3.1%	3.0%	2.8%	0.0%	-6.9%	-6.9%	0.0%	0.5%	0.5%	0.7%	Shrinking GDP
Adjusted Gross Income all individual taxpayers	$ 10,400	$ 10,712	$ 11,012	$ 11,012	$ 10,251	$ 9,543	$ 9,543	$ 9,591	$ 9,639	$ 9,706	
Corporate profits before income and payroll taxes	$ 3,051	$ 3,089	$ 3,128	$ 3,128	$ 2,912	$ 2,711	$ 2,711	$ 2,724	$ 2,738	$ 2,757	
Adjusted Gross Income top 5%	$ 3,574	$ 3,681	$ 3,784	$ 3,784	$ 3,523	$ 3,279	$ 3,279	$ 3,296	$ 3,312	$ 3,335	
Taxes paid by top 5%	$ 840	$ 865	$ 889	$ 1,892	$ 1,761	$ 1,640	$ 1,640	$ 1,648	$ 1,656	$ 1,668	
Net tax rate paid by top 5%	23.5%	23.5%	23.5%	50.0%	50.0%	50.0%	50.0%	50.0%	50.0%	50.0%	<<< Rising
Net tax rate paid by corporations	43.7%	44.4%	45.1%	60.0%	72.6%	72.6%	72.6%	72.6%	72.6%	72.6%	Tax rates
Total individual, estate, trust and excise taxes	$ 1,669	$ 1,719	$ 1,767	$ 2,769	$ 2,578	$ 2,400	$ 2,400	$ 2,412	$ 2,424	$ 2,441	
Corporate Taxes paid	$ 1,332	$ 1,372	$ 1,411	$ 2,271	$ 2,114	$ 1,968	$ 1,968	$ 1,978	$ 1,987	$ 2,001	
Total taxes net of refunds	$ 3,001	$ 3,091	$ 3,178	$ 5,040	$ 4,692	$ 4,368	$ 4,368	$ 4,389	$ 4,411	$ 4,442	
Total taxes as a % of GDP	14.6%	8.1%	8.1%	12.7%	12.7%	12.7%	12.7%	12.8%	12.8%	12.9%	
CBO Estimate Annual Spending	5.5%	5.5%	5.5%	5.5%	5.5%	5.5%	5.5%	5.5%	5.5%	5.5%	
Mandatory Federal spending ($T)	($2,851)	-$3,007	-$3,173	-$3,347	-$3,532	-$3,726	-$3,931	-$4,147	-$4,375	-$4,616	<<< Rising
Net Income after Mandatory Spending	$150	$84	$5	$1,693	$1,160	$642	$437	$243	$37	-$173	Spending

My analysis starts with the fact that nearly ALL of our federal income tax revenue is currently allocated to mandatory social spending and interest on the national debt, which increases like clockwork by 5.5 percent every year. This means that the rest of our government spending, including defense, education, research, environmental, etc., must be financed by issuing more debt, which in turn increases the mandatory interest payments on that debt. From that basis, the analysis in Table 6 shows a temporary five-year benefit from doubling taxes on the top five percent of earners and rolling back the Trump corporate tax cuts. After that, the gap between mandatory spending and tax revenue goes negative as far as the eye can see, which means ever higher issuance of national debt and the commensurate interest payments. Sound sustainable?

Many politicians assume the American people are dumb enough to believe that individuals and corporations will behave the same way in a rising tax environment. They don't tell you that everyone pays higher taxes in the form of lost jobs and opportunity as government spending crowds out the private sector economy. This defies history, modern economic theory, and common sense. The truth is, taxing high earners will not come close to solving our spending problem; in fact, it will make it a lot worse. Closing the long-term funding gap without cutting Social Security and Medicare benefits would require either, nearly doubling income-tax rates for every citizen, or eliminating nearly every remaining federal function as Table 6 illustrates.

Once again history provides the example. Confiscatory taxation was a main cause of the fall of the Roman Empire. For hundreds of years, Rome financed its burgeoning public expenditures by conquest. By the third century, the costs of defending the borders of their vast empire from the encroaching Barbarian hordes required massive tax increases to the point where farmers stopped working and abandoned their land in exchange for receiving public entitlements. When the government became aware of this behavior, they forced farmers to continue working their land under penalty of imprisonment. Some parents sold their children into slavery to avoid torture for non-payment of taxes. This ushered in a downward spiral with citizens losing trust in their institutions and many fleeing the empire or welcoming the Barbarians in dethroning their corrupt government.

Lower tax rates and regulations, on the other hand, always show their power when deployed. It worked for President Kennedy in the 1960s, Reagan in the 1980s, Clinton in the 1990s, and Trump now. As of this writing, the corporate tax reform package and reduction of the regulatory state has supercharged a previous low growth economy to one of the best economies in decades. Unemployment is at 3.9 percent, the lowest in decades, and the rate is the lowest in history for African Americans and Latinos. Annualized real wage growth stands at 3.1 percent, highest in nearly 10 years. The poverty rate is 12.3 percent, down from 14.8 percent in 2014. If we have any hope of closing our government deficit and strengthening our middle class, we need robust economic growth. Anemic economic growth will cause the entitlement math to crush us. The deficit will continue expanding, key programs will continue to be squeezed, and taxes will rise until politicians and voters finally confront the elephant in the room. Just after Barack Obama's election in 2008, his chief of staff, Rahm Emanuel, told an interviewer: "You never want a serious crisis to go to waste." I think this is revealing about how some politicians view the process of accruing centralized power.

Most of this doesn't go unnoticed by the American public, who have been steadily losing trust in their institutions for years. The harbingers of this are apparent everywhere, from the election of a populist and divisive president like Donald Trump, to British exit from the Euro, and the election of populist governments around the globe. A distrust of public institutions is a classic sign of an unravelling society. A September 2016 Gallup Survey revealed the following disturbing trends that seem to be getting worse:

- 82 percent of Americans disapprove of the way Congress is handling its job.
- 69 percent say they have little or no confidence in the legislative branch of government, an all-time high and up from 63 percent in 2010.
- 57 percent have little or no confidence in the federal government to solve domestic problems, exceeding the previous high of 53 percent recorded in 2010 and well exceeding the 43 percent who have little or no confidence in the government to solve international problems.
- 53 percent have little or no confidence in the men and women who seek or hold elected office.

Americans believe, on average, that the federal government wastes 51 cents of every tax dollar, up significantly from 46 cents a decade ago and from 43 cents three decades ago.

49 percent of Americans believe the federal government has become so large and powerful that it poses an immediate threat to the rights and freedoms of ordinary citizens. In 2003, only 30 percent believed this. [9]

All of this leads to an American political system that might be in the middle of a breakdown. This has happened several times in our past, and the correction of our present course will be messy and painful for many and a true test of the resilience of our country. It will likely be an "if you can keep it" moment. Keeping in mind that evolution is not an outcome but a process, the hope is we will show our historical resilience and continue to form that more perfect and *sustainable* union.

CHAPTER 2

Exploring Sustainability

Evolution starts
with sustainability.
Each species knows this.

I hope you'll indulge me for the next couple chapters as I dive into a little history and science. I want to bring you along some of my journey of discovery of ways to build sustainable government. Basically, what I found is that aligning the architecture of government with models of strength and durability in nature is a great place to start. Another good starting point is studying how our ancestors developed philosophy and science as tools to discover truth. These truths became the foundation upon which societies were built. The on-going evolutionary processes of science and philosophy sometimes revealed new truths that negated old truths which required that society adapt. Hopefully, you'll find this little sidetrack informative and entertaining, but I think it will put us on solid ground as we build the case for Locally Grown Government.

Evolution = Sustainability

Life is a wonder to behold – a phenomenon birthed by God, a divine creator, or maybe just a "one in a billion trillion squared" chance of certain atomic particles bashing together perfectly. Regardless of origin, biological evolution is a primary force of nature, just like gravity, electromagnetism, and the two nuclear forces. Even though early humans were physically weaker than many predator species they co-existed with, their survival was due to their most important advantage: their brains. They are outsized for our frames, and all that real estate has been used wisely, to imprint experience and pass it through the DNA (our biological read-only memory) to future generations.

When the consciousness light switch was flipped some 200,000 years ago, modern Homo sapiens possessed powerful brains that provided a deeper level of curiosity. We learned how to anticipate and manipulate our environment rather than react to it like our pre-human ancestors. As humans migrated from Africa to the "fertile crescent" of the Middle East, we began to manipulate the environment to suit our needs. The invention of agriculture and domestication of animals elevated us from a nomadic hunter-gather species to a richly diverse social network of tribes and villages that grew into empires. Along the way, humans discovered ways to interact with each other more efficiently and creatively. Written language emerged as an amazing innovation where we could store our thoughts for others to read at a later date. This is analogous to the way a computer writes from its memory to its hard drive where data can be accessed later. We described our lives and passed on hard-learned lessons to our progeny in a communal way. Thus, cultures were created with a new artifact called religion often at the center. Religion was a way to explain our origins and our purpose. It also was a means to codify desirable human behavior into traits and practices that produced the best outcomes in life. We wrapped that all in elegant stories about gods who represented the physical and behavioral world of human beings. These religions, like the evolutionary force that birthed them, were all about survival. With the growing complexity of the world, finding the proper sustainable balance between all the competing forces in the world was, and still is, the "great human undertaking." It's our job to be sustainable because sustainability equals survival.

If something is sustainable it persists, it keeps going on forever or at least a long period of time until an event occurs to test its resilience. If a system or species is not sustainable, then it dies. It becomes an extinct relic of the inability to adapt to changing circumstances. Whether diminishment of water or food or climate or predation, the biological fossil record is full of evidence of those species that didn't make the cut. Ideas that fail to adapt can also die because they are no longer sustainable. Since the ability to think is the most important human trait, it follows logically that the ideas that flow from that thinking are important too because all that mankind has created had to be thought about first. It is no surprise that once humans mastered the basics of producing adequate food and shelter, we moved on to deeper thinking about our role in the universe. Over the millennia, many of those ideas were transformed into rules that controlled societies and birthed the concept of government. Things like "the divine right of kings" initially served a purpose in building stability into societies with fixed social classes that couldn't normally be breached. Nobility was something passed on by blood, not achievements or skills. People knew where they stood and this was good to keep them focused and productive, while the noble upper class kept the peace by trying to redistribute some of the communal largess and keeping a large chunk for themselves. Nowadays, we look at that idea as ludicrous. A king or queen is no more descended from God than you or I. However, it took a lot of spilled blood over thousands of years to prove that point. That was an *unsustainable* idea that died because it concentrated too much wealth and power into the hands of a few. Some may point out that the idea of divine right survives in authoritarian regimes ruled by one person or a small group that just thinks themselves smarter or more deserving than everyone else. Regardless of the narrative, authoritarian regimes ultimately enforce their rules behind the barrel of a gun.

Morality is
a collection of tools for
cooperation.
– Adapted from the Evolution Institute

A critical part of the sustainability of our species has been our discovery of key behaviors that supported survival. One could imagine a small group of early humans figuring out that, if they saved some of the mammoth instead of feasting on it all immediately, they would be able to eat for a longer period without hunting. This practice of delayed gratification evolved into the notion of sacrifice and became viewed as a noble behavior that was celebrated in religious and cultural rituals. Parents sacrificed for their children to help them survive; warriors sacrificed their lives to preserve their tribes and their culture. Early humans also figured out if they shared their mammoth with a neighboring tribe that wasn't as lucky on their hunt, maybe that tribe would share when the tables were turned. In similar fashion, cooperation was celebrated as a noble behavior.

The Evolution Institute is a nonprofit think tank whose mission is using science to solve some of our most challenging social issues. One of their projects is analyzing a database archive of historical and sacred texts stretching back several millennia. They search for common moral and ethical themes amongst the world's different cultures. Their research concludes that morality, as a human construct, is just the "good behavior" that fosters cooperation in society. They identified seven moral rules that seem to be universal across cultures: "love your family, help your group, return favors, be brave, defer to authority, be fair, and respect others' property." [1] However, these rules were often emphasized differently among cultures. Asian cultures tended to stress "mutual cooperation and group solidarity" while certain African tribes highly valued the important warrior traits of bravery while others stressed reverence for one's elders and ancestors. Promoting the common good is a critical human trait, but it requires delegation of certain individual rights and the need for institutions that can be trusted to protect those individual rights. Done properly, these institutions help the community grow and prosper. However, this delegation can have a dark side as those institutions grow more powerful.

> *One second before*
> *The Big Bang, all science fails.*
> *That's where God lives.*

A web search of "definition of science" reveals the following: "the intellectual and practical activity encompassing the systematic study of the structure and behavior of the physical and natural world through observation and experiment." (Isn't Google astounding?) In its earliest form, science was indistinguishable from magic. Smart, nerdy alchemists and wizards conjuring understanding and control over the natural world must have been an amazing thing to see for the hoi polloi of the ancient world. Over millennia, great civilizations and empires invested resources into understanding the natural world because they thought knowledge would give them power. They were right. Knowledge is power. I'd consider that a natural law.

Until the mid-16th century, humans believed the sun revolved around the earth, and the most powerful and enduring institution of the previous 1,500 years, the Catholic Church, considered it blasphemy to believe otherwise. Imagine the surprise of the church leaders when Nicolaus Copernicus, a devout Christian himself, proved the earth orbited the sun. Neither heliocentrism nor a spherical earth were self-evident truths to humans until some smart people who knew math made it impossible to believe otherwise. It took nearly a century after Copernicus' death and validation by other scientists like Galileo for the all-powerful Church to accept heliocentrism as a scientific fact. The scientific method of observation, experimentation, theory formation, and peer review showed that an idea once believed to be an unassailable fact was false. Imagine the societal and intellectual upheaval from the realization that the earth was not the center of the universe?

Geocentrism proved to be an unsustainable human idea because it could not survive the changing circumstances of scientific inquiry. If you haven't read the book *The Day the Universe Changed* by James Burke, you should. It's a bit dated but awesome, nonetheless. It presents a wide view of the history of science, technology, and human civilization to discover moments in history when a change in knowledge massively changed man's understanding of his place in the universe. I remember after reading that book 30 years ago wondering what would be the contemporary "Day the Universe Changed" moment in my lifetime? I certainly didn't see the internet coming back then. But like many of my ancient forebears, I thought that if we found we were not alone in the universe, that would certainly qualify. The point is that biological evolution applies as much to ideas as it does with our bodies. When they become less useful or proven false over time, they shrivel and die. I'm guessing some future version of Homo sapiens won't have an appendix because it outlived its usefulness just like our tails. If a business or government's expenses consistently exceed its income, it dies. If we continue to upset the ecological balance of our earth, at some point we may die. Evolution is driven by sustainability and is the Fifth Power of the Universe. The more we understand it, the better.

CHAPTER 3

The Power of Nature's Laws

*Human behavior is
bound by the laws of nature,
just like the rose bush.*

O nce we separated ourselves on the evolutionary tree from all the other animals, humans became self-aware and pondered how the cosmos operated and their place in it. This new curiosity underpins our evolution and created the great ancient civilizations in short order. Thus, science was born as a powerful method to derive truth from nature. Ancient civilizations all contained the common trait of trying to understand and control nature to their own benefit. Throughout antiquity, science and philosophy were viewed as separate but equal tools to understand truth. Many of the greatest thinkers in history, like Galileo,

Copernicus, Newton, Boyle, and Kepler, were both scientists and devoutly religious people, some even clergy. They understood that philosophy, religion, and the arts were not at odds with science in the search for truth.

Throughout our history, humans learned from observing nature what was strong and sustainable and tried to apply those observed natural phenomena and structures to ordering our societies. This belief of being aligned with nature was a powerful driver for ancient civilizations. It provided comfort that this alignment would make their way of life sustainable. So began the building of the canon of natural law by our forebears. Natural law is a philosophy that observes certain rights are inherent to humans and are created by nature (or God) and can be comprehended by using logic and reason. They exist independent of laws created by any government or society. They are self-evident, meaning we can all see them for ourselves. If we are interested in solutions that can help the sustainability of our society, we should look to nature to understand how it manifests sustainability.

Pyramid power.
Timeless and enduring strength.
The ancient ones knew.

In that vein, it's no surprise that as the imperial Egyptian architect Imhotep looked out over the plane of Giza and thought about creating a durable monument to his king, he chose the pyramid. This shape is balanced and stable because the largest portions of the structure are closest to the ground and earth's gravity. We see how long pyramids have lasted. We see them in other cultures like the ancient Central American and Asian cultures half a world away. They must have seen the enduring nature of mountains and understood how nature creates strength and balance. If an ancient culture was going to invest in building a long-lasting structure as a metaphor for their civilization, it made sense that they picked examples of such structures from the natural world. It was self-evident to the ancients that the pyramid was a sustainable structure.

Just like their physical manifestation on the Giza plain, ancient Egyptian society was also shaped like a pyramid as shown in Table 7. At the top were the gods, such as Ra, Osiris, and Isis. Egyptians believed that the gods controlled the universe. Therefore, it was important to keep them happy. They could make the Nile overflow, cause famine, or even bring death. Pharaohs were usually elevated to status of gods in human form and shared the top of the pyramid with them while servants and slaves made up the bottom. Pharaohs were supreme rulers who had the last word on everything.

Table 7 – Egyptian Society Pyramid

Now some might argue that the pyramid concept really is the shape of all governments. Inherently, governments are small groups that rule the many. Most ancient societies consisted of a king or queen ruling under self-serving ideologies such as the "divine right of kings." Sure, there were a bunch of nobles under the king who ruled their respective locality and paid taxes to the king. However, the monarch was the final word on all matters and their word was law. So, although the physical shape of the society was a normal-looking pyramid, when you consider where the actual power resided, the pyramid was inverted as shown in Table 8.

Table 8 – Inverted Power Pyramid

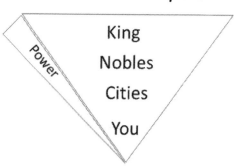

Unlike an upright pyramid, an inverted pyramid is very unstable. The same is true of monarchial and authoritarian governments that centralize power within a small ruling elite. These types of states ultimately fall prey to the natural tendency to corruption and self-servitude where there is little accountability. History has shown that over the long term they fail in bloody revolutions, civil wars, and wars between nations. Even the most enduring monarchial empires were characterized by the higher levels of autonomy at lower levels of the pyramid. One of the secrets to the longevity of the Roman empire was that it provided the opportunities for conquered peoples to become Roman citizens. This fostered a sense of common interest and provided access to all of the benefits of the empire.

> *Dharma for Hindus*
> *is the principle of the*
> *great cosmic order.*

Europe wasn't the only epicenter of modern human culture. Asian empires extracted wisdom from nature in somewhat different ways. The ancient cultures of India and China focused more on being aligned with nature than trying to control it. In the Buddhist and Hindu religions, "Dharma is the law that "upholds, supports, or maintains the regulatory order of the universe."[1] Its manifestation depends upon the purification and moral transformation of human beings and its natural laws are collectively referred to as the Dharma. It has become the spiritual and social infrastructure for 21 percent of the world population.

In his January 2019 Wall Street Journal op-ed, "How Hinduism Has Persisted for 4,000 Years", author and Indian member of Parliament Shashi Tharoor describes how Hinduism has persisted for 4,000 years because of its inherent flexibility. Unlike Christianity, Judaism, and Islam, it is non-dogmatic. The religion hinges on the idea that all the wisdom of the ages and knowledge of God cannot be contained in one book. The Hindu search for God is internal, not external, and is extremely flexible in that it allows individual interpretations of divinity and expressions of reverence for that divinity. It is inherently skeptical about single organizations and liturgy that claim to know everything. Instead it offers a buffet of choices of worship from different gods and books and nothing is ever discarded. It embraces difference and all forms of belief within it. A core tenet of Hinduism is encouraging introspection and intellectual inquiry. This flexibility and skepticism of centralized authority makes Hinduism a truly bottom-up sustainable way of life for billions of people over the eons. [2]

> *Those who do not learn*
> *history's lessons are all*
> *doomed to repeat it.*
> – Adapted from George Santayana

A sine wave is the form taken by all forms of energy in the universe. They are wave patterns that occur in nature, including wind waves, sound waves, and light waves. They are smooth periodic oscillations or continuous waves defined by the mathematical sine function. Sine function math is applied in the fields of physics, engineering, signal processing, and many others. As illustrated in Table 9, sine waves have some basic characteristics. The amplitude is the distance from a peak or trough from to the midpoint of the wave. The frequency is the number of oscillations or cycles that occur for each unit of time. Lots of cycles means higher frequency. Higher frequency (shorter) waves can contain a lot more information but can only travel shorter distances because the material world (trees, mountains) interferes with the signal more readily. Lower frequency (longer) waves can carry less data but can travel longer distances.

Table 9 – Sine Waves

Music on the car radio is either AM (amplitude modulation) or FM (frequency modulation). FM stations broadcast at higher frequency for better music quality and less static, but as you travel further from the radio station, the signal breaks up and eventually you lose it. By contrast, AM radio stations broadcast longer waves that can be picked up hundreds of miles away from the broadcast signal and contain lots of static, but you still can listen. AM is much less impeded by the mountain ranges and forests than FM. Despite its drawbacks, I was an FM guy because those radio stations just played the cool music. Anytime I was close to Boston, it was mandatory to tune into WBCN with Charles Laquidara and the Big Mattress Show.

Sine waves, and the mathematics that describe them, are natural laws. Energy is oscillation and oscillations are sine waves. The bio-electrical signals firing in my brain as I write this travel along my neural network as sine waves. I consider the sine wave a fundamental building block in physics, and by extension, biology. Its main feature is that the form repeats over time, making it a dynamic natural shape. Sine waves are a means to transport energy and information over distances. So, like solar waves that make life on our planet possible, why wouldn't evolution choose this natural feature to communicate thought waves in biological organisms?

An interesting hypothesis of how the cyclicality of the sine wave shows up in human behavior is the subject of the 1997 book *The Fourth Turning* by Neil Howe and William Strauss. It transposes human history across a rhythmic continuum and sees repeating patterns emerge. Generations have personalities, like the individual people who comprise them. Generational archetypes like "The Hero Generation" are best exemplified in Anglo-American history by the generations who fought the great wars. This generation interacts as a loosely coupled group with the three other generational archetypes through the four seasons of their lives. As depicted in Table 10, a full cycle (called a saeculum) is roughly the length of a long human life. The cycle is divided into four segments or "turnings."

The First Turning is a high, a period of societal unity and accomplishment. The Second Turning is an awakening where the values of the previous generations are challenged. The Third Turning is an "unraveling" where people lose trust in their institutions, which steadily weaken. And the Fourth Turning is a calamity where a new order replaces the old order. One of my favorite songs by the Who, "Won't Get Fooled Again," comes to mind. "Meet the new boss. Same as the old boss."

The general shape of this historical repetition is, of course, the sine wave, with each part of the wave representing the four seasons of the earthly cycle. The social friction between these human generational archetypes and their different personalities is what creates human history. Parents in the 1960s and 1970s called this the "generation gap." Table 10 shows the historical sine wave that winds through the four seasons (turnings) of our lives.

Table 10 – Cycle of History

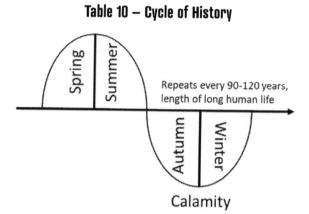

The book describes co-mingling of four generational archetypes; Nomad, Prophet, Artist, and Hero. Prophets are spoiled as children, become self-absorbed evangelists as young adults, then concentrate on moral growth as mature adults and finally become wise elders. Nomads are unprotected as kids who grow up as detached skeptical pragmatic adults, reminiscent of the "latch-key" kids of the 1970s. Nomads finally emerge as desensitized, pragmatic elders in the post-crisis world. In contrast, Heroes grow up protected in reaction to the failure by society to protect the young Nomads. They grow into young adulthood as team players during a crisis, which fuels their confidence (and hubris) in midlife post-crisis. The most recent example is the Hero generation who fought WWII.

My father was the youngest of 11 kids growing up in an immigrant Italian household in Massachusetts. Four of his brothers went off to war and one didn't return. These Heroes came back from war and fueled one the great economic expansions in history. Heroes then became the elders who their kids, the Baby Boomers, tried to overthrow. Finally, the Artists are overprotected children during the crisis who become careful, thoughtful young adults, evolve into free yet tentative mature adults, and then finally become empathetic elders. These two components – generational archetypes and the four turnings – form a pattern of cyclical social change.

The key concept of *The Fourth Turning* is understanding time as cyclical rather than linear. Buddhism and Hinduism would be comfortable with this outlook. Naturally, if a phenomenon is characterized by a repeating pattern over a time, it can be understood by mathematics. If the authors are correct, there should be some predictive power in recognizing those patterns in our current society, and they are not shy in stating that we are in the middle of a fourth turning now. Yikes!

> *Most don't understand*
> *the exponential function.*
> *They miss great power.*
> –Adapted from Albert Bartlett

I remember a story I read years ago that really cemented my understanding of the word "exponential." Bear with me if you've heard this one before.

The story goes that the ruler of India was so pleased with one of his palace wise men, who taught him the game of chess, that he offered him a reward of his own choosing, and he said to the man: "Name your reward!" The man responded: "Oh, Emperor, my wishes are simple. I only wish for this: Give me one grain of rice for the first square of the chessboard, two grains for the next square, four for the next, eight for the next, and so on for all 64 squares, with each square having double the number of grains as the square before." The emperor agreed, amazed that the man had asked for such a small reward – or so he thought. After a week, his treasurer came back and informed him that the reward would add up to an astronomical sum, far greater than all the rice that could conceivably be produced in many centuries! [3]

How much rice? The number of grains of rice on the last square can be written as 2^{63}, or 2 times itself 63 times, or 18.446 quintillion grains of rice! We are all like the emperor in some ways – we find it hard to grasp how fast functions like "doubling" makes numbers grow. These functions are called "exponential functions."

We live in an era that is often characterized as exponential change. I think most people understand exponential to mean "really fast" but fail to understand exactly how fast. Al Bartlett, a scientist who worked on the Manhattan Project, coined the phrase that I adapted in my previous haiku: "The greatest shortcoming of the human race is our inability to understand the exponential function." [4] Technically, if something is changing at an exponential rate, mathematics describes it as: $f(x) = 2^x$, a function whose value is a constant raised to the power of the argument. Think of "exponential" as nonlinear growth or decay. Table 11 shows an exponential curve that begins with slow growth that eventually hits an upward inflection point where the growth is no longer linear.

Table 11 – Exponential Curve

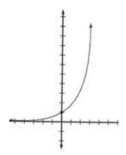

There are many examples of exponential growth and decay in our universe. One example is observed in bacteria. There are types of bacteria called prokaryotes that multiply very rapidly. If we put 100 bacteria in a petri dish and recorded the size of the population each hour, we'd measure 200 after the first hour, 400 after two hours, 800 after three hours, and so on. The bacteria population doubles each hour. This is exponential growth. Eventually the growth tails off because the environment is no longer able to support the massive bacteria colony. This constraint of exponential growth is in an important natural law in biology. You cannot be larger than your container.

Another example of exponential growth is Moore's Law, named

after Gordon Moore, a cofounder of Intel Corporation. Moore first published what later became known as Moore's Law in a 1965 *Electronics Magazine* article called "Cramming More Components onto Integrated Circuits." [5] Basically, Moore's Law states that CPU processing power doubles about every two years for the price of $1,000. Over the last 50 years Moore's Law has proved amazingly accurate. The typical mobile phone we carry is many times more powerful, less expensive, and smaller than the most powerful computers running our companies when I started my career 38 years ago. Moore's Law has increased the processing power of microchips exponentially and allowed technology to permeate nearly every aspect of modern life. Microsoft and the FAANG companies (Facebook, Amazon, Apple, Netflix, Google) would not be possible without the power of Moore's Law. Despite it being one of the main forces driving our history, most people fail to comprehend the profound implications of this exponential function.

The most important and controversial implication of Moore's Law has often been described by futurists such as Ray Kurzweil, who believe that exponential growth trends such as Moore's Law will eventually lead to a "technological singularity." Singularity posits that the invention of artificial superintelligence (ASI) will trigger exponential technological growth, resulting in unthinkable disruption to human civilization. Imagine a point where our already existing self-learning computer programs begin a "runaway reaction" of self-improvement cycles, resulting in a powerful superintelligence that surpasses all human intelligence.

This seems like a crazy claim, but are there other examples of exponential growth in human experience that can add context as to whether singularity is possible to achieve? Before we answer that question, it might be helpful to agree what constitutes a truly important historical achievement. Many people consider agriculture and domestication of animals as very important achievements. The dog was the first species domesticated by humans, around 14,000 BC. It took another 6,000 years before we domesticated and started breeding horses, then oxen as we transitioned to agriculture. Agriculture created a reliable food supply that enabled larger human settlements and then cities with bustling commerce. Cities became targets of conquest, so a list of important human developments should probably include great wars that enabled great empires to emerge. Soon after modern humans became self-aware, they began pondering their place in the cosmos to ascribe deeper meaning to existence.

As we began to satisfy the lower tiers of "Maslow's Hierarchy of Needs" [6] (e.g., food and shelter), we had more time to devote to ponder our existence. Armed with a unique and powerful form of self-awareness, human thought began a rapid track of self-learning. In the 1940s, German Philosopher Karl Jaspers coined the term "Axial Age" to characterize the period 800-200 BCE when the great minds of Buddha (563-483 BCE), Confucius (551-479 BCE), and Socrates (469-399 BCE) all lived close to one another in time, but not in place. Jaspers calls this era "a deep breath bringing the most lucid consciousness" where these philosophers brought transformative schools of thought to three major civilizations: Indian, Chinese, and European.

These and many more are all great examples of transformative human achievements, but they still didn't result in "exponential" human development. In *Why the West Rules – For Now,* author Ian Morris tries to normalize achievements across many millennia to develop a consistent measure of the relative contribution of each to human growth. As he writes, "reducing the ocean of facts to simple numerical scores has drawbacks but it also has the one great merit of forcing everyone to confront the same evidence – with surprising results. In other words, if we want to know which developments bent the curve of human history, it makes sense to try to draw that curve."

Morris uses a modified version the Human Development Index (HDI), a statistical tool developed by the United Nations used to measure a country's overall achievement in its social and economic dimensions. The social and economic dimensions of a country are based on the health of people, their level of education attainment, and their standard of living. That curve shows that modern human population grew very slowly for over 99 percent of its duration as a species. Even with the innovations of agriculture, animal domestication, religion, science, and philosophy, the unpredictability of our natural environment still suppressed growth. Then in 1775 the Industrial Revolution was unleashed with the perfection of the steam engine by British engineer James Watt. You can see from the Table 12, *that's when human population went exponential.* The Industrial Revolution ushered in a golden age of technological improvement that bent the arc of human history radically upward. [7]

Table 12 – Industrial Revolution Unleashes Exponential Population Growth

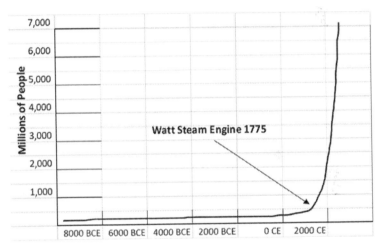

Are we really nearing the upper bound of our evolutionary amplitude in the longer eternal sine wave? Afterall, our great technological revolution has provided us weapons with the capability of destroying most life on the planet, and we know exponential growth is not sustainable forever. Maybe the technology that drives our rapid progress will become the upper bound of our development in the near term. If history moves in a cyclical sine-wave fashion and we could "zoom in and out" to view our trajectory, we might see smaller waves are just part of a larger sine wave – lots of smaller exponential events that revert back to the mean in a larger context, as shown in Table 13.

Table 13 – Sine Waves Are Really Connected Pyramids

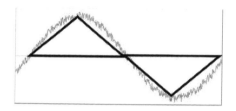

If we zoom into the curve, we see two identical triangles (a 2-D form of a pyramid). The peak of the wave is an upright triangle and the trough is an inverted triangle. It seems that the wave peak is consistent with our idea of prosperous peaceful times. However, the trough of the sine wave is associated with instability and calamity. Maybe just coincidence? As I see it, human history is a continuum of smaller cycles within a larger cycle. The smaller cycles sometimes can resemble exponential spikes for a period of time before they collapse under their own weight and settle back into its trough where the energy from the larger wave pushes it to rebuild another peak. Whether upright or inverted, the pyramid-triangle is at the center of it all as empires build and then collapse. By ordering the power in our societies from the bottom up, we inherit the sustainable nature of the pyramid. I think our wise Founders knew this when they formed our nation.

CHAPTER 4

The Nature of Power

*Power always thinks
it's wiser and more moral
than those it controls.*
–Adapted from John Adams

The Tension Between Inherent and Delegate Power

Understanding the characteristics of power is critical to appreciating the relationship between "we the people" and our government. To begin unpacking this, we need to understand the Founders' concept of natural law. All of us are created equal with free will to express ourselves and pursue happiness as we see fit as long as it doesn't directly infringe on another person's ability to do the same. Our Founders believed this was the natural state of humankind that is obvious or "self-evident." In other words, each of us differs from all others on the planet because we have free will and the ability to turn our thoughts into something tangible and concrete. Since each person has this power, it follows that the true source of human power is the individual. In *Common Sense Revisited*, author Clyde Cleveland refers to this as "indigenous power." He states, "All other forms of human power like corporations and governments derive their legitimacy from indigenous power." [1] I like to refer to this as "inherent power." Like the power of the sun, which is the source of all life on our planet, inherent power is primary and indivisible, a natural phenomenon that "simply is."

Inherent power is contrasted with what Clyde calls "surrogate power," which I will refer to as "delegate" power. Anytime people get together to form an organization, whether a club or business or government, they delegate some of their inherent power to another person or group. The mission of any organization is to promote the common interests of its members whether those are selfish interests, like a corporation's stockholders, or a charitable organization helping the poor. These common interests are enshrined in some form of bylaws or constitution laying out the specific powers the delegate has with rules that are understood, agreed to, and supervised by all. However, if one or more members decides to exercise more power than has been delegated, the organization can become corrupt.

A government is the ultimate delegate organization since its citizens realize there are many functions that can be provided more effectively when citizens combine their resources for the common good. In early rural America, farmers had a mutual understanding that if someone's barn burned down, their neighbors would band together to build a new barn for them. These "barn raisings" became the precursor to the mutual insurance company, a delegate organization that exists today. However, government becomes corrupt if it usurps the inherent rights of its citizens and then uses coercion, intimidation, and dishonesty to institutionalize the theft of inherent power.

A Brief History of Western Power

The Enlightenment was a philosophical movement mostly in Europe in North America, during the late 17th and early 18th century. The main characters passionately believed they were energizing and expanding human intellect and culture after the "dark" Middle Ages. Aspects of the Enlightenment include the rise of reason, liberty, and the scientific method. Enlightenment philosophy was skeptical of religion – especially the powerful Catholic Church – monarchies, and hereditary aristocracy. Enlightenment philosophy was influential in ushering in the French and American revolutions and constitutions.

The Scientific Revolution was ignited by Nicolas Copernicus and his scientific proof that the sun revolved around the earth versus the other way around, as was commonly believed. Science and liberal thought exploded during the Renaissance with the likes of Galileo, Kepler, Locke and Hobbs, Isaac Newton, and Adam Smith. The scientific method also influenced the way philosophers and statesmen thought about societal structures. They saw how the old monarchial order and the Church wrought hellfire and brimstone for centuries in Europe. Could they apply a little science to identify behaviors and civil codes that produced the best overall outcomes both economically and spiritually? From this era, we get the first principles of individual liberty, universal education, religious toleration, separation of church and state, and the use of reason and science rather than blind faith.

History is full of examples of what happens when people lose trust in their institutions. The modern nation-state was born from 17th century European religious warfare between forces loyal to Catholic Rome and the emerging Christian religious denominations born of the Protestant Reformation. The Renaissance thinkers were looking to classical forms of reason and science for guidance while the Protestants believed that the road to Heaven didn't go through Rome but rather through the soul of each individual and their relationship to the Creator. This idea is ironically more aligned with Hinduism and Buddhism. For centuries, people slowly lost faith in both the Catholic Church and the feudalism that had ruled Europe, and this culminated in the bloody 30 Years War (1618-1648) between Catholics and Protestants. The Treaty of Westphalia in 1648 could arguably be considered the birth of the modern nation-state. The resolution to the war allowed German princes to decide the official religion of their regions whether it was Catholic, Calvinist, or Lutheran. More important throughout Europe, the treaty solidified the notion of state sovereignty where each king would be the sole sovereign of his domain. Sovereignty is that power for which there is no higher appeal. While the general understanding was that God was the sovereign and that rulers governed as God's ministers, there was the attempt by some to sever government from the domain of heaven.

Such was the effort of the English political philosopher Thomas Hobbes (1588-1679). In his work *Leviathan* (1651), Hobbes lays the foundation for a ruler who is not under God but is still the absolute ruler in his domain. Hobbes' view of the state of man is one based on fear of chaos and disorder. Therefore, man's only recourse is to surrender his natural rights to a monarch who will protect him from chaos, but he must obey him absolutely. Hobbes' monarch was an absolute ruler who imposed order, in top-down fashion, upon his domain. This belief stemmed from the central principle of Hobbes' philosophy that human beings are essentially selfish. According to Hobbes, if man is placed in a "state of nature" with no government, we would be constantly at war with one another. Without government, Hobbes viewed life as very difficult. Hobbes' opinion of human nature was heavily shaped by the English Civil War (1642-1649), which ended with the beheading of King Charles I. Hobbes saw the resulting chaotic leaderless period afterwards to be as close to that basic state of nature as humans could get. Hobbes was a true top-down government advocate.

Enter John Locke, the 17th century English philosopher and physician who believed that natural law emanated from a divine creator and it governs both the material and spiritual world. He founded the concept of "empiricism," a theory espousing that knowledge comes mainly from sensory experience or what can be observed in the physical world. It emphasizes the role of empirical evidence in the formation of ideas rather than traditions like the Divine Right of Kings.

However, he also argued that traditions come from the common experiences of large groups of people over time and are important in establishing firm ground from which new ideas can be tested.

Locke's experience as both a scientist and a philosopher are typical of many "enlightened thinkers" in history and it gave him the ability to see the link between the physical and spiritual worlds. His ideas around natural law and natural rights were the underpinnings of the Glorious Revolution in England. The ideology of our Founders asserts that the individual is a divinely created being with free will and inalienable rights based on natural law. In this belief system, only the individual has inherent power. The individual is the sovereign master and the government is the delegated servant. He believed a country's constitution is the ultimate law and laws that are not aligned with it are legally void. The main role of government was to increase the freedoms of its citizens, and there should be a separation of powers to act as check on unbridled power that might infringe on those freedoms. From this main idea came the formation of England's first parliament in 1801. It's clear that our Founders read the writings of John Locke.

Given Locke's role as a scientist and physician, he understood how truth was revealed by applying reason to an issue or hypothesis. Locke supported using the scientific method developed over time by Greek, Roman, Muslim, and Renaissance scholars. That is the basis of how we gather knowledge today about our universe: gathering evidence, creating a hypothesis, testing and measuring the hypothesis through experiments, and then drawing conclusions. Primary to the scientific method was that all hypotheses must be tested against observations rather than resting only on "a priori" reasoning, intuition, or revelation. John Locke believed that natural law governed both the spiritual world and the world of men. These natural laws were translated as inalienable natural rights of Life, Liberty, and Property that can't be taken away by any government, institution, or religion.

In the mid-18th century, Jean-Jacques Rousseau expanded on Hobbes' philosophy and originated the idea that human beings were essentially products of their environment. He claimed that natural law was a primitive condition where men were constantly in competition with one another. In his view, natural law was without morality and humans essentially left that condition for the benefits of a cooperative civil society. As societies developed, the division of labor and private property required people to adopt institutions of law. By joining together into civil society through a social contract, Rousseau believed people can both preserve themselves and remain free. This is because submission to the general will of the people through a strong government guarantees individuals against being subordinated to the wills of others and ensures they obey the laws because they, collectively, are the authors of the law. He believed that the primary role of the government was to create equality for its citizens. However, Rousseau did not believe in the political equality that Locke and the American Founders believed in; he believed in the equality of material outcomes created by a strong central government that redistributes wealth.

It was also in the mid-18th century that Adam Smith expanded on Locke's theories of natural law. In *An Inquiry into the Nature and Causes of the Wealth of Nations (1776)*, Smith laid the foundations of classical free market economic theory. In this and other works, he developed the concept of the division of labor and described how rational self-interest and competition leads to economic prosperity. In his view, "the invisible hand" of the market was part of natural law as it guided a myriad of self-interested decisions by people into collective well-being for all. *"Wealth of Nations"* continues to be required reading for economists.

> *Government is not*
> *reason, it's not eloquence,*
> *it is simply force.*
> – Adapted from George Washington

Fast forward about 100 years, and the tug-of-war between the individual and the state continued as Karl Marx and Friedrich

Engels expanded on the Hobbesian Theory of Materialism with dialectical materialism. It accepts the evolution of the natural world and that government was part of that evolution. In 1848 while the world around them was erupting in conflict, Marx and Engels published the *Manifesto of the Communist Party*. It states that the source of all human conflict, and human history, is ceaseless class struggle. Given the massive economic growth of the Industrial Revolution in Europe and America, and the subsequent political conflict resulting from the stark income inequality it wrought, it is not hard to see how a book offering a blueprint for the working classes to fight back would be appealing. As a result, socialism became a fast-growing political idea during the tumultuous events of the 19th and early 20th century. It was a natural counterpoint to the dominant free market system that, at times, could seem cruel and immoral in its exploitation of human labor.

For however awful free market capitalism seems to some people, I believe history has shown capitalism has substantially increased the living standards of average citizens over the past 300 years. Communism on the other hand led to the concept of the state as the supreme authority resulting in the brutal regimes of Vladimir Lenin and Joseph Stalin in the Soviet Union and their satellite European states, Mao in China, Hoh Chi Minh in Vietnam, Pol Pot in Cambodia, the North Korean Kim dynasty, and the Castro dynasty in Cuba. In these regimes, tens of millions of people were murdered or imprisoned as enemies of the state. All of these were socialist governments that purported to support the plight of workers, but all the outcomes of their policies resulted in loss of freedom, poverty, and death for their people. Millions more were imprisoned and brainwashed by their governments' fear of inherent power. Meanwhile, the living standards of the average person degraded terribly as centrally planned economies slowly collapsed while their counterparts living in free market countries flourished.

Does this mean that all those who believe in communist policies are knowingly part of the deception? Absolutely not. Few people really understand the nature of what is happening when they vote for candidates who support policies that increase the power of federal government. Many Germans voted for Hitler, who ran on a platform that sounded like some modern-day American politicians, including anti-smoking laws and a national registration of firearms. There are those who consider socialism to be separate from communism and point to successful economies in European countries that embraced socialist policies. To those people I would answer, European countries still vote for their governments in orderly transitions of power, have somewhat open economies although with lots of import protectionism, and rely on the United States military umbrella for their national defense. Still, policies of free college and free healthcare, and an expansive social safety net, have translated into unwieldy and even dangerous levels of sovereign debt and slow economic growth. The power of the European central government grows with no practical limit to its intrusion into the lives of its citizens. How long before a crisis forces this slowly creeping socialism into a more authoritarian form? Britain has had enough of this infringement on its sovereignty and decided to exit the European Union, effective October 31, 2019. As I write this book, the world is watching how quickly the Chavista regime of Venezuela turned from promises of equality and prosperity into a collapsed economy on the brink of civil war in 20 short years. The authoritarian socialist regime of Venezuela only exists because of support from its military leaders and the communist regimes of Cuba and China. It's worth remembering the words of Vladimir Lenin. "The goal of socialism is communism."

> *Societies that*
> *choose equality over*
> *freedom get neither.*
> – Adapted from Milton Friedman

Like many of our American Founders, Thomas Jefferson (1743-1826) was deeply influenced by Enlightenment thinking. He and James Madison were primary authors of the Declaration of

Independence, which stressed Enlightenment ideas such as liberty, fundamental human rights, and equality. I concede that this vision unfortunately did not include slaves or women, serious defects that were corrected later. Before we fought a war and severed ourselves finally from the yoke of the English monarchy, our Founders were conceiving and building their ideas around the best, most sustainable form of government that embodied those principles of the Enlightenment. In 1776, our Founders eloquently put their stake in the ground with our declaration of sovereignty and the primacy of inherent natural rights:

> "We hold these truths to be self-evident, that all men are created equal, that they are endowed by their Creator with certain unalienable Rights, that among these are Life, Liberty and the pursuit of Happiness. – That to secure these rights, Governments are instituted among Men, deriving their just powers from the consent of the governed, – That whenever any Form of Government becomes destructive of these ends, it is the Right of the People to alter or to abolish it, and to institute new Government, laying its foundation on such principles and organizing its powers in such form, as to them shall seem most likely to effect their Safety and Happiness."

It took all of "four score and seven years" for this proposition to be severely tested. In my opinion, the American Civil War was on par with the founding as the most important event in our history. It settled a passionate disagreement that already existed between the free and slave colonies but was tabled for later in order to get all colonies on board with the Constitution. The politicians in the southern states believed the federal government had become corrupt by usurping state power and outlawing their choice of slavery. They built a false narrative that slaves were not considered fully human and therefore not "men" as indicated in the Constitution. However, it's not that slavery wasn't part of founding discussions. The 1787 Constitutional Convention contained the "Three-Fifths

Compromise," which allowed slave states to count each slave as three-fifths of a free man for the purpose of allocating US Congressional districts for the House of Representatives. Unfortunately, this gave slave states an inordinate amount of power, and they dominated federal government until 1861. However, there seemed to be logical inconsistencies. On the one hand, southern states viewed slaves as property, no different than a horse or shovel. On the other hand, for the purposes of collecting power, slaves were three-fifths human. Which is it? Convenient double standards like this are still a common practice among politicians. This mind exercise didn't account for the obvious, self-evident evil of slavery. When a critical mass of Americans, mostly in northern states, finally rediscovered their moral compass and saw that black people were as human as they were, and that their inalienable rights were being completely violated, the battle lines were drawn. The Enlightenment-era "first principles" of ethics were the foundation of the Constitution, and the institution of slavery spat in the face of that. Thankfully, the Union prevailed, and we amended our Constitution to correct the hideous institution of slavery.

The Founders also knew it was much easier for a government to seize the inherent power of the citizens if it is geographically separated from them. There are many studies showing people behave much differently when they talk face to face as opposed to on the phone, anonymously online, or in a crowd. There is strong correlation showing that the further removed a person is from a person they are communicating with, the less likely they are to be truthful. [2] While there were no electronic communication devices in the 18th century, the Founders still understood the nature of human behavior and concluded that it's better to have strict limits on government entities that are farther away from its citizens. That's why state governments have constitutions that limit their power, but the national constitution places more strict limitations on the federal government, which is even farther away from the people.

The Founders also created a constitutional republic, not a pure democracy. They knew that it was too easy for the majority in a pure democracy to violate the inherent rights of the individual. As Jefferson stated, "A democracy is nothing more than mob rule, where fifty-one percent of the people may take away the rights of the other forty-nine." Their intention was to do everything possible to put into place a form of government that could not usurp inherent power from the people. The only way to keep government from usurping inherent power is to structure it from the bottom up.

In his 1985 book *The State*, Hungarian economist Anthony de Jasay, who fled his communist homeland at 23 years old, posits that ideology really doesn't matter despite citizens wringing their hands about the pros and cons of being ruled by the right or the left. Twentieth century Scottish philosopher Alasdair McIntyre summed it up nicely: "Whoever you vote for, the government wins." Whether Nazis, communists, military authoritarians, democratic socialists, conservative oligarchs, or monarchies, the type of government doesn't really matter because the mission is the same: to increase government power. Governments take on a life of their own.

Anthony de Jasay uses the example of a business with shareholders, managers, and employees as an organizational metaphor. They sometimes have competing interests, but economists agree that the main goal is to maximize profits. Profitable companies are sustainable while unprofitable ones are not. A similar dynamic exists in government where different agencies and groups compete for resources to increase their power. Jasay believed redistribution was "addictive" for politicians because giving away freebies in exchange for votes appeals to the basic human behavior of seeking the shortest distance between two points. Votes are the most important thing for politicians because it keeps them in power, and with power comes money. It allows the political class to swing between the DC government and the interest groups that compete for DC influence. I think most Americans see this phenomenon for what it is.[3]

If politicians proclaim that a form of redistribution is a basic right, citizens naturally won't want to be deprived of that right and will demand redistribution. They don't care how it's paid for or what the larger economic repercussions might be; they vote for those candidates who promise to protect the newly created rights. For decades, Social Security was described as the "Third Rail of Politics," because any politician trying to touch it would be toast. Most citizens in this country believe Social Security is their right no matter what.

Most people also don't understand the true cost of the things they believe they get for free, and politicians are adept at obfuscating that cost. Done on a larger scale, redistribution changes the nature of society and skews the price signals in the economy. Companies start to spend more money on lawyers and lobbyists to influence policy to benefit them rather than investing those dollars hiring new employees and creating new products. Jasay maintains that a strong constitution is required to check this natural behavior and ensure governments balance individual freedom with the common good.

Most of the people I've met who work in government are dedicated public officials who really aren't in it for the money. They are mostly behind the scenes, so you rarely see them on TV or social media. But I think it is natural human behavior to want the organization you work for to be important. So, it's perfectly natural for career politicians to have a personal interest in making government more important. Politicians who favor more centralized power have a personal stake in their decisions. George Mason University professor and economist James Buchanan was awarded the Nobel Prize in Economic Sciences in 1986 for his development of Public Choice Theory. In his 1962 book *The Calculus of Consent* (with Gordon Tullock), he focused on how politicians and government bureaucrats act in their own self-interest, the same way as consumers and businesspeople do in private sector. Buchanan used both economics and political science to develop his Public Choice Theory. The same principles used to understand private decisions in the free market also apply to voting, lobbying, campaigning, and even candidates. A person's first instinct is to make decisions based upon their own self-interest. Buchanan explains his theory as "politics without romance" because many political promises appear to be concerned with the public interest, but in reality have selfish motives. He believed that by examining the behavior of voters and politicians, you can predict their actions and therefore outcomes. The common-sense version of Public Choice Theory is observing the dominance of career politicians in government at all levels and the preponderance of those who become wealthy in a field where you're not supposed to make a ton of money because you are theoretically working in the public interest.[4]

Take it or leave it.
The illusion of options.
This is Hobson's Choice.

A Hobson's Choice refers to a bargain where only one real option is offered. There is an appearance of choice because the person considering the offer can choose to accept the offer or refuse. This is technically two choices but really one. This saying was attributed to Thomas Hobson, a stable owner in 17th century England, who offered his travelling customers the horse closest to the door of the stable or none at all. He discovered it was efficient and profitable to limit the choices of his customers. A weary traveler, faced with the "take it or leave it" deal, took the deal more often than not.

These sorts of bargains are famous. I'm of Italian descent and love the *Godfather* movies even though they are less than flattering for my Italian American brethren. They are still iconic American stories. In the first *Godfather* movie, Don Corleone is approached at his daughter's wedding by his godson, the famous Sinatra-like crooner Johnny Fontane. Johnny's serial philandering with movie starlets has put him sideways with one of Hollywood's most powerful moguls, Jack Wolz, who refuses to give him the lead role in a film that was a perfect fit for him. After a quick "schiaffo in faccia" (smack in the face) to stop Johnny's embarrassing sob fest, Don Corleone assures him everything will be taken care of. When Johnny asks how he is going to convince a big Hollywood producer, Corleone replies, "I'm gonna make him an offer he can't refuse." Voila. Another poignant

Hobson's Choice. The problem was that the producer, Jack Wolz, really didn't understand the offer when he refused and sent consigliere Tom Hagen back to New York emptyhanded. But that's a horse of a different color.

During the writing of this book, I was called to jury duty in my residence county of Indian River, Florida. After reporting at 8 a.m. with 150 other citizens, waiting for three hours while the courts were in process, and speaking to my daughter's high school biology teacher who was also called, I was among 40 people who made it to the final step in the selection process: the interview by the judge and the attorneys on both sides of the case. It was a criminal matter where the standard for ruling guilt or innocence, beyond a reasonable doubt, is higher than for civil matters. The defense attorney was a charming and capable woman who asked questions to about half of us (including me) based on our answers to a pre-selection questionnaire. Essentially, she was offering different forms of Hobson's Choices to reinforce our understanding of "innocent unless proven guilty." For example, she asked if we would be okay with only the prosecutor presenting evidence and she and her client did nothing in their defense. Several who were asked that question said "no," that they should hear both prosecution and defense cases before deciding. After all, common sense and fairness dictates one should hear both sides of an issue to reach an informed conclusion. The people who said "no" felt there was no other choice in order to be perceived as "fair-minded." In reality, the answer is "yes"; you should be able to adjudicate without hearing from the defense because the entire burden of proof falls on the state prosecutor. Having never served on a jury, I was a bit sad I wasn't chosen to be among the six jurors because I was fascinated watching the process of a critical government "common good" function being done by a completely random selection of citizens from our county: rich/poor, old/young, male/female, white/black/brown. Other than my stint of military service, this is the most egalitarian process I've witnessed.

The Hobson's Choice has become an effective means of control by clever people in all walks of life. Buy my product, ride my train, hire my labor union, vote for my candidate or you are either crazy, stupid, racist, or worse. Although the person on the other side of the bargain may have other choices, they have been boxed into a corner intellectually, so they believe there is only one choice. The Hobson's Choice is the key component of "political correctness." Nobody wants to be labeled as a bigot or stupid, so they relent to the pressure to publicly accept all kinds of bad ideas. In this way, businesses gain control over their clientele and governments gain control over their citizens. It's important to understand that Mr. Hobson or other monopolists didn't have the ability to restrict their customers' choices from the outset of their enterprises. It takes time for a monopolist to grow their power. In the early years, customers have real choices from many companies competing for their business, but as the monopolist lobbies government for concessions favorable to them, they continue to grab market share and slowly eliminate their competition.

America has a rich tradition as a republic, not a democracy. Yes, we have democratic elections, but government power is carefully circumscribed, and the primacy of inherent power is upheld in our Constitution. We have a long tradition of checking government power with our judicial system that decides conflicts between government and individual power. In every country, pure democracy always starts with good intentions but then devolves to collectivism and socialism as the costs of meeting voter demands increases. Politicians who feed off this offer the ultimate Hobson's Choice: *Vote for me or your gravy train stops!* This is how, after several generations of a growing entitlement state, America has become a country where the number of people receiving government redistribution has increased rapidly and the number of people paying taxes has decreased equally rapidly.

According to a 2018 Gallup Poll, more than half of America's largest demographic segment, young millennials, have a positive view of socialism. [5] With this backdrop, it's no surprise that young voters turned out in droves in the 2018 fall midterm elections where the Democratic Party reclaimed the majority of the House of Representatives led by a cohort of young activist representatives touting an agenda of radical change for America. A pillar of this plan is called the Green New Deal and it focuses on re-ordering economic activity to address climate change and substantially increasing already unsustainable government entitlements. The Green New Deal calls for the following goals to be accomplished in 10 years:

- Eliminating usage of ALL fossil fuels
- Modifying ALL buildings in the country for energy efficiency
- Eliminating the flatulence of cows
- Changing our transportation system to be ALL electric with a focus on high-speed rail to replace air travel
- Guaranteed income for ALL Americans whether someone chooses to work or not
- Free healthcare for ALL Americans
- Free college for ALL Americans
- All of the above infrastructure would be built by government employees, not the private sector
- Lots of other goodies too many to mention [6]

Estimates of the cost of this range from $93 trillion [7] over 10 years to *the entire GDP of our planet*.[8] When asked how this would all be fundedsupporters state that the government would simply borrow from the Federal Reserve and that we shouldn't be worried about deficits when it comes to things like climate change. They support a 70 percent top income tax rate on incomes over $10 million, which would likely raise less than $15 billion per year according to one estimate. This means that the cost of the Green New Deal will really be borne by working-class Americans.

I agree with the science behind climate change but have questions about the scope and timeframe of its effects. I don't think that the planet will be doomed in 12 years if we don't shut down our economy now as Green New Deal proponents claim. In fact, according to a May 2019 Washington Post interview [9] with Saikat Chakrabarti, Chief of Staff for Rep. Alexandra Ocasio-Cortez, the

Green New Deal was never about climate change. Chakrabarti surprisingly disclosed, "The interesting thing about the Green New Deal is it wasn't originally a climate thing at all. We really think of it as a how-do-you-change-the-entire-economy thing." Unfortunately, this confirms one of the common criticisms about climate change activists. That it's less about climate than it is about power.

Already we are seeing the cost of renewable energy sources becoming competitive with fossil fuels and renewables usage growing rapidly. We had sensible regulation of coal-fired energy plants under the Obama administration that has all but shut down usage of coal. According to a May 2019 study by the IMF, [10] the fossil fuel industry receives $649 billion in direct and indirect subsidies in the United States. In my view, the government should stop ALL fossil fuel subsidies. However, as large as that amount seems, the US ranks 19th of the 25 countries the IMF measured in terms of energy subsidies as a percentage of national GDP. Pretty good compared to Russia and China at 40.3 percent and 11.4 percent, respectively. Even better when you consider we are the world's largest economy and largest energy producer. It is a good thing for the US and the world to reduce its reliance on fossil fuels. However, we do not need to shut down our entire economy to address climate change concerns.

The Green New Deal wouldn't be a real concern if it weren't gaining support among members of Congress and some of the 2020 presidential candidates. [11] If you don't support them, you are a climate denier. Then there is President Trump saying if you don't support him, you are a fake news, unpatriotic, deep-state loving Marxist. How's that for a Hobson's Choice?

In the United States and around the world, there is a steady menu of Hobson's Choices from leaders who bamboozle otherwise smart people into giving away their inherent power. It's political illusionists who summon the magic of cognitive dissonance to get citizens to willingly vote against their interests. This form of coercive power is how a republic deteriorates into mob rule democracy and then to a socialist nanny state and then finally to an authoritarian police state.

Most citizens won't realize when their country is at the tipping point, nor do they appreciate the power of Hobson's Choice. The deception is that there aren't many choices, only two and one is clearly unacceptable. Those offering the bargain are not compelling you to do anything specific; they're simply guiding your mind so that you won't see any other choices except the one they want you to take. Senator Padme Amidala said it best in the movie *Star Wars: Revenge of the Sith*. As the Sith Lord addresses the Senate, he states that the Republic would be reorganized into a new centralized galactic empire in order to guarantee a "safe and secure society." To that, Padme replies: "So this is how liberty dies...with thunderous applause." Who wouldn't want safety and security? Mr. Hobson would be proud.

CHAPTER 5

What Do We Mean by Local?

*The butcher, baker
and the candlestick maker
is locally grown.*

America's Constitution spends a lot of time delineating federal powers. As the 10th Amendment confirms, "powers not delegated to the United States by the constitution, nor prohibited by it to the states, are reserved to the states respectively, or to the people." The "people" are the citizens living in America's cities and towns. If the premise of this book is rebalancing our government toward more local rule, it is only fair that we spend some time talking about what we mean by local. I think to most, it's the city or town where we grew up or currently reside in. I grew up in Lunenburg, Massachusetts, a sleepy little town first settled in 1718 that was surrounded by lots of other similarly small towns. Massachusetts is a collection of 351 cities and towns. Being a primary geography in America's founding, Massachusetts' governing constructs became models for other colonies to follow. States subdivided into counties and then cities and towns. The power relationship between towns-counties-states was often defined in either state constitutions or statutes. In Massachusetts, cities and towns had much more autonomy than counties. Counties were confined mostly as a common registry of deeds and licenses and courts. County police departments don't exist. The situation is quite different in my current home state of Florida where county government is quite powerful, often exceeding the power of the cities and towns contained in it. In addition to the traditional functions, the county handles inspections, collects all taxes, has a robust police force, runs the schools, and more.

Boston is one of our oldest cities and the county *is* the city. There is no other city or town in Suffolk County other than Boston. The state abolished the last of any administrative county functions in 1999. In its earliest days Boston expanded by annexing neighboring towns like Dorchester, Brighton, and Mattapan, but early on, the state stepped in to stop further annexation in its effort to control the powers of cities and towns. By the mid-1800s, the country was growing at such a fast rate demographically and geographically, there were many political and jurisdictional collisions between them. Then came a landmark ruling in 1868 from the Federal 8th Circuit Court, led by Justice John Dillion that affirmed:

"Municipal incorporations owe their origin to, and derive their powers and rights wholly from, the legislature. It breathes into them the breath of life, without which they cannot exist. As it creates, so may it destroy. If it may destroy, it may abridge and control." [1]

This became known as Dillon's Rule. At the time, many states and municipalities followed the theory of "home rule" whereby jurisdictions within the state could exercise significant autonomy for governance as long as it was within the bounds of the state and federal constitutions. Several states' constitutions explicitly affirmed home rule. Then in 1871, the chief justice of the Michigan Supreme Court wrote in a concurring opinion that "local government is a matter of absolute right; and the state cannot take it away." The Supreme Court has not ruled definitively between the two decisions but has since upheld parts of Dillon's Rule while permitting states to write legislation allowing any city or town that is a target for being annexed into a larger city the right to accept or reject annexation. Today about 40 of our 50 states observe Dillon's Rule in some form while 10 states have written home rule into their state constitutions. It's no surprise to me that my home state of Massachusetts is one of the 10 home rule states. [2]

My analysis doesn't reveal any major patterns between the home rule and Dillion's Rule states. But in his 1993 book, *Cities without Suburbs*, author and former Albuquerque, New Mexico Mayor David Rusk says the thing that matters most is a city's elasticity. Those with the ability to expand their borders (elastic) tend to be more affluent, with less crime and higher bond ratings. Cities like Birmingham, Alabama (inelastic) and Charlotte, North Carolina (elastic) illustrate the issue. Birmingham is surrounded by 34 other municipalities in Jefferson County that are smaller but more affluent suburbs with better public infrastructure. During the 1950s to 1990s, many families fled the problems of inner cities for a better life in suburbia. None of these wealthier suburbs wanted to be annexed by Birmingham, and the state permits Dillon's Rule at the county level. Counter examples are Charlotte and Austin, which have grown tremendously over the past decades and met their growth needs by annexing adjacent towns. North Carolina and Texas are both hybrid states that have elements of Dillon's Rule and Home Rule. They encouraged borders to accommodate the economic growth of both these cities. This provides more land to build homes for new citizens moving in. It increases the tax base, saves money on duplicate infrastructure, and keeps cities more diverse. These are places where people want to work and live. Today, Charlotte and Austin have two-thirds higher median income, one-third lower unemployment, and half the poverty rate of Birmingham. The simple takeaway is that bad state laws that make city borders unchangeable are at a disadvantage. [3]

So, for cities hobbled by the inability to expand, what are some of the ways they can address their plight? Let's start with lobbying their state legislators to make necessary changes. Short of that, it's up to a county or region to plan how merging works out to everyone's mutual benefit. A 2018 *Economist* article, "*Why American Cities are so Weirdly Shaped*", cites Pittsburgh as one of 130 cities and towns in Allegheny County, Pennsylvania, that worked with its neighbors to cooperate on joint projects to make the area a growing technology hub. It also describes how Louisville merged with the other 92 cities and towns in Jefferson County to form "Greater Louisville." [4]

A great visceral way to understand what a city's natural borders looks like is by looking at a satellite image at night. Wherever you see a hub of lights, that's the city! When you put a political map overlay on that satellite image, they don't match up. Greater Los Angeles operates economically as a unified region mostly, and yet there are 17 different congressmen that represent the county. The shapes of the districts are odd, of course, due to gerrymandering for political advantage. Currently, there isn't too much that can be done about this as the US Constitution explicitly provides for the House of Representatives to be allocated according to population, but maybe a constitutional amendment can be proposed to regulate this partisan but important political gerrymandering process. Each of the 435 US Congressional districts contains about 711,000 people. There are 17 Congressional districts that comprise greater Los Angeles.

Another way to express the idea of "local" is through the construct of the 383 metropolitan statistical areas (MSA) for the United States defined by the US Office of Management and Budget (OMB). An MSA is a geographical region with a relatively large population density and close economic integration throughout the area. They are not legally incorporated municipalities, but rather are an analytical construct used by various government agencies to better understand economics and demographics.

At the center of an MSA is usually a large city like New York or Los Angeles that is the economic hub of the region. Some MSAs have more than one major city, like Minneapolis-St. Paul and Raleigh-Durham. OMB also tracks economic data for lower-level MSA components called core-based statistical areas (CBSA). These are defined as clusters of counties or equivalents where at least 50 percent of the people reside in urban areas of at least 10,000. Not to further complicate matters, but the OMB also delineates 536 micropolitan statistical areas (MSA) as a cluster of counties with at least one major urban area, where the population is between 10,000 and 50,000. Table 14 shows the 955 CBSAs and 383 MSAs plus seven in Puerto Rico in the US. As you can see, most of the US land area and population is covered by this statistical construct. The point is that we already have in place concepts of local entities larger than the thousands of incorporate cities and towns and smaller than states that could provide a solution to the dilemma of how a city expands beyond its existing borders to maintain economic viability.

Table 14 – United States Map of MSAs/CBSAs

Another phenomenon that is changing the nature of our local cities and towns is described in the 2009 book *The Big Sort: Why the*

Clustering of Like-Minded America Is Tearing Us Apart. The author, Bill Bishop, talks about how Americans are self-sorting into cities and towns and even neighborhoods that are culturally and ideologically similar to them. Parents tend to want to live in places with other likeminded citizens with churches and schools and institutions that they can count on to teach their children in a manner they approve of. Certainly, America affords its citizens the freedom to live and associate wherever and with whomever they want. However, Bishop argues that the consequences of all of us living in our own little echo chambers is that we are increasingly intolerant of dissenting views. This could be catastrophic to our democratic republic. We already see this happening now with the polarization of our citizens, which is exacerbated by intellectually cloistered media that feeds the intolerance. *The Economist* addressed this phenomenon in a June 19, 2008 article, "The Big Sort":

> "When a group is ideologically homogeneous, its members tend to grow more extreme. Even clever, fair-minded people are not immune. Cass Sunstein and David Schkade, two academics, found that Republican-appointed judges vote more conservatively when sitting on a panel with other Republicans than when sitting with Democrats. Democratic judges become more liberal when on the bench with fellow Democrats. Voters in landslide districts tend to elect more extreme members of Congress. Moderates who might otherwise run for office decide not to. Debates turn into shouting matches. Bitterly partisan lawmakers cannot reach the necessary consensus to fix long-term problems such as the tottering pensions and health-care systems." [5]

Can it be true that Americans are "choosing" *not* to get along with each other? I don't think so. As the country has grown and changed demographically, people have made the best choices for them. If they have kids, it's natural to want them being raised in an environment they agree with. However, the danger is that we shield each other from the very diversity that has driven evolution for millions of years. In its earlier forms, our cities and towns were more mixed and egalitarian where kids of all backgrounds went to the same public schools. I attended a public school like that.

Maybe if we fix the nature of where we live, town by town, the country can heal the political virus of ideological polarization. Maybe it starts with education. With all the new money that will pour into local coffers from our recommended increased level of federal budget transfers, we can improve public schools so they will be more attractive to wealthier citizens who might otherwise send their kids to private schools. Maybe we should consider a constitutional amendment that creates a rational fair process for determining congressional districts that encourages diversity rather than leaving it up to state legislators who gerrymander away diversity when their party is in the majority.

There are important national organizations of local government that are working on common problems like these and sharing best practices. The Big Seven is a group of nonprofit organizations comprised of state and local government officials. These groups include the National League of Cities (NLC), Council of State Governments, National Governors Association, and National Conference of State Legislatures. They are constantly lobbying the federal government on issues that affect their local interests. [6] As Locally Grown Government becomes a tangible movement working on the solutions outlined in this book, I expect to there to be a natural affinity with these organizations.

CHAPTER 6

Locally Grown Principles

Local government.
Politicians will not pee
where they eat dinner.

Locally Grown Government is driven by two main principles: adherence to the US Constitution and sustainability. We think the structure of the Constitution was designed to be sustainable. It has allowed America to adapt to changing conditions while still remaining mostly true to the constitutional principles of bottom-up government and primacy of inherent power. However, the flexibility of the Constitution also provides enough room for bad policy to be implemented that could ultimately tip the balance away from sustainability. It seems to me we are at that tipping point. This is why we double down on sustainability as a core principle. Let's cover my Locally Grown principles in more detail:

- Adheres to the US Constitution
- Bottom-up, decentralized self-organizing
- Bias to individual rights vs. equality
- Transparent and accountable
- Flexible
- Sustainable
- Evidence-based
- Promotes citizenship
- Bias to double-bottom line
- Enabling
- Compassionate
- Infuses public dialogue with meaning
- Harnesses excess capacity
- Promotes work
- Bias to simplification
- Incentivizes negotiation
- Technology-enabled

Constitutionally Bounded

Locally Grown Government is committed to the 17th and 18th century Enlightenment principles of individual dignity, open markets, limited government, and faith in human progress brought about by debate, science, and the search for truth. Our Constitution is based on these principles. We strongly believe that the historical evidence points to the success of this worldview over the past three centuries in America and much of the rest of the world. Certainly, history has shown that ideologies like communism have failed to make life better for its people, not to mention murdering millions of them. In September 13, 2018, *The Economist* magazine published an article titled "The Economist: A manifesto for renewing liberalism" for its 175th Anniversary. It was just in time to eloquently support the liberal world order that has come under assault. They said:

"Global life expectancy in the past 175 years has risen from a little under 30 years to over 70. The share of people living below the threshold of extreme poverty has fallen from about 80 percent to 8 percent and the absolute number has halved, even as the total living above it has increased from about 100 million to over 6.5 billion people. And literacy rates are up more than fivefold, to over 80 percent. Civil rights and the rule of law are incomparably more robust than they were only a few decades ago. In many countries, individuals are now free to choose how to live—and with whom. This is not all the work of liberals, obviously. But as fascism, communism and autarky failed over the course of the 19th and 20th centuries, liberal societies have prospered. In one flavor or another, liberal democracy came to dominate the West and from there it started to spread around the world." [1]

The Economist declares the need for the liberal world order to reinvent itself in our times. They identify the troubling lack of trust citizens have for their institutions in the USA and in liberal democracies around the globe. I highly recommend reading this article.

By this time, stating that Locally Grown Government is constitutionally bounded may seem a bit redundant. Of course, we are constitutionally bounded. By definition, every action our government takes must be constitutional, right? We have a Supreme Court to watch over these things, right? But when there are politicians seeking to increase delegate power, they can find ways to make legislation seem constitutional. And if we have an increasing body of federal law that selectively ignores the constitution, judges begin to rely on that constitutionally compromised case law to justify further encroachment on inherent power. It becomes a self-reinforcing system. People get comfortable outsourcing more of their inherent power to politicians eager to accept it. They vote for government to give them things that they are told are rights. Over time, a culture of dependency develops that feels normal, feels constitutional. And when things go wrong, even for relatively insignificant things, people increasingly look to the federal government for solutions.

I think our founding document, as amended, is properly constructed and sufficiently flexible to adapt to our rapidly changing times, while remaining true to our principles. It enumerates the powers of the federal government while stating that any powers not specifically granted to the federal government automatically inure to the states. We have a massive body of case law that mostly supports this, but the bias has been for more powers being given to the Feds. Others may argue that changing circumstances have required more central control, and this debate over where power resides is central to the current political climate. Still, we retain the fundamental bottom-up structure created by the Founders while allowing flexibility to adapt to changing circumstances.

Bottom-up

A democratic republic like ours requires the consent of the governed. Our elected representatives must embrace this fact, or the system fails. Democracy cannot be forced upon citizens by a central authority, nor can it emerge bottom-up from mayhem. Rather, it is the result of a negotiation between citizens of what constitutes the common good. It works because it allows citizens the freedom to create meaning and purpose in their lives while ensuring the common good is respected.

In contrast, top-down government requires force to maintain its power. Dissent can't be tolerated, and fear and coercion become the indispensable tools to ensure the rabble falls in line. Bottom-up government is founded on the inherent power of the individual citizen whose basic organizational unit is the family. Families are based on love. Parents are endowed with the biological instincts of selflessness in caring for their families. Family is really the most basic and ancient form of government, and if families are not stable, nothing will be stable.

Decentralized

It's a legitimate question to ask that, with all the responsibilities and tasks involved in governing, how can a decentralized structure get anything done? It would seem there would be too many competing interests and no higher authority to adjudicate over the inevitable disputes that arise. Well, our Constitution doesn't exactly permit full decentralization of power. It reserves for the federal government important exclusive powers like establishing a national currency, national defense, justice system, regulation of interstate commerce, foreign affairs, and immigration. That's a lot of power that doesn't typically affect the daily lives of ordinary people who are understandably happy to delegate these responsibilities upstream. But how can politicians in Washington, DC, know what's best for people living in Topeka and Chicago and Los Angeles? We are a huge and diverse country, and legislation that tries to be "one size fits all" is bound to be less effective and more contentious.

There are many examples of the effectiveness of widely distributed power. The Federalist Papers, which are part of America's founding tradition, describe the benefits eloquently. Federalism is a metaphor for decentralized power, and it serves as a model for many emerging countries that have diverse populations. In some countries, federalism is adopted as a means of giving different ethnic and regional groups some autonomy and control over their own affairs. In a 2004 paper, "Why Decentralize Power in a Democracy", author and Stanford professor Larry Diamond makes this point:

"The thinking is that if different ethnic and religious minorities have some autonomy, some ability to determine their own local affairs with respect to education, culture, and economic development, they will feel more secure, and be more willing to accept the authority and legitimacy of the larger national state. If a republic is to survive, it cannot be a winner-take-all system, particularly if one party is always going to win, and thus take all. When some governing responsibilities and resources are distributed to lower levels of authority, and when there are a lot of different provinces and municipalities whose governments will be chosen through elections, parties and groups that cannot win control of the central government may win the opportunity to exercise power in some of the lower-level governments. This increases their confidence in and commitment to the political system, and the sense among citizens that the system is fair and inclusive. If groups with strong bases of support in the country are completely and indefinitely excluded from any share of political power at any level, they are likely to question and even challenge the legitimacy of the system. In short, decentralization is increasingly being demanded from the grassroots, and is embraced for its potential to enhance the depth and legitimacy of democracy." [2]

Viruses need hosts,
organic or digital.
Centralized system.

A decentralized but interlinked network also provides an important natural firewall against the spread of bad things. According to the US Center for Disease Control (CDC), each year in the United States, at least two million people become infected with bacteria that are resistant to antibiotics and at least 23,000 people die each year as a direct result of these infections. Many more people die from other conditions complicated by an antibiotic-resistant infection. Food-borne illness affects 48 million Americans each year.[3] These are staggering numbers of people affected by harmful organisms that are literally everywhere looking to invade a host species. A host is a relatively homogenous environment with characteristics that encourage growth. In the organic world, it is a larger organism like a bird, a vegetable, or a human. Once the organism invades, it quickly infects the host, causing sickness and even death. Since animals and humans are social creatures, they are in constant contact with one another, providing the micro-organisms an opportunity to jump to other hosts through the air and physical contact. Humans and animals have natural antibodies that fight these micro-organisms, but many of the bugs spread so fast they overwhelm our physical systems. Over the last century, we have devised ingenious treatments to fight these infections by developing vaccines that supplement our natural defenses and even immunize us from becoming infected in the first place. But the bugs are determined. They are life after all, and their simple mission is to survive and grow, so they adapt. Vaccines must be constantly updated to handle new, more resistant strains of bacteria and viruses. Sometimes it feels like we are losing the war.

In similar fashion, computer malware depends on a common host in the form of a homogenous digital network to spread. A piece of malware is written for the underlying operating system upon which the software it infects is built upon. Black Hat hackers wanting to invade Apple products build their malware specifically for the iOS operating system. It generally won't function in a Microsoft Windows environment. The different operating systems become a natural firewall. Isn't it fascinating to see digital software code behaving just like living organisms? Both are programmed to be mobile, stealthy, and self-replicating. Given that human computer engineers can create software code that behaves biologically, it's not hard to imagine a future world where machines might become self-aware.

So, what do the commonalities between organic and computer viruses have to do with crafting more responsive and sustainable government? The answer is diversity. The more diverse systems are, the less likely they are to be invaded by intruders. If a government becomes too top-heavy, meaning that the level of involvement in people's lives increases, the command and control mechanisms become standardized so that economic and social "shocks" to the homogeneous system spread quickly. In economic and political systems that rely heavily on central planning by a few allegedly smart people, the risk increases that a wrong decision will have far worse impact on the entire country than a network of many states, or cities and towns making similar decisions but whose effects are walled off by political boundaries. The geographic borders of many lower-level government entities act as a natural firewall for bad decisions.

Self-Organizing

Bottom-up and decentralization are important but together not sufficient features of a sustainable democratic republic. Governing at the base of the power pyramid requires immense flexibility. Yes, all the layers of government are bounded by a national constitution, but how do we manage the day-to-day issues of the diverse cities and towns where life is lived? The answer is to allow the base of the power pyramid to be self-organizing. Each diverse component of the base will have cultural idiosyncrasies that only citizens living there will know best what will work and be respected as law. And this can differ significantly from town to town. In the US, some local governments organize as cities, with elected mayors and city councils who create and enforce local ordinances and laws governing diverse issues like real estate development, business licensing, and schools. Other smaller municipalities organize as towns with an elected town council and a greater emphasis on public town meetings. All these local forms must conform to the laws of the state they belong to as well as federal laws.

A great example of self-organization is Visa International Inc., the largest global credit card provider. As of 2018, Visa had 323 million customers, 40 percent more than its nearest competitor. Dee Hock founded the company in 1968 with a list of principles gleaned from a lifetime of observing nature. In his 2005 book, *One from Many*, Hock describes:

> "The amazing thing about Visa was that nobody could find the center of the company. The center was like a non-coercive enabling organization that existed only for the purpose of assisting owner members to fulfill their activities with greater capacity, more effectively, and at less cost."[4]

Hock thought of his company as a "chaordic" organization, which embraced both the chaos of competition and the order of cooperation. In his earlier book,

The Birth of the Chaordic Age, Hock describes the principles behind a chaordic organization:

- It should be equitably owned by all members.
- It must not force uniformity.
- It should be open to all qualified members.
- Power, function, and resources should be distributed as much as possible.
- Authority should be fairly distributed within each governing entity.
- No individual or group should be able to dominate or control decision-making.
- It should introduce, not compel, change.
- It should be flexible yet durable.[5]

At the core of Hock's formula is the organization as an "enabler" rather than "controller." Many effective leadership theories are based on this critical concept. "Lean" is a management practice that seeks to remove constraints and simplify business processes so that they are more efficient. It recognizes that many answers to hard problems come from people on the front lines doing the work, not from people in the front office theorizing about and controlling the work.

Finally, a general principle that should guide the distribution of power is that societal units must be large enough to allow diversity; small enough to encourage community; flexible enough to promote innovation; and strong enough to counterbalance tribalism, globalism, corporatism, and chaos. An architecture such as this must constantly weigh the cost and benefits of scale. We live in a time of multinational corporations, transnational trade agreements, global capital shifts, and near-instantaneous communication. The forces of globalism on one hand and tribalism on the other threaten to pull apart nation-states. Will our democratic response be limited to the United Nations and street protests in Seattle? So given this discussion, here is an updated take on our Power Pyramid in Table

15 showing our existing three-tier governing structure that is right-sized for power at the appropriate levels.

Table 15 – Locally Grown Power Pyramid

Bias to Individual Rights

The most important feature of the US Constitution is the guarantee to its citizens of the right to mostly control their own lives. It accomplishes this by affirming the inherent power previously established in the Declaration of Independence: "Life, Liberty and the pursuit of Happiness." Using that foundation, the Constitution enumerates specific powers to the federal government where the common good takes precedence over individual liberty. It limits federal power by stating all other powers not specifically enumerated automatically inure to the states and individuals. This means that there must be a high bar for government to infringe on any individual right. An example that elegantly exposes the tension between individual rights and the common good is privacy. Although the Constitution contains no express right to privacy, the Bill of Rights addresses relevant aspects including privacy of beliefs through freedom of speech and religious worship in the First Amendment; privacy of the home against forced quartering of soldiers in the Third Amendment; privacy of the person and possessions as against unreasonable searches in the Fourth Amendment; and Fifth Amendment protection against self-incrimination, reflecting the privacy of personal information. In addition, the Ninth Amendment states that the "enumeration of certain rights" in the Bill of Rights "shall not be construed to deny or disparage other rights retained by the people." The meaning of the Ninth Amendment is a bit squishy, but some Supreme Court justices have interpreted the Ninth Amendment as justification for a broad reading of the Bill of Rights to protect privacy in ways not specifically provided in the first eight amendments.

With the rapid incursion of technology into our lives, our personal data is all over the place. Some say there should be no expectation of privacy when you use the internet. However, the federal government, in its exercise of delegated power to "defend the United States against all enemies, foreign and domestic" argues that collection of personal data is essential in detecting and deterring crime and foreign attacks. After all, terrorists and hackers are all using the most advanced technology to attack individuals, companies, and our government. Certainly, citizens have a common interest in protecting against nefarious actors. In the aftermath of the 911 tragedy, the FBI developed software to monitor and analyze our internet traffic. This program, called Carnivore, required telecommunications and internet companies to provide back doors to sweep all digital traffic into a common government-controlled database. Not just the bad guys, but all of us. In 2013, Edward Snowden, a contractor hired by the National Security Agency (NSA), revealed the existence of this program through Wikileaks. He was equally hailed as a patriotic whistleblower and a traitor, but he most certainly violated US espionage laws and remains a fugitive living in Russia. I am conflicted about what to think about Mr. Snowden. On one hand, I am all for transparency and am glad I know that the federal government is collecting all this data on us. On the other hand, the method he used to expose this fact was clearly criminal and most certainly has helped our adversaries evolve their techniques, which endangers us all. At the end of the day law is law, and he should face the consequences of his actions. After he has served his time, maybe we should organize a parade for him.

The government defended its right to collect personal information as part of the enumerated power of common defense. It further qualified that Carnivore was not reading any personal communication unless an individual is the subject of an investigation. In this case, the government must request access to the massive database it already possesses, from the Foreign Intelligence Surveillance (FISA) court. With judges appointed by and overseen by the chief justice of the Supreme Court, the secret FISA court reviews the evidence and either grants or denies access. For many, given the power of technology, it is hard to believe that the database is not being analyzed by the government outside of specific FISA court authorizations. Privacy advocates are rightly concerned that this power to monitor is a slippery slope that could be used to stifle speech or attack citizens for political reasons. It is my opinion that this level of government data collection is not constitutional and is a perfect use case supporting the primacy of individual rights over common good in the gray areas of life. However, there are legitimate concerns on both sides of the issue and a consensus has not yet emerged.

Locally Grown Government supports that when an issue becomes a close struggle between individual rights and the common good, deference should be to the individual rights.

Transparent and Accountable

By most standards, the American political system is the most transparent and accountable in the world. After all, we have open and fair elections that people trust, which permits us to have orderly transitions of power. The freedom of speech guaranteed by the Constitution's First Amendment underpins "the fourth estate," meaning the media. While not formally recognized as part of our political system, the media wields significant influence in shaping public opinion and acting as a check on government power by making some of its activities transparent. Many countries marvel at how Americans "air their dirty laundry" for the rest of the world to see. While some may view this as a sign of weakness, it really is a source of our strength.

Still, in a nation where local, state, and federal government comprises millions of employees and 37 percent of our national GDP, there is much that happens that is neither transparent nor accountable. Now certainly, there are areas like national security where it's not appropriate for activities to be made public, but there is plenty of room where shining a little daylight on government activity will expose corruption and incompetence and enhance efficiency.

Such a powerful and exalted position in American culture also comes with responsibilities. While news organizations and individual journalists often have their own codes of ethics, most share the basic principles of truthfulness, accuracy, objectivity, impartiality, fairness, and public accountability. While enjoying wide latitude to publish what they want, print media still are bounded by libel and slander laws that prevent them from knowingly defaming a person's character and publishing false advertisement. In contrast, broadcast media are regulated by the Federal Communications Commission (FCC) through its licensing power. It can fine broadcasters for violating public decency standards on the air and can even revoke a broadcaster's license, keeping it off the air permanently. The FCC also enforces the following rules for political campaigns.

- The Equal Time Rule, requiring broadcasters to provide equal time to all candidates
- The Right of Rebuttal, requiring broadcasters to provide an opportunity for candidates to respond to criticisms made against them
- The Fairness Doctrine, requiring broadcasters who air a controversial program to provide airtime for opposing views [6]

These are common sense regulations that have been in place since 1934 and have served our country well. They are a good example of the proper role of federal power. However, something changed in 1996. The Communications Decency Act of 1996 included the all-important Section 230, which states: "No provider or user of an interactive computer service shall be treated as the publisher or speaker of any information provided by another information content provider." Silicon Valley lobbied hard for the inclusion of this section, which shields Google, Facebook, and any other "internet company" from liability for what their users post on their platforms. In the early heady growth days of the internet, this seemed like an easy call to foster innovation. However, with Google now representing over 92 percent of the global search engine market [7] and 67 percent of Americans citing social media as an important source of their news, [8] the effects of Section 230 have taken on new meaning. These companies make money from all sorts of horrible, false content produced by some of their users. The Russians famously tried to influence the 2016 election by paying to post "fake news" content on Facebook, Google, and other platforms.

By contrast, traditional news organizations have no such government protections, which has contributed to the reduction of their market share and influence in our society. There are loud voices lined up to decry any levelling of the playing field between traditional news organizations and online platforms. They shout slogans like "

Support Section 230 or kill the internet" [9] or "Kill net neutrality, and you kill the internet." These are classic Hobson's Choices delivered by monopolists and their proxies. The internet isn't going to grind to a halt if we add a little common-sense government regulation to rein in obvious excesses. This is the proper role of government to uphold the common good.

Our principle of bottom-up is a natural support of transparency and accountability. Again, Stanford Professor Larry Diamond elegantly expresses the principle in his 2004 paper, "Why Decentralize Power in a Democracy?"

"When government is closer to the people, it is more likely to be held accountable by them for its successes and failures in the provision of basic services, the maintenance of order, and the fair resolution of local issues and disputes. Government tends to be more responsive when it is closer to the people. That's why democracies are increasingly embracing the principle of subsidiarity: that each government function should be performed by the lowest level of government that is capable of performing that function effectively. Finally, decentralization of power provides an additional check against the abuse of power. Of course, checks and balances are needed within the central government itself. This is why there must be an independent legislative and judiciary, and effective auditing and counter-corruption mechanisms."

Locally Grown Government believes that the duty of transparency and accountability of government extends beyond elections and that the rules governing a free, fair, and truthful press must extend to online information platforms.

Flexible

Species that are flexible and learn from experience survive. Those that aren't don't. Our nation's Founders struck a balance between unchanging natural law principles and the flexibility to adapt, which is readily apparent when you look at the 27 constitutional amendments that proceeded the original document. The amendment process was designed to be a high bar requiring that an amendment be proposed either by the Congress with a two-thirds majority vote in both the House of Representatives and the Senate or by a constitutional convention called for by two-thirds of the state legislatures.

Given the stark divide in American politics these days, it feels like we are overdue for further amendments to clarify the tensions between individual rights and the role of government. I support evidence-based decisions in crafting amendments but recognize that it is ultimately a political process that sometimes can be less than rational. As citizens, we implicitly agree to abide by these new rules because that is itself a form of supporting the common good. Support for new amendments have been gaining in recent years including term limits, mandatory balanced budgets, and clarifying the definition of citizenship. Organizations like the "Convention of States in Action" are working with state legislatures to convene a Constitutional Convention to propose new amendments. As of this writing, a resolution to convene has passed 14 state legislatures with significant support in 10 more states. Thirty-four states are the magic number, and they are organized, growing, and likely to reach the threshold. I can imagine what a raucous affair that might be! [10] *Locally Grown Government holds that the Constitution is sufficiently adaptable to changing circumstances and that a significant backlog of issues has developed to warrant a new Constitutional Convention.*

Sustainable

The first chapter of this book focused on sustainability for good reason. It is at the exact center of all we are talking about. If an idea is not sustainable over the long term, it has little value. We apply the sustainability test to all that government does. Much of this has to do with money and the commitments made over the long term. We have shown in previous chapters how the financial health of our government, at all levels, is getting worse by the year. A continually weakening financial condition will have terrible long-term impacts on all levels of our society. It weakens us economically and invites adversaries to be more aggressive. As Americans, we fancy ourselves as being the "indispensable nation," the world policeman, creator of the post-WWII world order. We are all those things, but that status is not guaranteed forever.

Locally Grown Government considers sustainability as THE most important feature of a well-functioning society.

Evidence-Based Policy Making

Evidence-based decision making is critical to just about every modern discipline from business to baseball to government. Policy should look at the outcomes generated by past decisions to inform future decisions. If the purpose of a government program is to reduce poverty, it should do that. If it doesn't, the policy should be modified or scrapped. The modern effort to cure poverty was born when President Lyndon Johnson declared in his 1964 State of the Union address, "This administration today, here and now, declares unconditional war on poverty in America." Yet according to a 2017 study by the Heritage Foundation, the government has spent $22 trillion of US taxpayer money fighting poverty since 1964. This spending (not including Social Security or Medicare) is three times the cost of all military wars in US history since the American Revolution. And there's been little to show for it. The poverty rate in American was about 15 percent in 1965 and was still at 15 percent in 2014, only recently dropping due to improving economic conditions, according to the US Census. [11] That's a disturbing level of ineffectiveness.

If policy doesn't change in the face of clear evidence that it doesn't work, there must be some other reason why the policy is in place. Unlike the business world, government policy often defies conventional logic. One wonders why politicians ignore the evidence. It follows that the policy must be serving some other goal that's different than what is being publicized. In most instances I am familiar with, those goals are to increase delegate power of a small number of people.

Locally Grown Government highly values evidence-based decision making and past experience, with all its triumphs and tragedies. It is the rich soil from which the new flowers of human progress are grown.

The Double-Bottom Line

Double-Bottom line (DBL) is an idea that extends the conventional bottom line that measures financial performance in business. It adds a second bottom line to measure performance in terms of positive social impact. Besides generating an adequate financial return, many investors look for ways to put money to work contributing to the common good. Things like reducing poverty, increasing affordable housing, improving the environment, improving food quality and availability, and expanding access to clean water are all areas where startup activity is vibrant. Several years ago, the federal government established a new corporate entity called a B-Corp, which must include as part of its mission contributing in a verifiable, transparent, and accountable support for social good that balances profit and purpose. In short, it's doing well while doing good.

An example of a double bottom line company is Plastic Bank, which has developed a blockchain-based software platform that enables exchange of plastic for money, products, or cryptocurrency. This enables recycling around the world and stops the flow of plastic into our oceans while helping people living in poverty build better futures. People collect the plastic and bring it to special recycling centers, where companies pay for the plastic to reuse in manufacturing more plastic products. The company has a sustainable economic model while cleaning up our oceans and providing economic opportunity for those in poverty. [12] That's kind of a triple bottom line, and we should all love those!

In politics, DBL often takes the form of Public-Private Partnerships (PPP) with a wide range of forms varying in the extent of involvement of and risk taken by the private party. The terms of a PPP are typically set out in a contract or agreement to outline the responsibilities of each party and clearly allocate risk. Public utilities are great example of PPPs. They are highly regulated but also protected monopolies that guarantee a stable rate of return for investors while the public gets reasonably priced electrical power. Public infrastructure projects – like highways, airports, and dams – are other examples.

A fast-growing area of venture capital investing is food technology. In 2018, VCs invested over $2 billion in food tech. This has ramped up from less than $100 million in 2008. IWI Life extracts protein from algae and uses it as a healthy food additive. [13]

Safe Traces makes edible bar codes that are embedded in food to pinpoint the sources of tainted food. [14] Apeel creates sprayed-on food wrappers you can eat that triples shelf life to reduce food waste.

Making money while contributing to the common good is good for business.

Locally Grown Government seeks to take advantage of double-bottom line opportunities wherever they exist.

Promote Citizenship and the Common Good

> *Our citizenship*
> *is worthy competition*
> *with our ancestors.*
> – Adapted from Tacitus, Roman historian

Article 14 of the Constitution defines citizens as "All persons born or naturalized in the United States." Pretty straightforward. Either you're born here or you emigrate from another country and go through a "naturalization" process. But what does it mean to be a citizen of the United States of America? If you analyzed the answers from 100 different people, I suspect you'd get a scatterplot with a fair number of outliers but also, hopefully, some convergence around a mean. There would be things like "born in the US," "obligated to fight for our country," "entitled to speak and worship freely," "entitled to own guns," "entitled to vote," "obligated to care for the poor," "entitled to free healthcare and school." In short, a collection of individual rights and obligations. I'm guessing the survey would also show a lot more entitlement or rights than obligations. Some of the answers you'd find in the Constitution and others not so much. The Declaration preamble summarizes inherent rights of citizens: "Among these are Life, Liberty and the pursuit of Happiness." The Constitution's preamble then defines the general features of the common good and a system of government with delegated power to secure these rights.

Despite recent flirtations with trying to invert our sustainable power pyramid, the United States has created more opportunity, wealth, innovation, and rising living standards for a greater number of people than any other country or empire in history. We have immense land mass, incredible natural resources, amazing public infrastructure, the best colleges and universities, and the most powerful military in the world. This all belongs to "we the people." What if we could boil this down to dollars and cents and divide it among all citizens? It's probably an impressive number. To be protected by the strongest military and be able to live freely and pursue your dreams with the greatest resources available is priceless. To those who would rather focus on America's shortcomings, I'd ask them if America is so bad, why are hundreds of thousands of people from other countries trying to cross our borders each year?

But America's success is not possible without the work of millions of citizens. All of us working together in a market-economy creates our GDP; we pay our taxes for the common good and keep the rest for ourselves. The more we get to keep, the more freedom we have. But democracy cannot emerge from the total of our individual wants and desires. For our democratic republic to succeed, we must look beyond ourselves to the common good some of the time.

Common good reflects our aspirations where we dream and search for meaning and band together around shared ideas that reach beyond our lives. We are all born into relationships starting with our families that soon extends to our communities, workplaces, and leisure time. From this, we extract what Robert DeNiro refers to in the film *Meet the Parents* as "the circle of trust." [15] We trust our friends and family who have our backs as we have theirs. A well-functioning democracy also requires these interdependent relationships and circles of trust. These relationships enable us to have civil conversations about how to achieve greater liberty and opportunity. But how are these relationships formed? Not from outside authority, but because we choose to live in relationships with each other. At this point, the political class gets nervous when the common good transitions from an idea to concrete actions by citizens. As a force beyond government control and partisan politics, common good becomes something complex and threatening to the established political order because it belongs to no one and to everyone at once, infusing our relationships with meaning and our politics with hope.

But over the past decades, Americans have increasingly outsourced their inherent power to government. It used to be that elders lived in multi-generational households where they played an important role in providing wisdom and an extra set of hands for daily chores. This created a more cohesive society with most citizens sharing the value of taking care of their elderly parents. Now we increasingly look to government programs like Social Security and Medicare to shoulder the burden. Those costs come from the common good, which increasingly is viewed as "not my pocketbook." Someone else pays theoretically. Many of us view our tax dollars as our sole contribution to the common good and therefore look to the government to do the heavy lifting. This might be workable if everyone paid taxes, but our tax base is getting smaller every year.

In a recent national online poll of 800 full-time college students, respondents were asked for their opinions of capitalism and socialism. While 45 percent said they had a favorable view of capitalism, 31 percent expressed an unfavorable view.[16] Not exactly a ringing endorsement of the property rights that have made the United States the most prosperous nation in history, pulled millions of people out of poverty, and enabled funding of the great universities they attend. What's more, these respondents reported that they felt uncomfortable if their views differed from the political views of their professors if their professors were left leaning.

A 2018 study by Mitchell Langbert, an associate professor of business management at Brooklyn College, reviewed the political party affiliations of nearly 9,000 tenured, Ph.D.-holding professors at 51 of the top 60 liberal arts colleges. It found that there are more than 10 professors affiliated with the Democratic Party for every faculty member who is a registered Republican. A 10-1 ratio. [17] Now whatever your political affiliation, hopefully we can agree that diversity of opinion is essential in our democracy and our schools. If students are only learning one point of view in school and dissenting views are not tolerated, education morphs into indoctrination. This isn't a good model for producing well-informed citizens to maintain a functioning democracy nor is it a model for uncovering the truth.

We need to re-establish the value of citizenship for all. Those who benefit more from the common good should be grateful rather than feeling entitled. Those who earn more should be grateful for living in a country that has provided the opportunity for them to become wealthy. We need to pry a lot of functions of government that used to be performed at the state and local level from the fortified walls of Washington, DC. This shift to performing some government jobs at a lower level will be more visible and appreciated by citizens as they are front and center in their communities. All sectors of the community can get involved and restore relationships that cross social and economic boundaries. As Chicago University professor and philosopher Jean Bethke-Elshtain put it:

> "The common good requires us to agree on at least one shared value; the presumption that one's fellow citizens are people of goodwill who yearn for the opportunity to work together rather than continue to glare at each other across racial, class, and ideological divides."

Locally Grown Government believes citizenship is the most valuable asset on the balance sheet of each American. The freedom to speak, worship, and work as we desire that is guaranteed by our Constitution is unique in the world and the root of our individual and collective success.

Enabling

In my view, a key role of government is being a reasonably transparent archive of important data and basic science. The, EPA, NASA, NOOA, CDC, DOD, and other federal government agencies perform valuable roles as providers of primary research data. This is often provided free of charge to companies that build products from those shared resources. We think this is a great double-bottom line function that should be expanded to include enabling a federally maintained archive of best practices in government so that zip codes and states can learn from each other faster. Using evidence-based decision making, we can identify what the good and bad policies are. Copy the good and delete the bad. Like our brain has been doing with human behavior for a million years. By combining and modernizing the Bureau of Labor Statistics (BLS) and other valuable data sources and adding a collaboration platform for municipalities, government can further enable innovation. We could use new technologies like blockchain to ensure that privacy and security is maintained.

In startup land, we rarely build software from the ground up. Instead, we knit together pre-built code components into interesting new combinations. It would be a poor use of venture capital for a startup to write credit card processing code from scratch when you can simply pull pre-built code from the Open Source Commons, obey the Commons agreements, and be off to the races. We think that federal government can expand its existing role as a basic research archive into an Open Source Commons for state and municipal government software and best practices.

This enabling feature of federal government can foster innovation and growth in all dimensions of life: political, moral, and social, not just economic. Lower levels of elective office can become an arena for training and recruiting new leaders, including women, minorities, and young people who have not previously had a role in public life. And these lower levels of democracy provide a more accessible means for citizens to become active in public affairs. When multiplied across 20,000 cities and towns and 50 states, government can become self-organizing to better serve the common good.

Locally Grown Government believes a key role of sustainable federal government is being an easily accessible repository of data and best practices which enables local and state government to be more effective.

Infuse Public Dialogue with Meaning

When we speak in public, we should do so with some restraint and thought to the kind of society we wish to create. We must look for opportunities to create dialogue and discourse rather than diatribe and disagreement. Argument, yes; empty posturing and mindless sloganeering, no. Over the past couple decades, the tone of public dialogue has grown coarser and more confrontational. It used to be we could agree on the big things and people understood what it meant to be an American citizen. Nowadays, it seems there is a growing faction that believes America is the main problem in the world. They view our history as one of exploitation of people and resources in favor of a wealthy capitalist class and that the main role of government is to equalize the economic outcomes of people as much as possible. Other factions believe the government is the enemy and don't think they should pay taxes that are simply redistributed to others "who don't work hard." Still other factions lament the loss of cultural traditions and believe America's role in maintaining the global order has come at the expense of sovereignty and job losses at home. Political leaders contort themselves trying to appeal to whatever subsets and cross-sections of these factions that can be assembled into a coalition of voters to keep them in power. All of this adds up to a toxic brew where public dialogue devolves into emotional personal attacks rather than informed civil dialogue. If everyone becomes a single-issue voter, our future is pretty grim indeed.

What's needed is a process of working upstream from the myriad of ground-level issues (abortion, race relations, environmental regulations, immigration, taxation) until we arrive at common ground. I propose there is no more important common ground than sustainability because it's in everyone's best interest to survive. What good is making common good promises that are unaffordable and will bankrupt the country in the long term? By the same token, what good is great economic growth if it comes at the expense of having an environment that becomes unlivable? Or having great economic growth but with the benefits inuring to relatively few people so everyone else requires public benefits to make ends meet? Sustainability in all its forms should be something we can agree on, and making sure it drives our public dialogue seems like a good place to start.

Locally Grown Government believes that public dialogue must be infused with shared meaning if our nation is going to heal the political divide.

Promotes Work

What is work? I think most would say something like "the activities we must do to earn money so we can buy things we need to live." In the days before complex society, humans were hunter-gatherers like all the other species on the planet. Over time, we invented agriculture as a better mousetrap to feed everyone. We ate better and more often, and our brains grew ever larger and more complex, storing and analyzing experience to figure out other ways to improve our lot. I'd wager that today most Americans don't have the foggiest notion how to feed themselves outside of a supermarket or restaurant. Relatively very few people hunt or grow food anymore. We pay others to feed us so we can be accountants, lawyers, auto mechanics, computer programmers, and the like. It has all been woven into an efficient virtuous economic matrix yielding tremendous benefits.

In 1962, a US economist named Arthur Okun observed a relationship that states that "for every one percent increase in the unemployment rate, a country's GDP will be roughly two percent lower than its potential GDP." Later coined as

Okun's Law, this shows a virtuous multiplier effect by decreasing unemployment and increasing GDP. [18] His research quantifies what I believe to be self-evident: That productive work is contagious in a good way which also aligns with the evolutionary need to feed, clothe, and house ourselves.

Families are the oldest and most important governmental form. Families form the base of the power pyramid. People in a family should all have a clear view of the common good: loving and doing whatever possible to ensure the health and safety of its members. As such, most activities in family qualify as work, whether explicitly paid or not. Stay-at-home moms and dads are quite busy raising their kids, shuttling them to school and playdates and sports practices and games, volunteering for PTAs and coaching their teams. It's actual work and it's not paid. Caring for elderly parents is not paid but critical, nonetheless. We can easily see the value of this work in the marketplace when we try to outsource it. Elder care is a $400 billion industry growing over 6 percent annually,[19] while childcare is a $38 billion industry growing at a similar rate.[20] This is certainly work and it's valuable, and I don't know too many old citizens who wouldn't prefer being cared for by their kids in a family home setting or children who wouldn't rather be with their parents than a day care center with strangers.

But work provides another critical benefit to each of us and society at large. It represents the primary source of self-esteem. Accomplishing something others recognize as valuable builds us up, gives us confidence, gives us status, makes us feel important, and plugs us into the greater social network. People who are disabled or unemployed for a long period of time have higher rates of depression, substance abuse, and illness compared to those who work. Older people who continue working or actively volunteer rather than retiring to a sedentary life tend be healthier with lower rates of dementia. Think of all the excess capacity we could unlock if we could mobilize our elderly. It might be the mother of all double-bottom line events. Society gets tremendous experience while bending the cost curve for healthcare and proliferating the generational knowledge that is often lost as our institutions change over time.

We are social creatures, and work requires interacting with others, learning new things, and solving new problems. Whether you're a janitor, carpenter, lawyer, waitress, or Fortune 500 CEO, work is a primary source of self-esteem. This is as it should be. You cannot replace honest work with a handout and expect to get the same result either individually or in the greater society. The chants for universal basic income by a growing cadre of politicians are mistaken if they believe it will be an uplifting phenomenon in our country. There are better ways to attack income inequality than taking away the opportunity and pride that only comes from being a self-sustaining citizen. Anyone who tells you different is misinformed.

None of this is to say that Locally Grown Government principles don't include an effective social safety net to raise those less fortunate out of poverty. We simply believe that it should not be provided primarily by government, and we will provide some alternatives later in this book. Before there was ever government welfare, there was a robust network of private charitable and religious institutions that provided an effective safety net. Institutions like the YMCA, Salvation Army, Goodwill Industries, and Habitat for Humanity are still more effective than government programs.

The early 20th century preacher William J. H. Boetcker said it best in his 1916 pamphlet entitled "The Ten Cannots":

- You cannot bring about prosperity by discouraging thrift.
- You cannot strengthen the weak by weakening the strong.
- You cannot help the wage earner by pulling down the wage payer.
- You cannot further the brotherhood of man by encouraging class hatred.
- You cannot help the poor by destroying the rich.
- You cannot keep out of trouble by spending more than you earn.
- You cannot build character and courage by taking away man's initiative and independence.
- You cannot help men permanently by doing for them what they could and should do for themselves. [21]

Locally Grown Government promotes work as essential to life and the source of human dignity. To be more successful, charities, government, and private sector business must work together to include a work component within safety net programs. We cannot deprive people of their dignity.

Harness Excess Capacity

Excess capacity is an economics concept used to describe a situation where a company is producing at a lower output than it has been designed for. For growth companies, like the startups I've been involved with, you intentionally build excess capacity because you expect the market demand will be there. For mature companies, not having enough capacity to meet demand is something you want to avoid. You can't sell what you don't have, and being constantly in a backorder eventually turns off customers and they buy elsewhere. Economists refer to excess capacity as "slack" when referring to the collective economy. Eventually, excess capacity over the longer term indicates a poorly managed company that probably won't last long.

Excess capacity as it pertains to individuals is not usually good or bad. If you own a car, you aren't driving it all the time. According to the American Automobile Association (AAA), Americans spend about 13 percent of their daily time in a car. That's a little over three hours. The rest of the time the car is idle. Uber and Lyft have figured out how to grow multibillion-dollar business using this excess capacity. Airbnb has harnessed the excess capacity of people's homes and apartments to generate revenue for owners. Business schools teach courses on identifying and monetizing excess capacity. In my opinion, the most valuable and ubiquitous reservoir of excess capacity in our nation is our elder population.

There is no doubt we are racing toward a future with a lot more elderly. According to the US Census, 2035 will mark the first time in our nation's history that the number of people 65 years or older will exceed the number of people 18 years or younger. [22] This might come as a shock to a nation that has fancied itself a hub of youth and opportunity, but America mirrors a global trend where people are simply not getting married or having babies at the same rate as previous generations. In wealthier nations with rising expectations, the cost of raising and educating children has risen much faster that the ability to pay for them. This is becoming a massive problem in most of the developed world where countries have made significant financial promises to old people with the expectations that young workers will continue to work and pay taxes to finance them. This is setting us up for a future dominated by fights over declining resources between the old and the young.

Without diminishing the challenge, there are reasons to be optimistic because the needs and capabilities of the generations are complementary. Evolutionary developmental psychology is a field of study that applies the basic principles of evolution to understand the development of human behavior. Researchers in this field believe that old and young are designed to help each other. As people age, they have a strong desire to be needed and wanted, especially by young people. Just ask any grandparent. They want to be wanted. They have a desire to protect, nurture, and guide younger people. The earliest evidence of religion in humans came in the form of ancestor worship where ancient Mesopotamian cultures began to bury their dead, in many cases near their living quarters. The elders of the tribe were keepers of the tradition, the human databases that passed on wisdom to the youth. Grandmothers especially played a key role in helping with childrearing and daily chores. Old people balance the selfishness of children as they pass on virtues like patience and emotional control to ensure the next generation survives and prospers. In exchange, younger people respect and revere their elders both in their life and after their death. At least, this is how it's supposed to work.

Despite the seemingly powerful fit between the needs of the old and the young, the connections required for this to work seem to be mostly broken in our current age. The primary means of communication between young people these days is digital. Instagram and Snapchat are private rooms with "Adults not welcome" signs on the door. Meanwhile, most octogenarian grandparents have neither the ability nor desire to communicate in that fashion. As of this writing, I watch as the Democratic Party is birthing its own version of the GOP Tea Party with mind-blowing speed. Rep. Ocasio-Cortez is posing a legitimate threat to the elder leadership of her party. Nancy Pelosi, the 78-year-old Speaker of the House, has been in politics for

31 years and has fewer Twitter followers than Rep. Ocasio-Cortez, who has been in politics for about a year. She is shouting down Pelosi as she and her colleagues seek power. That doesn't seem like respect for one's elders.

And who can blame her? Mrs. Pelosi's generation has built the wall between old and young on the back of our government budgets. Pensions and elder healthcare programs account for almost 38 percent of our entire spending across all levels of government. And these programs are growing much faster than our economy and the rate of inflation. The older generation has glorified the dream of retirement and is moving from their hometowns for the sun and fun of Florida, Arizona, and the Carolinas and they expect younger workers to pay for it.

It didn't use to be like this. Until the early 20th century, most Americans lived in multi-generational households. People were not nearly as conscious of age since everyone had a job to do in the household and was respected for that job. Grandma and Grandpa were simply members of the nuclear family, not an occasional visitor that their grandchildren roll their eyes at as they return to the cultural wasteland of their digital devices. As the eldest of six children from a father who was the youngest of 11 children of Italian immigrants, I remember the multi-generation household. We all worshipped my grandparents, who deserved our adoration. They were better than we were, and we knew it.

So how can we harness this great excess capacity resource of our aging population? Elder citizens own the majority of household wealth in America not to mention a firm claim on 39 percent (and growing) of the nation's tax revenue between Social Security and Medicare. That's where the money is. They also possess great knowledge, which they are willing to share freely with nearly anyone who asks. But nobody is asking. Imagine the value we could unlock for society if we could reconnect the ancient bond between generations by unlocking this excess capacity of knowledge, money, and compassion?

Singapore provides a working example, harnessing the excess

capacity of the elderly. As described by the Civil Service College of Singapore, the country has taken a holistic approach to an aging society by creating a "Kampong for all ages." The project invests in multi-generational villages that support seniors as continuing participating members of society. There are multi-generational living quarters adjacent to playgrounds and schools where seniors and children interact. They enlist a host of stakeholders to ensure fast-track zoning requirements and access to capital for these environments. [23] There are similar projects popping up in the US such as Gorham House in Portland, Maine, an assisted living community built in proximity to schools and playgrounds where the community shares healthcare and other services. [24]

In 2016, two MIT grads founded Nesterly with a mission to "tackle the two big challenges of housing affordability and aging in place with one simple solution." The company pairs elder homeowners with spare rooms in their house with university students who need affordable housing. The students get reduced rent by helping the elder homeowners with household chores.[25] In Florida where I live, there are many ad hoc relationships like this already. I moved my family from Jackson, Wyoming, to Florida to help my parents and am so lucky that my wife Kati was happy to do this with me. Yet another example of me punching way above my weight when I convinced her to marry me.

In his book *How to Live Forever: The Enduring Power of Connecting the Generations*, author Marc Freedman sums it up nicely.

> "Of all the things that divide us, the gap between old and young is arguably the most bridgeable. Connecting across generations is not only pragmatic, it's an essential part of the human experience and a key to the cycle of life. After all, the young will soon be the old – likely faster than they ever imagined."

Locally Grown Government believes there is massive societal value to unlock by harnessing the excess capacity of our elder citizens.

Bias to Simplification

One of the important lessons in business I've learned happened in my 40s from a guy I hired to run my company, Enservio. When Bain Capital invested in Enservio, they reached out to one of its alumni (they have a large and fantastic network) who had cofounded and sold a company in the insurance space. Unbeknownst to me, Jon McNeill began checking my client references through the back door. Thankfully, companies like The Hartford and MetLife waxed eloquent about our products, and Bain Capital Ventures led our Series A funding round. Shortly thereafter, Mike Krupka, the managing partner at Bain and an Enservio board member, mentioned that Jon was a big skier like us and had a place near Sugarbush Mountain in Vermont. He wanted to meet me. Any chance to ski I was down for, so Jon and I met, and we hit it off immediately. Shortly after our connection, I realized Jon was a better guy than me to scale the company. It made perfect sense that I could continue my R&D work and Jon would be CEO. This was another huge business lesson for me. Don't let pride stand in the way of accomplishing your goal. Let the best decision rise to the top, especially when it comes to making money! I like to say that Jon was the smartest person I ever hired and the best boss I've ever worked for. Enservio has since been acquired and Jon moved on to run Sales for Tesla and then, most recently, to Lyft as their COO.

Early in his tenure at Enservio, Jon introduced the concept of Lean into our company. For those not familiar with it, Lean emerged as a popular and effective business process optimization discipline that focuses on eliminating waste in the process of delivering a product or a service. It's the art of simplification, just like haiku. The first serious practitioner of Lean (though it wasn't an organized methodology then) was Henry Ford with his innovative auto assembly line. Just after WWII, Toyota founder Kiichiro Toyoda observed Ford's success and started to coalesce those observations into a set of principles that he instilled at Toyota, which went on to become one of the world's largest and most profitable auto companies.

In 1996, James Womack and Daniel Jones further distilled the methodology in their book *Lean Thinking*. Fundamentally, Lean is the process of removing production constraints and waste. Waste muddies up the water. Removing it makes things clearer, easier to see. It finds the shortest distance between two points, which is kind of common sense but in an organized, disciplined, repeatable way. With Lean, everyone on the "production line" is integral to the process.[26] In fact, the workers run the process and are constantly on the lookout for waste in production. Lean was a wild success at Enservio, making us profitable much faster, with better customer service and a great team culture that resulted from it. We also ran our software team using Agile, a Lean version for engineering teams. Here are the key easy-to-understand principles of Lean as distilled in the book *Lean Thinking*:

- Specify the value desired by the customer.
- Identify the value stream for each product, providing that value and challenge all of the steps necessary to provide it.
- Identify and remove wasted steps.
- Make the product flow continuously through the remaining value-added steps.
- Introduce pull between all steps where continuous flow is possible.
- Manage toward perfection so that the number of steps and the amount of time and information needed to serve the customer continually falls.

One could only imagine how powerful Lean would be if we applied it to government at all levels. Let's just start with the rampant functional overlap between various federal government departments. Take the Department of Agriculture, whose mission is to regulate and support farms.

Over 70 percent of its budget goes to food programs for the poor like food stamps. It also spends over $6 billion on forestry, which you would think would be better situated in the Department of the Interior. It also spends $1.4 billion on rural rental subsidies, another welfare program.[27] Shouldn't that be situated in the Department of Housing and Urban Development?

There is no better place to focus a Lean exercise than with entitlement programs since we spend 67 percent (and rising) of our entire federal budget on these. It follows that we should add to that amount two-thirds of the interest of national debt, which consumes six percent of the budget (and rising). So, 71 percent of our entire federal budget goes to transfer payments to more than 50 percent of Americans.[28] Between the math of automatic increases and our national demographics, entitlement spending is the storm that will sink our ship if left unchanged.

Let's just start with direct subsidy programs for the poor. Medicaid, food stamps, cash welfare, rental subsidies, and earned-income tax credits are run by different cabinet departments. They all have differing eligibility cutoffs, which can interact with one another and cause poor Americans to face marginal-tax rates of 95 percent in some cases. Just eliminating the duplication of programs from where they logically belong would save a ton of overhead. Service would improve and we would get better reporting transparency from avoiding having to pull numbers buried in many departments. Some might argue that this lack of transparency is a feature, not a bug, designed by politicians to obfuscate true costs and accountability. The ability to simplify is a treasured skill. Those who can make products that are easy to use, present ideas that are easy to understand, and simplify processes are valuable people in our society. They make a difference almost everywhere they go, and usually make plenty of money along the way.

Locally Grown Government believes that the shortest distance between two points is a straight line. Simplifying complexity is a mission that produces exponential benefits to stakeholders.

Win-Win Negotiation Is a Lost Art

A win-win agreement is where the parties reach a deal after considering each other's interests and each party gets as much benefit as possible when considering opposing views. Nobody gets everything they want but each party gets some of what they want. Doing this effectively is another super-power along with being a simplifier and a positive enabler. Great negotiators are highly prized people. Unfortunately, it's becoming a lost art, especially in politics where it's needed most.

Notice I prefaced negotiation with "win-win." There are myriad examples of negotiations that have happened that were great for one party but not the other. I've witnessed these from both sides of the table during my career. But relationships get damaged when one side finds out they were taken advantage of. It's not a sustainable long-term practice because people of this ilk get a reputation that ultimately hurts their long-term prospects. Here are some simple principles for win-win negotiation.

Win-win requires real effort to understand the other side's motivations, interests, emotions, priorities, lines in the sand, etc. That means each side needs to be reasonably open about what they want. Bad deals happen when there is information asymmetry, where one party has better information than the other.

Win-win requires that both sides operate in good faith. This means you actually intend to do a deal. We've seen many times in politics where one political party pretends like they want a deal but really have some ulterior motive where "no or yes" is a foregone conclusion. They want to be seen as willing to negotiate to improve their appeal to voters. A good example of this is immigration policy. Both sides of the aisle pay lip service to wanting reform but won't budge on any key points because they see value in keeping it as an election issue. If I am going to say "no" to everything you want, that's not really a negotiation. Win-win requires each side to prioritize their list of "wants" and the list of "wants" of the other party. This requires good-faith discovery with the other party.

Win-win requires both parties to assign weights to their priorities. Once these prioritized lists have been weighted, it becomes somewhat a matter of math to determine the optimal outcome for both sides. I would argue that this is the only principle that doesn't require full transparency. Each side should be biased to the best deal for them. The ranking allows each party to compare bundles of priorities against each other to find the right combination that works best for them. Personally, I am a Pareto guy. If I can get 80 percent of what I want, that's my deal-making sweet spot.

Finally, you cannot be afraid to walk away. No deal is better than a bad deal. If possible, always agree to meet again if circumstances change.

Locally Grown Government considers win-win negotiating to be a core skill needed by leaders in all dimensions of our society, especially in politics.

CHAPTER 7

Locally Grown Is Technology Driven

*AI will rule us
if we let it, so let's not.
Let's use tech wisely.*

Technology is a locally grown principle important enough to warrant its own chapter because it is driving the arc of history in a way that must be addressed. No one can argue that science and technology has been a major contributor to our evolution. From the first stone tools to control fire, domestication of animals, agriculture, medicine, and creation of industrial machines, we have used technology to become the most dominant species on the planet. Our growth finally spiked during the Industrial Revolution of the 19th century and has continued that exponential growth curve with the advent of the digital revolution of the past 60 years. Now, we can create software algorithms that mimic some human thinking behavior, learn from that behavior, then modify itself to achieve better outcomes. AI has become a technology that sparks human imagination as we see a future where we coexist with intelligent machines. Apple uses AI to power its voice-recognition software, SIRI. Google and Amazon use AI to predict what products you're interested in or where you might like your next vacation to be. AI applications are also proving to be groundbreaking in the fields of investing and medicine, and it seems that no industry is immune from its effects. AI promises to create solutions to some of humanity's most difficult problems, but there is a growing community of technologists and thinkers also warning of a dark side to AI.

One of the best-known critics is tech entrepreneur Elon Musk, who calls AI systems "the biggest risk we face as a civilization," comparing AI to "summoning the demon." He fears that when humans create self-improving AI programs whose intelligence dwarfs our own, we will lose the ability to understand or control them. Another famous tech venture capitalist and early Facebook investor, Roger McNamee, has just written a new book, *Zucked: Waking Up to the Facebook Catastrophe*, where he asserts that Facebook's usage of customer data and its algorithmic methods of keeping users engaged has created an addictive brew that is toxic to our culture. Many famous Silicon Valley entrepreneurs significantly limit the screen time for their kids at home and educate them at places like the Steiner-Waldorf school that don't allow technology into the classroom until age 12. These tech icons create some of the most disruptive technologies in human history, create trillions of dollars of wealth in the process, but are wary of overexposure for their own children. What do they know that we don't?

In his recent book, *Sapiens: A Brief History of Humankind*, historian and author Yuval Noah Harari states that an interesting feature of AI is that it effectively centralizes decision making. He is another voice in the pessimist camp who feels that "Homo sapiens as we know them will disappear in a century or so." Pretty grim outlook but hard to argue with as we see the growth of AI in places like China. From his book:

"Democracy processes information in a distributed way. It distributes information and the power to make decisions among many institutions, organizations and individuals. Dictatorships, on the other hand, concentrate or attempt to concentrate all the information and power in one place. Given the technology of the 20th century, this was very inefficient. Nobody could process the information fast enough and make good decisions, and this is one of the main reasons why the Soviet Union lagged far behind the United States. AI and machine learning might swing the pendulum in the direction of centralized systems. Think about the revolution in genetics. The United States may not be allowed to build a medical database of all US citizens, for reasons of privacy, individualism and human rights. But if China builds a national genetic database and enters all the medical records, school records and everything about all its people, they could make breakthroughs in genetic research." [1]

Imagine China, with a long history of human rights abuses, being the world leader in AI. It's hard to conceive a future of intelligent Chinese Terminators ravaging our planet, but AI will disrupt our economic and political systems, nonetheless. Then again, with the help of America's most powerful tech companies the Chinese may just well achieve their objective of global hegemony. Google, for example, has publicly and loudly refused to use its resources to help the US Defense Department but instead is helping the Chinese government better monitor and oppress its citizens. I find this unconscionable for a company whose motto is "Do no evil."

As more jobs and industries fall victim to AI, the income inequality gap will only get worse. However, many historians suggest that out of the ashes of economic destruction rises the phoenix of whole new categories of jobs and productivity gains that have always created societal benefits that far outweigh the costs. The steam engine and electrification created more jobs than they destroyed, by breaking down the job of one worker into smaller tasks that could be performed by many other workers in the assembly line. Still, it is difficult to compare those innovations with the scale of what happens when AI is deployed more fully in our global economy. The AI revolution will dwarf the Industrial Revolution since it replaces both cognitive and physical labor and does so rapidly across a global digital ecosystem.

In an essay adapted from his book, *AI Superpowers: China, Silicon Valley and the New World Order*, author Dr. Kai-Fu Lee adds to the bleak outlook for society as artificial intelligence proliferates:

"We can't know the precise shape and speed of AI's impact on jobs, but the broader picture is clear. This will not be the normal churn of capitalism's creative destruction, a process that inevitably arrives at a new equilibrium of more jobs, higher wages and better quality of life for all. Many of the free market's self-correcting mechanisms will break down in an AI economy. The 21st century may bring a new caste system, split into a plutocratic AI elite and the powerless struggling masses. Recent history has shown us just how fragile our political institutions and social fabric can be in the face of disruptive change. If we allow AI economics to run their natural course, the geopolitical tumult of recent years will look like child's play. On a personal and psychological level, the wounds could be even deeper. Society has trained most of us to tie our personal worth to the pursuit of work and success. In the coming years, people will watch algorithms and robots easily outmaneuver them at tasks they've spent a lifetime mastering. I fear that this will lead to a crushing feeling of futility and obsolescence. At worst, it will lead people to question their own worth and what it means to be human." [2]

Despite the dystopian future warned by some, count me in the optimist camp. While I think there is definitely a need for legislation to protect consumer privacy and healthy market dynamics, I believe technology will continue to improve human life in ways we cannot imagine now. Most experts think it will take decades for AI to be able to handle a meaningful chunk of the myriad tasks performed by humans. Simple human tasks like facial recognition and understanding human gestures and emotions are extremely difficult problems for AI. While there is no doubt that repetitive jobs and many knowledge jobs will disappear as AI is applied to them, there are many jobs AI won't replace. Work like corporate strategy, product design, caring for the elderly, teaching children, and construction. Jobs that require empathy and caring, such as therapy and home healthcare, are unlikely to be disrupted by AI. AI will not replace well-paid trade jobs like plumbers and electricians. There is a long list of jobs that will survive AI.

There are suggestions for some form of Universal Basic Income (UBI) to replace lost livelihoods of AI victims. This appeals to many Silicon Valley folks who look for technical solutions to messy social problems while they continue to build software products that make themselves rich.

Andrew Yang was a 2020 Democratic presidential candidate who's "Freedom Dividend" proposed paying $1,000 per month to all US citizens over 18. He would pay for it with a value-added-tax of 10% along with consolidating some existing social programs.[3] At least he is trying to pay for it by transforming some of the existing social safety net. Still, UBI feels anathema to a country like American built on the value of work both as the source of economic prosperity and individual self-esteem. A better solution is to pay citizens for jobs that are often unpaid that enrich our communities such as elder and childcare. These jobs are typically performed by family members for other nuclear and extended family members out of love and empathy. We have already established how important morality has been to human development so why not celebrate moral behavior in the most recognized way possible in a capitalist society? Pay the people. This can supplement or replace already established volunteer channels.

Job destruction by automation has always existed and will always exist. As long as markets remain open and free, competition will continue to be the great leveler that replaces tech companies that might seem unassailable. Remember how we thought of AOL, Yahoo, eBay, Netscape 20 years ago? The FAANG companies are not impervious to competition. Technology will continue to unleash new human potential and could be the basis of a new social contract where it continues to work for us rather than the other way around. Let's wade a little deeper into some specific examples of ways that technology can help.

Tough problem to solve?
Ten heads are better than one.
The wisdom of crowds.

If you have a hard problem to solve, do you think you have a better chance of solving it with a hundred smart people working on it or just five smart people working on it? In his book *Politics*, written 2,400 years ago, Greek philosopher Aristotle was probably the first person to recognize the "wisdom of crowds." I paraphrase:

> "It is possible that the many, though maybe not individually good men, when they come together to be better, collectively, just as with public dinners to which many contribute, are better than those supplied at one man's cost." [4]

Crowdsourcing provides a platform for users to collectively work to solve problems, often by breaking them into smaller tasks. Wikipedia is one example of a crowdsource information platform that permits users to curate and publish regular content while holding the community responsible for quality and accuracy. Here's Wikipedia describing its own operating model:

> "The wisdom of the crowd is the collective opinion of a group of individuals rather than that of a single expert. A large group's aggregated answers to questions involving quantity estimation, general world knowledge, and spatial reasoning has generally been found to be as good as, and often superior to, the answers from any of the individuals in the group." [5]

In recent years, crowdsourcing has taken hold as an important technology business model. Websites like Kickstarter and GoFundMe focus on raising money from many smaller individual investors for startups and nonprofit ideas. Phylo is a company that combines crowdsourcing and gamification to help genetic disease researchers. Juries are a form of crowdsourcing whereby a diverse group of people, after hearing legal evidence presented at a trial, will usually make a better decision than a single judge or juror.

Our Founders knew something about the wisdom of crowds as they constructed our Constitution and bottom-up government. They knew you have a better chance for wiser and more responsive government addressing the needs of its people when it is done at the state and local level. However, the steady upward flow of power from the many to the few in our federal government is exactly the opposite of crowdsourcing. It concentrates decision-making with a few politicians. If the federal government is operating within its constitutional boundaries, this form of centralized decision making is efficient and necessary to maintain our republic. However, as the federal government does more that it should, we run the risk of poor decision-making because we leave out too many smart minds from the process.

The Federal Reserve System is case and point. Created in 1913, it has been allowed to control an increasing portion of our economy. It is a private company, not a true part of our government, and has a monopoly on creating and controlling the money supply for the most powerful nation on earth. It has limited accountability to the government that created it; Fed governors are appointed every four years and there isn't a lot of turnover. Now granted these are very smart people. They collect massive amounts of economic data in their efforts to understand our economy and control inflation and maximize employment. They are making decisions every quarter that affect interest rates and the actions of other central banks around the world. Despite all this intellectual firepower and monetary tools at their disposal, they represent a tiny fraction of all the smart people on the planet who engage in financial transactions every day. They also have a terrible record of predicting and preventing economic recessions and depressions. A common joke is: "The Fed has predicted nine of the last five recessions." The point is that if you concentrate most decision making with small, homogenous groups, you are almost guaranteed suboptimal decision making. We can apply crowdsourcing technology to help solve a host of social challenges starting with the biggest challenge of all: shifting a large chunk of our federal government functions to the many states and municipalities.

> *Blockchain is really*
> *just tokenized consensus.*
> *Let's restore the trust.*

The founder (or group of founders) of Bitcoin, Satoshi Nakamoto, created the first cryptocurrency in response to the 2008 Financial Crisis and the failure of government central banks. In October 2008, Nakamoto published his paper, *Bitcoin: A Peer-to-Peer Electronic Cash System.* In January 2009, he launched the software network, and the first units of the cryptocurrency, called Bitcoins, were created or "mined." The general technical architecture of Bitcoin is called blockchain, which allows digital information to be distributed but not copied. [6]

For millennia, the value of money was always been tied to something reasonably scarce like gold and silver. But when President Nixon decoupled the US dollar from gold in 1971, the dawn of modern fiat money began. The Bitcoin founder was skeptical of fiat money (e.g., US dollars, Euro, Yuan) that could simply be printed anytime, giving the government's immense power to "inflate" their currencies to more easily pay their debts while unintentionally eroding the value of people's savings. His Bitcoin solution limited the total supply to 21 million, and to date about 15 million Bitcoins have been mined with the math puzzles that need to be solved to acquire them, getting increasingly more difficult with each new coin. The last of the 21 million Bitcoin should be mined sometime around 2065 at the current mining rate.

This limited supply created the scarcity effect Nakamoto believed was a required feature of a stable currency long-term. The utility of a global digital currency with a fixed circulation that is cryptographically secure, anonymous, and convertible to any fiat currency was an alluring proposition for speculative investors beginning in 2016, and they started piling in. Being able to store wealth on a thumb drive that was essentially untraceable by governments seemed a lot easier than moving around other such assets like gold and fine art. However, as the price bubbled up to a frothy $17,549 per Bitcoin in late 2017, it began to look more like the 17th century Dutch Tulip investment bubble rather than a stable currency alternative. At this point, governments started to pay more attention to cryptocurrency as a potential disruptive force, and some like China began to crack down. In the US, the SEC has stepped in to declare cryptocurrencies would be taxed on capital gains and losses the same as any asset class. These events collectively pricked the bubble and, as of this writing, the price of Bitcoin and most other cryptos became volatile in early 2019. Still, Bitcoin's value has risen from a few pennies in 2010 to $10,368 as of August 1, 2019, demonstrating that, at least as an asset class, it is here to stay. Table 16 shows how the value of Bitcoin has changed since it was created.

Table 16 – Bitcoin Price Over Time

Despite the growth of cryptocurrencies in a short period of time, the real value of Nakamoto's groundbreaking idea is the blockchain infrastructure that undergirds these systems. Think of the blockchain as a spreadsheet that is copied many times across a network of computers where the spreadsheet is regularly updated. If I changed something on my spreadsheet, the network automatically updates all the other spreadsheets on the network. However, before my changes are accepted, all the other computers collectively validate my identity, and if at least 51 percent of the computers cannot verify who I am, my changes are not updated. It is almost impossible for the blockchain to be corrupted because it would require a huge amount of computing power to override the entire network. Corrupting the network would have the effect of destroying the value of the information it contains. This is a kind of "mutually assured destruction" for networks.

So, a key feature of the blockchain is crowd-sourced encrypted security. This method of using a network has clear benefits. The blockchain database isn't stored in any single location so there is no single point of failure and no centralized information exists for a hacker to attack. Hosted by thousands of computers simultaneously, its data is accessible to anyone on the web. Since it was created in 2009, the Bitcoin blockchain has operated without significant disruption. None of the small performance problems have been due to hacking or mismanagement. The internet has been quite robust for nearly 30 years, a track record that bodes well for blockchain technology as it continues to develop.

One drawback of blockchain is the extremely high energy consumption by the vast arrays of computer servers required to support the network, which is why most large blockchain companies operate in geographies with low energy costs, but there are innovations that are being developed that make the algorithms more efficient and in turn less expensive to operate. Another typical drawback of blockchains is that the rate of transaction throughput is slow relative to other types of validated transaction. For example, the Visa network processes credit card transactions more than 20 times faster than Bitcoin, a limitation that will prevent it from being a true currency. However, there are a number of other cryptocurrencies like Ethereum that are working on technical modifications that will make it much faster.

Blockchain is an institutional technology more than the typical information technology. Unlike platforms like Facebook and Google that are designed to exploit the personal data of its users, the blockchain starts with an assumption of privacy. This is a simple but hugely important difference. This means most of our current centralized infrastructure can be replicated in terms of functionality but can be decentralized using blockchain. Users starting with a presumption of privacy could enable a reorganization of society and economy. This feature of blockchain can enable new Decentralized Autonomous Organizations (DAO). Organizations within society rarely operate in isolation but rather function as parts of ecosystems with societal benefits created by the flow of value throughout the ecosystem. It's not Samsung that delivers our mobile phones; it's a huge, globally collaborative supply chain. In contrast to our current institutions, the blockchain optimizes value within the entire ecosystem, offering a much greater value for society.

Blockchain Is Already Being Implemented by Government

It's not only the private sector that is hopping on the blockchain bandwagon; governments see the possibility to make themselves more efficient and responsive to their citizens. Estonia was the first country to use blockchain at a national level with their E-Citizenship program to create their own identity system. The results have been impressive with increased citizen satisfaction and trust and bureaucratic efficiency. Now almost all public services in Estonia are digitized and accessed through secure digital identities. For example, Estonians have their healthcare registry on the cloud, where they can log in and see when medical professionals have looked at their data. Any government official that accessed their data improperly can be prosecuted. Plus, their entire medical record is available to them. [7]

India has introduced a nationwide centralized ID database and largely eliminated physical currency. They started by introducing the Aadhaar biometric database that gave 95 percent of the population a digital proof of identity (POI) in 2016. This also provided identity to a lot of people in India who were without any ID. Any person without an ID could receive an Aadhaar ID if another person already registered with Aadhaar vouched for the person's existence. This provides those who previously had no ID the ability to get mobile phones and open bank accounts.[8]

The state of Illinois launched a pilot trial of a blockchain-based registry system for secure personal identities. They partnered with a blockchain startup company, Hashed Health, through the Illinois Blockchain Initiative in order to streamline the process of issuing and tracking medical licenses. The state of Arizona passed legislation in early 2018 to authorize acceptance of cryptocurrencies for payment of taxes.[9] Other states are exploring similar legislation as well as applications of blockchain tech within their operations.

Facebook Tries to Replace VISA as the Biggest Payment Platform on Earth

Having worked in Silicon Valley during the Web 1.0 Dotcom boom, Bitcoin's price volatility kind of felt the same to me. Just like the Dotcom bubble bursting created tons of carnage (including the startup I worked for), there were astounding technologies and companies that rose from the ashes that have literally changed our world. Some of those early internet companies like Google and PayPal are quietly investing (and Facebook not so quietly) in cryptocurrency and other blockchain projects. Like those disruptive companies of Web 1.0, I believe blockchain technologies will be equally disruptive and we are in the early innings.

Facebook's introduction of its Libra crypto is further confirmation to me that blockchain is here to stay. The company is positioning Libra as a new global payment system that will be more like PayPal than Bitcoin. In fact, PayPal is one of over 24 partners that includes Visa, Mastercard, and Coinbase. While Libra is technically a cryptocurrency, it is different in that a group of 100 corporate partners will invest $10 million each so that the cryptocurrency is backed by $1 billion hard money to start. Also different is that transactions will be validated on the blockchain by a centralized governing body, the Libra Association, rather than the much larger anonymous distributed network of miners on the Bitcoin platform. This makes Libra a hybrid blockchain. Facebook's base of 2.4 billion active users gives Libra tremendous global reach right out of the gate. However, Congress and others, including me, have their doubts about Libra, especially given Facebook's mishandling of user data and privacy. We will see.

Other Blockchain Opportunities

Here are some other examples of blockchain-enabled institutional support of inherent power already underway:

- *Sharing Economy:* By enabling peer-to-peer payments, blockchain enables direct interactions between people without intermediaries, resulting in a decentralized sharing economy.
- *Crowdfunding:* Crowd-sourced venture capital funds.
- *Supply Chain Auditing:* The distributed ledger is an easy way to certify the provenance of products and their components. Think ethical diamonds – and authentic organic food.
- *Social Networks:* Instead of Google and Facebook harvesting all the financial value of the personal information we share and content we create, cryptocurrencies can compensate the creators and user for sharing. People can finally gain control of their personal information and decide who and when to share it with and be compensated accordingly. This acts like a form of royalty payments similar to what exists in the entertainment industry.
- *Prediction Markets:* Wisdom of the Crowd applications will compensate contributors for successful outcomes.

- *Protection of Intellectual Property:* Smart Contracts can protect copyright and automate the sales of creative works online, eliminating the risk of infringement.
- *Identity Management:* Authentic, digital, irrefutable, secure proof of who you are. Think of the efficiencies that can be harvested with this capability in the global economy.
- *Registry of Deeds:* Blockchain is tailor made for securely managing property titles and mortgages.
- *Philanthropy:* American individuals, estates, corporations, and foundations gave a total of US $410 billion in 2017 to nonprofits, faith-based organizations, and other charities, according to the Giving USA 2018 report. [10] Accountability has become a critical component of giving. Blockchain can provide donors end-to-end visibility of how their gifts are being used and how effective they are.
- *Volunteering:* There are so many important jobs performed in our society that are not compensated. People who volunteer their time do so for reasons other than financial gain, which typically reflects their religious or ethical beliefs. It is the ultimate embodiment of the common good when people volunteer their time. Unfortunately, only 25 percent of us donate time at least once per year. Imagine a volunteering app where you could compensate people with cryptocurrency for their volunteer efforts. From adult caregivers to their elderly parents, to helping build a Habitat for Humanity house, to working at the local food pantry, imagine how transformative for society it would be if we could double volunteering to 50 percent of our population?

CHAPTER 8

Locally Grown Money

Bad money always
seeks to drive out good money.
This is Gresham's Law.

The above Haiku is based on a quote attributed to Sir Thomas Gresham (1519-1579), an English financier during the Tudor dynasty. The concept of "good money" was that there was little variance in the face value of a coin and the commodity value of the metal it was made from, usually gold or silver. In contrast, "bad money" has a commodity value less than the face value of the coin. In the past, governments would debase their currency by substituting base metals in their coinage; for example, adding copper to gold and creating an alloy that has the same face value. Another word for this is fiat money, and it's what we have today in most countries. Physical paper currency and the diminishing amount of coins in circulation contain no precious metals.

It didn't use to be this way. As part of the Federal Reserve Act of 1913, the Fed was obliged to keep at least 40 percent of the outstanding currency in circulation in gold. The new central bank was a great innovation in response to the Panic of 1907, when a deep economic recession led to a run on deposits and the failure of many banks. After much debate between political factions aligned with the big Wall Street banks and those representing rural interests, a great compromise was reached that created the Federal Reserve system to guarantee liquidity in the US financial system. Still, this liquidity machine was required to back the US currency it issued with gold.

In 1944, while WWII was still raging, 44 allied nations gathered at the Mt. Washington Hotel in New Hampshire to create the international monetary system including the International Monetary Fund (IMF) and the World Bank. The main feature of the Bretton Woods Agreement was to maintain a stable rate of exchange between national currencies that was tied to gold. The United States became the guarantor of the global system, and the US dollar was redeemable for gold by anyone.[1] As the postwar world recovered and the US share of global GDP declined, government entitlement obligations grew rapidly and so did the US public debt. The Federal Reserve responded by printing more money, causing rapid inflation. The US found it had nowhere near the gold required to redeem its dollars if demanded by other countries. In 1971, as a result of these economic pressures, President Nixon cancelled the convertibility of the dollar into gold and thus began the era of fiat currency. The ancient Gresham's Law was upheld once again as the bad money chased out the good money.

The money we earn from our jobs, save in our banks, and use to pay for our lifestyles is just a form of "tokenized trust." We trust that a dollar is worth something because our government says so, and if everyone believes it, things are wonderful. We exchange our labor for this fiat money to pay for the things we need to live. Everyone is in on the game. But when government continues to print more money to pay its bills, the resulting inflation reduces the value of the currency. Left unchecked, the government seizes inherent power by plundering private wealth. Freedom is handed over without resistance and paid for by taxation and use of debauched fiat money. It is nearly impossible for citizens to retain their inherent power when they permit politicians to borrow unlimited amounts of money.

The US Treasury publishes an executive summary of the federal government's financial condition each year. Table 17 shows the state of our financial condition as of December 2017. One of the most important financial measures used in the private sector is net worth: assets minus liabilities. When it goes negative, you're teetering on the edge of bankruptcy. The net worth of the US government, by its own accounting agency, is –$20.4 trillion as of FY 2017. [2] Does this sound sustainable?

Table 17 – Federal Government P&L and Balance Sheet

	2017	2016*
Financial Measures (Dollars in Billions):		
Gross Costs	$ (4,609.3)	$ (4,515.7)
Less: Earned Revenues	$ 431.9	$ 383.9
Gain / (Loss) from Changes in Assumptions	$ (356.5)	$(273.3)
Net Cost	$ (4,533.9)	$ (4,405.1)
Less: Total Taxes and Other Revenues	$ 3,374.6	$ 3,345.3
⊞ Unmatched Transactions and Balances	$ 2.8	$ 8.1
Net Operating Cost	$ (1,156.7)	$ (1,051.7)
Budget Deficit	$ (665.7)	$ (587.4)
Assets:	$ 3,480.7	$ 3,534.8
Less: Liabilities, comprised of:		
⊞ Debt Held by the Public & Accrued Interest	$ (14,724.1)	$ (14,221.1)
⊞ Federal Employee & Veteran Benefits	$ (7,700.1)	$ (7,209.4)
Other	$ (1,472.7)	$ (1,401.1)
Total Liabilities	$ (23,896.9)	$ (22,831.6)
Net Position (Assets Less Liabilities)	$ (20,416.2)	$ (19,296.8)
Sustainability Measures (Dollars in Trillions):		
Social Insurance Net Expenditures	$ (49.0)	$ (46.7)
Total Non-Interest Net Expenditures	$ (16.2)	$ (10.6)
Sustainability Measures as Percent of Gross Domestic Product (GDP):		
Social Insurance Net Expenditures	(4.0%)	(3.8%)
Total Non-Interest Net Expenditures	(1.2%)	(0.8%)
Fiscal Gap	(2.0%)	(1.6%)

So, who is on the hook for all these liabilities? The answer is "all of us," or at least the shrinking portion of American citizens who actually pay taxes. In the long term, a growing debt burden becomes a big problem for everyone. The World Bank says a country reaches a tipping point when the debt-to-GDP ratio approaches or exceeds 70 percent. That's because GDP measures a country's entire economic output. When the debt is greater than the entire country's production, lenders worry whether the country will repay them. In fact, they did become concerned in 2011 and 2013. That's when Tea Party Republicans in Congress threatened to default on the US debt.

That was a foolish attempt to limit government spending. Why? Because the Constitution gives Congress the ultimate authority to spend. Congress developed a budget process that's worked for years, but over the past 20 years, deficit spending has become the modus operandi since it can have mild and temporary stimulating effects on the economy. But just like steroids have a short-term effect on reducing pain, the effects diminish with each successive use over time until they don't work at all. Of course, politicians get elected for creating jobs and growing the economy and lose elections when unemployment and taxes increase. As a result, Congress has little incentive to reduce the deficit.

We got a taste of this with the 2008 financial crisis as the real estate asset bubble burst, fueled by US Government housing policies, Fed easy money policies, and corporate greed. It was in the aftermath of the near failure of our banking system that Bitcoin was created to become a cryptographic monetary medium of exchange that didn't rely on central banks to control it. Like its fiat currency counterparts, it is also a form of tokenized trust, but unlike fiat money, it has limited supply with a maximum of 21 million Bitcoin that can ever be created.

While I am not advocating that the US convert to a crypto version of its currency, it's worth considering a return to some asset-based backing or limitation on printing of the currency. Because the Federal Reserve operates independently of the government, the only accountability that currently exists is the presidential appointment of the seven governors to staggered 14-year terms and the chairman of the Board of Governors every four years. This intentional insulation of political concerns is an important feature of the Fed but also gives it vast unchecked powers over our economy, and it is often wrong on its policy decisions.

There are many examples of those brilliant minds at the Fed getting it wrong, but here's one that most of you should remember. In 2003 then Fed Governor and future Chairman Ben Bernanke said that "disinflation i.e., where asset values drop, risk will remain a concern for some time," and the Fed kept its easy money policies in place as the economy was expanding at a multiyear three percent GDP growth rate. This was a primary contributor for inflation and the housing bubble. As the bubble was bursting in 2007, Mr. Bernanke still wasn't worried, saying the "financial system will absorb the losses from the subprime mortgage problems without serious problems." We all know what happened, and it was the opposite of what Bernanke had predicted.

The Federal Reserve considers its policy of setting target interest rates an important signaling tool for the market. It prefers to keep the Fed Funds rate (the rate at which banks can borrow from the Fed) between two and five percent. In this range, they believe the economy grows between two and three percent annually with unemployment four to five percent. This is their "goldilocks" state. The problem is that target rates are an inefficient and error-ridden tool to create stable money. In its effort to unwind its unprecedented "quantitative easing" policy in response to the Great Recession of 2008-09, the Fed cut and maintained the benchmark Fed Funds rate at .25 percent, effectively zero. In addition, they purchased a massive amount of Treasury debt and inflated their balance sheet to a high of $4.5 trillion as of September 2017. The idea was this policy effectively creates free money and rekindles risk-taking "animal spirits" and increases asset prices. It certainly increased prices for those that had assets, but GDP growth remained stubbornly sluggish throughout most of the Obama presidency. GDP growth is what creates jobs. Alas, all good things must come to an end and the Fed is trying to unwind this policy (i.e., reducing its balance sheet by selling Treasury debt and increasing interest rates). Abundant and relatively low-cost capital enables more risk-taking, which creates wealth. More capital drives innovation and creates jobs. Interest rates are the cost of credit, not a measure of capital. Under current Fed policy, credit may be cheap, but capital is scarce, especially relative to labor. Low taxes and stable money create economic growth and wealth.

It's time for citizens to demand some changes in the country's relationship with the opaque private banking network with which they entrust their currency. The only way to create more Fed accountability is through new legislation or a constitutional amendment. While there are loud voices on both the left and right that call for the dissolution of the Fed, I think doing so would be a mistake. I would instead prefer a modification of the existing Fed mandates of maximizing employment, stabilizing prices, and moderating long-term interest rates. I believe that maximizing employment should be removed from the mandate as it is often at odds with the other two mandates, which should really be the primary concern. If the Fed stays focused on stable prices (i.e., moderating inflation) and stable interest rates, the employment level should take care of itself as it is a byproduct of the other two policies. We have spent a lot of time in this book pointing out the folly of too much central planning, and government trying to control employment levels is an egregious example. Only businesses can collectively determine the right levels of employment to meet market demand.

Locally Grown Government supports either legislation to modify the Federal Reserve mandate or a constitutional amendment that details the role of the Federal Reserve, including eliminating full employment from the current mission.

CHAPTER 9

Locally Grown Architecture

Local government.
It's needed more than ever.
True people power.

Distributed vs. Centralized Architecture

Look at a satellite view of most large cities and you will see lights arranged in a hub and spoke shape. City center is brightest with all roads leading to middle. Table 18 shows an example of Paris, the famous City of Lights. This shape reflects how human civilization organized and grew. It is a natural shape just like a solar system or the neuron, which enables our ability to perceive the world around us. The emperor and his government were at city center in their grand palaces, assembly halls, and religious institutions. This is where the action was. Consistent with the "divine right of kings," the ruler was at the center of everything. Centralized decisions were made, and edicts were radiated outward through the spokes of the wheel. It was a very efficient way keep an empire together for a while as long as your communication network was robust and efficient.

Table 18 – Paris at Night

However, a centralized system of government degrades over time because it can't scale efficiently as its geographic reach grows and the demands of a large empire weigh down the central authority. Roman law had less power the further you were away from Rome. Over time, garrisons of a few hundred troops weren't enough to protect its vast borders and keep a local population of many thousands in line. However, up to a certain size, the centralized governing model is effective and probably required to create the cultural and legal cohesion necessary to have anything resembling a city or empire.

So, it makes perfect sense that at the dawn of computing, engineers borrowed their architecture from how human societies initially organized. The human architects of our digital world unconsciously endeavor to build a better version of human thinking. Starting with Alan Turing's famous machine that broke the German codes in WWII, computers performed basic tasks much faster and more accurately than humans. Centralized mainframes defined the first phase of network computing. My first computer classes in college consisted of monochromatic dumb green screen terminal "nodes," connected to a host server that prioritized central resources (i.e., memory and hard drives) to handle inbound requests as in Table 19.

Table 19 – Centralized Model

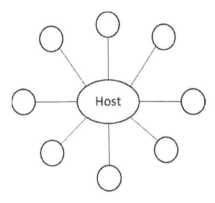

We refer to this computing architecture as "client-server," and it ran large and small organizations around the world for decades starting in the 1950s. If you needed more computing power, you simply added more CPUs and RAM and storage in the existing host server. This is called "vertical-scaling." For 20 years, all that existed were "dumb terminal nodes" that only functioned when connected to the host server. In the mid-1970s, the personal computer revolution redefined the nature of computing with the likes of IBM, Microsoft and Apple who distilled centralized computing into one relatively small box that people could use without being part of a network. All the components were in one place and fit neatly on your desk. As elegant and simple as centralized architecture is, it has some important disadvantages. Chief among those is: if the host server goes down, the entire network goes down. Next, client-server is highly dependent on the network connectivity (cables, Wi-Fi, etc.) The system can fail if the nodes lose connectivity since there is only one central host. Client-server networks can become overloaded if the volume of requests exceeds the ability to process those requests. Finally, centralized computing cannot "scale up" after a certain limit is reached. Adding more hardware and software capabilities doesn't improve performance enough to justify the cost.

Centralized computing is great for running Bank of America, Ford Motor, Proctor & Gamble, and the five million small businesses in America, but what happens when they all want to talk to each other? Well, in mid-1990s along came this incredible new computing network called "the Internet" that turned centralized computing on its head. It introduced a new concept called a "distributed system" where every node makes its own decision. The behavior of the system is the cumulative decisions of the individual nodes rather than a centralized host. All nodes are peers of each other and work towards a common goal in a "peer-to-peer" network as shown in Table 20.

Table 20 –Distributed Model

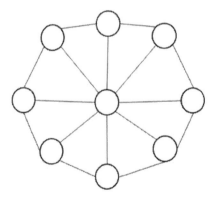

Distributed systems address the key weaknesses of centralized systems, which makes them much more robust. First there is no single point of failure. If one or several nodes go down, the system continues to operate without those nodes since each node has everything it needs to process a request or do a transaction. This fully autonomous capability of each node permits the system to scale horizontally, meaning you can simply add new computer nodes and the power of the network increases. As with client-server networks, distributed systems permit vertical scaling by simply adding CPU, RAM, and storage to the nodes. Network engineers use both scale methods to design optimal network efficiency. Finally, distributed systems operate much faster than centralized systems because of their high geographical spread. There simply is less physical distance for your request to travel to a node that can respond.

Some nodes can become server nodes for the role of coordinating traffic between the other nodes. In fact, the first version of a distributed system was networks of personal computers connected through a host that managed traffic in the network and provided access to shared resources. This solved the problem of not being able to work if the network had problems, which was often in the early days. You could get work done on your PC, which contained "local" applications from pioneering companies like Microsoft and Apple. Nearly 50 years later, this version of distributed computing still underpins our digital ecosystem.

Another version of a distributed network is Google. When you search for "Declaration of Independence" on your web browser, Google provides an amazing 141 million results in a few milliseconds. What appears to be one system fulfilling the request is really thousands of computers crawling the web and delivering results to your device. Google search is really many computers working together to accomplish a single task. However, in an ironic twist, Google's internal distributed architecture doesn't carry through to most of their consumer-facing products, like their productivity tools that mimic the long-time market leader Microsoft Office. Here Google goes "back to the future" by forcing you to have an internet connection to use their G-Suite applications that reside on their "virtualized central server." It's just a fancier version of that old green screen mainframe network that I began my career with, except way more efficient and powerful.

Most technology companies have adopted this new form of centralized computing and have cleverly rebranded it as "The Cloud." Yes, it has its advantages of pooling resources more efficiently, but it still has the same serious drawbacks as the legacy centralized model. I will add another serious drawback that has finally roared to the front of public consciousness: privacy. As it turns out, these "Cloud companies" spy on us and use our personal data to make gobs of money while doing a poor job of protecting that data from malicious hackers. Even worse, these Cloud companies use our data to manipulate how we buy, how we consume information, and how we vote. Even worse than that, there is evidence that Google is working with the Chinese government to help them improve their massive citizen surveillance system. So much for Google's motto of "Do no evil."

My vision of a true distributed system is much closer to the reliable PC-based client-server model than to the Cloud model. I don't use G-suite but rather prefer working with Microsoft Office on my laptop, where I can decide what data to share through or store on the Cloud. I can still get lots of work done, like writing this book, disconnected from the network.

Locally Grown Government Is a Distributed System

As originally defined in our Constitution, America is a good example of a distributed system. What's left of our original three-tier government structure is still somewhat of a distributed architecture. The original founding architecture lays out a few enumerated powers as the exclusive province of the federal government. Any other powers not specified are retained by the states and "the people." That means most of what we would recognize as government was *not to be performed at the federal level.* That means there are 50 state nodes and 20,000 local nodes that are to do most of the governing. To me, this distributed governing model is very similar to my preferred version of distributing computing, the PC-based client server model. The PC nodes are local governments that are fully equipped with the "applications" to perform their jobs whether the network of higher government is running or not. The states are server nodes that have their own operating rules and are repositories of shared resources between the nodes. The federal government should theoretically have far fewer rules than the state server clusters and local nodes. Its "host role" is limited to executive functions like protecting the entire network (i.e., defense), who to let into the network (i.e. immigration), regulating network traffic (i.e., judiciary and commerce), and being a repository of shared resources (i.e., Bureau of Labor Statistics and Census). In fact, the "network" *is* the body of federal and state laws that connect all the local nodes. And just like high traffic volumes can slow down the performance of digital networks, so does a high volume of state and federal regulation and taxes slow down an economy.

In order for most of government to be performed at lower-level nodes, those nodes must have all the resources they need to carry out the defined governmental roles. The Founders built that capability into our design. States and cities have their own budgets and rules to meet many of the demands of its citizens. They tax and spend just like the federal government. When the federal government transfers money to the state and local level for the many social welfare programs it has created, that money comes with rules about how it is to be allocated. The problem is that state and local governments don't always follow the rules. Why is that?

I think the problem starts with the fact that the federal government mandates that these big programs *must* be performed. For example, states *must* implement Medicaid and the federal government subsidizes between 50% and 73% percent of the total cost depending on the state needs.[1] This means states must raise and spend their own tax revenue to implement the program that is forced upon them. Organizations act like people. If you make folks spend their own money on something they may or may not want, most will damn sure try to do things their own way. In other words, people, and organizations, do what is in their best interest as nature designed. For programs like Medicaid, that takes the form of states not enforcing things like eligibility rules to the benefit of favored political constituencies, which is why these programs have become unsustainable. A better way is to reduce the rules, so state and local nodes have more autonomy to customize the safety net to meet their own needs. Also, by replacing the current "open checkbook" approach in favor of block grants for federal money (i.e., fixed annual amount), states will have more incentive to be efficient. Please don't confuse me as being against our social safety net. The purpose of this book is to reconfigure how government in general, and the safety net in particular, can be implemented more efficiently using our three-tier architecture.

Centralization Within Distributed Architecture

You'll recall that I described the centralized model as being a valuable way to organize smaller systems or systems that have specific characteristics that require central authority. Digital computing architecture allows clusters of sub-systems that require centralized command and control to perform their functions while still remaining part of the overall distributed network. A good example of this is "authentication," which controls who is allowed to use the system. Think of it as where a user logs in to an application. A large distributed network will typically use clusters of authentication servers to serve a fixed number of nodes in a "hub and spoke" architecture. One government analog for this is the Defense Department. The very nature of its role requires uniformity that is established by a hierarchical chain of command. There isn't a lot of autonomy in the military. You have a job to do whether you like it or not. It's the centrally decided mission that matters, not your opinion of that mission. So important is this structure to its effectiveness, the military requires its members live under a different set of laws than non-military citizens, called the Uniform Code of Military Justice (UCMJ).

In my opinion, most of the constitutionally enumerated functions of the federal government should be organized in a centralized model. However, before doing that, Locally Grown architecture calls for rationalizing the myriad federal functions and placing them in the correct "server nodes." This means relocating functions that don't belong within their current federal departments to other departments where the functions are more similar. It eliminates duplication of function. For example, why do we have a massive agency mostly dedicated to providing healthcare to military veterans when we have another even more massive agency delivering healthcare to the elderly and the poor? We are all humans after all. Illness doesn't distinguish between veterans, the elderly, or poor. If we rationalize the federal government from a functional perspective, we would find that several federal departments and agencies become shells of their former self. For example, once you remove the $100 billion SNAP (food stamp) program from the Agriculture Department, there isn't much left except a federal bureaucracy with not much to do. It then makes much more sense to merge the antiquated and pork-laden Department of Agriculture with the Department of the Interior. The following is a sample list of prospective functional consolidations that would improve the operating efficiency of our federal government.

- Eliminate the Department of Veterans Affairs.

  - Merge the healthcare portion of Veteran's Affairs to HHS. A special function within HHS can be set up to handle special military-related injuries.
  - Remainder of Veterans Affairs is merged with the Department of Defense.

- Eliminate the Department of Agriculture.

  - Merge the SNAP program with HHS.
  - Merge the $6 billion forestry function to the Department of the Interior.
  - Merge farm subsidies to the Department of the Interior.

- Eliminate the Department of Labor.

  - Merge data-gathering functions like the Bureau of Labor Statistics into the Department of Commerce, where similar functions like the Census are performed.
  - Merge labor law enforcement with the Department of Justice.

- Merge the Department of Transportation into the Department of Commerce.
- Merge the Department of Housing and Urban Development with HHS.

Most of our current federal organization chart was created for good reasons, but over time it has become subject to politics and the overall Hamiltonian momentum of federal government expansion. The above list is a mere smattering of the opportunities to improve the efficiency of the federal government by consolidating duplicate functions.

Table 21 is a snapshot of how the federal government could be reorganized within a more distributed architecture. The constitutionally enumerated functions are lighter-shaded and the "general welfare" function is darker-shaded.

Table 21 – Federal Government in a New Distributed Model

The consolidated functions are unshaded. As you can see, the enumerated functions are organized in a centralized hub and spoke architecture. As much as possible, I have consolidated the "general welfare" functions in Health and Human Services and shaded that blue to indicate that is a non-enumerated department, meaning that the functions are not specifically defined in the Constitution but rather considered part of the "general welfare" clause of the preamble.

Three-Tier System Architecture

We are a demographically and geographically diverse nation with a three-tier government hierarchy that supports this diversity. The problem is, there has been a steady delegation of our inherent power upstream to the point where the federal government is becoming a single point of failure in our societal system. Citizens have come to depend on federal government to solve too many problems that are meant to be handled at lower tiers. The more people get comfortable with a big brother government, the more they will look to big brother to solve their problems. Federal power still depends on a relatively small group of politicians and bureaucrats to make the right decisions on a myriad of complex issues, and they often don't make the right choices.

Locally Grown Government seeks to reverse the upward-delegation bias that has taken hold by "distributing" more authority to the state and local tiers. This rebalancing of the governmental "load" will yield more efficient, responsive, and scalable government by crowd-sourcing hard problems in our many state and local laboratories and sharing solutions among them. I'm sure there will be critics out there who will be skeptical that state and local government will be able to do as good of a job that the many federal functions do now. To that I say it's tough to do worse than the 10-20% of waste, fraud, and abuse that riddles many of our largest federal programs. I see how distributed architecture has vastly improved performance and scalability of computer networks, which makes it self-evident to me that returning to the original distributed architecture of our Constitution will yield similar results. We just need the will to make the transition.

Of course, there will still be states and local governments

determined to self-destruct by over-promising, over-taxing, and under-delivering to its residents. Even now we have several states and large cities that are running out of options to fund their bloated governments. I'm sure there will come a time in the not too distant future when one or more of these states will reach the end of their rope and look to the federal government for a bailout. When the time comes, I hope "we the people" rise up and demand those states bear the consequences of their poor and corrupt decision-making. We have robust bankruptcy laws that permit the slate to be wiped clean so re-organization can create a smaller, more efficient, sustainable city or state. As painful as this process may be for a large state (and the country), it would likely change bad behaviors in other unsustainable cities and states so they can avoid a similar fate. And as bad as this may be, the entire system won't buckle as the healthy nodes continue to operate without the failed nodes. Once fixed, the failed nodes can join the system again and increase the power of the overall network. For me, this is a much better outcome than waiting for the entire system to crash as the federal host cannot handle the burdens of failed state and local nodes in addition to its own unsustainable burdens. This dystopian future is reminiscent of my earlier example of how the exponential growth of prokaryotic bacteria eventually collapses because it has consumed all the resources of its environment. Remember, a thing cannot be larger than its container.

Three-Tier Node Architecture

Everything that our government and its citizens does is bounded by a large, constantly growing body of laws enacted by political delegates. These laws are supposed to be bounded by the state or federal Constitution but are often challenged in our judicial system, which decides on a law's adherence to one or both constitutions. Decisions by lower courts can be appealed through our hierarchy of federal courts all the way to the US Supreme Court, and the buck stops there. All of the decisions rendered by the courts become part of what is referred to as "case law," which is used as primary research for each new legal case. A primary function of an attorney is trying to match the facts of the current case with those of previously decided cases. Any matches become important facts to be considered by judges and jurors in the current case. Ideally, cases with similar facts as previously decided cases should be adjudicated similarly. This critical legal principle is called "stare decisis," Latin for "already decided."

This growing body of laws and already-decided cases form the foundation of our tradition of the "rule of law." Ironically, this massive corpus of case law is just a collection of words in documents with links to other documents, similar to how Hypertext Markup Language (HTML) digitally links related web pages. In fact, measuring the number of links between web pages was the brilliant "ah-ha" innovation that powers Google search relevancy. In similar fashion, we can organize our national case-law database as a network of "stare decicis" hyperlinks and apply AI to it to deliver relevance and predictive power that would improve the efficiency of our judicial system. In fact, there are already many software applications that employ AI that can be modified to do what I am suggesting.[2]

To summarize, the US Constitution, state constitutions, and the all-existing federal, state, and local laws are the first of three components of each autonomous node in our system. They function similar to computer Read-Only Memory (ROM), which is a set of semi-permanent instructions in memory that can be read at high speed but can't be changed by programs that use it. Of course, "AI Legal" can never replace human attorneys, judges, and juries. Stare decisis is fallible as evidenced by the overturning of precedents such as *Dred Scott*, which supported slavery, and *Minor v. Happersett,* which supported denial of women's voting rights. However, we can help unclog our court system by using AI Legal predictions of the case outcome as a threshold that must be overcome in pre-trial hearings in order for a case to proceed to a jury. Many courts already do the manual version of this when caseloads start to clog the system. AI Legal can help in corporate product design and legislation at all tiers of government to increase the certainty that a product or law is legal.

The second major component of Locally Grown Government is

reforming and standardizing our decision-making infrastructure starting with how citizens and their delegates vote. Here we propose using blockchain technology to build an election system that guarantees the authenticity of votes and eliminates any potential for corruption while enabling a more active, informed citizenship. Restoring the public trust in our voting is the important to restoring trust in our public institutions.

The third major component of Locally Grown architecture is restoring the art of finding consensus in our political dialogue so that government can avoid gridlock and get things done for the people. Again, we envision applying technology rooted in Game Theory mathematics to determine optimal buckets of legislative priorities that can actually get passed by our three levels of government. Think of it as a mashup of different priorities similar to omnibus bills in Congress, which include pork for both sides of the political aisle.

Table 22 illustrates all three major components working together in a node. Again, nothing radical here, just a technology-enabled better version of how American government is already working. Each node has everything it needs to make decisions: the "constitution and case law rules database," "the consensus algorithm," and a "voting system."

Table 22 – Locally Grown Government Node Architecture

Constitution Law corpus
Entire system must be bound by Constitution.

Blockchain Blog, Survey, Voting
Anonymized Big Data

Consensus
Determine Nash EQ for different priority lists from Big Data

When a local node decides something, it shares the decision details upwards to the state node that shares it with all other local nodes connected to the state. Then each state node shares its collective decisions upwards to the federal node, which then shares all the state decisions downward to the other states. In this way, each node consumes the lessons learned from all the other nodes to feed a continuous improvement model. An example of a full system architecture is depicted in Table 23.

Table 23 – Locally Grown Government System Architecture

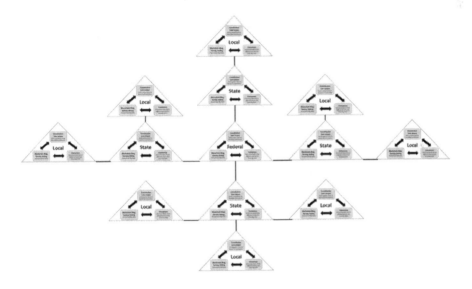

So local is where we start and build upwards to state government and then eventually to federal government. We envision devolving a significant portion of the current scope of our federal government (and the tax revenues that go with it) downward to its proper constitutional position. Over time, we envision lots of interlinked Locally Grown Government pyramids building to a more sustainable, stronger, distributed system of American government as shown in Table 23. In the following chapters, we will detail how this improved architecture is deployed across our nation.

Constitutional Amendments

*Constitutional
amendments were ingenious.
The great safety valves.*

The US Constitution was carefully crafted by our Founders to include an amendment process that provides the ability for government to adapt to changing circumstances. Though amendments appropriately must meet a very high bar to guard against "the passions of the moment," our Constitution has been amended 27 times. This is a small number considering more than 10,000 amendments have been proposed since 1787. Proposals have included such things as requiring Congress to balance the budget each year (i.e., the Balanced Budget Amendment), term limits for Congress, and a ban on flag burning. The last time a proposed amendment to the US Constitution was passed was 1992, when the 27th Amendment preventing Congress from giving itself immediate pay raises was ratified by the states. The process of amending the Constitution in this case took more than two centuries, showing the difficulty and reluctance among elected officials and the public to change a document that is so revered.

For an amendment to be considered, it must receive a two-thirds majority vote in both the House and Senate, or in a Constitutional Convention voted on by two-thirds of state legislatures. Once an amendment is proposed, it must be ratified by at least three-fourths of the states to be added to the Constitution. Most proposed constitutional amendments deal with the same few topics, like the federal budget and freedom of speech, and have gained some traction in Congress. I support some of the existing proposals as well as some new ones that would go a long way to making us a more sustainable, free, and fair society. Given the difficulty of getting Congress to act on these, we support the effort by organizations like the Convention of States in Action. They are a grassroots movement that is gaining traction, with 15 of the required 33 state legislatures having officially voted to convene a constitutional convention of states. Here are some of the proposals I'd lobby for when we get there:

New Amendment – Proof of Citizenship in Elections

In my opinion, the election process should be as standardized as possible across all jurisdictions, but we recognize there may be valid reason for differences between local, state, and federal. However, no matter where the election takes place across the thousands of polling places in the US, the federal process should be the same everywhere, and proof of citizenship should be required to vote in a federal election. Because most government elections are typically a mashup of federal, state, and local candidates, Proof of Identity (POI) can serve all three. If for some reason a polling place refuses to require POI, then it shouldn't be permitted as a polling station for federal elections. Some citizens then could be faced with the inconvenience of needing to go to two separate polling stations to vote for federal and then everything else. Local election officials would then be faced with the prospect of explaining to their constituents why they are not requiring ID.

There are some who object to requiring an ID to vote on the grounds that it represents voter disenfranchisement similar to how poll taxes resulted in disenfranchisement of poor minority voters during the Jim Crow era. This is a valid concern, though it is important to point out that we have come a long way from that. According to the Federal Office of Highway Policy Information, 87 percent of the driving-age population (age 16 and over) has a license. That means that 87 percent of eligible voters already possess sufficient ID to vote. When you add the many other forms of ID accepted by states for voting including military ID, student ID, hunting/fishing licenses, tribal ID, state and federal employment ID, welfare ID and birth certificates, we are really talking about a very small minority of citizens for which this could be a problem. If those citizens want to vote nearly all states can provide a special voter ID at city hall.

Every state except North Dakota requires eligible citizens who plan to vote in a federal election to register in advance. There are many public and private efforts to get citizens registered, like the Federal Motor Voter Act of 1993 requiring departments of motor vehicles to offer voter registration as part of any motor vehicle or license transaction. Churches, community groups, and nonprofits all have had well-organized voter drives for decades. Some states offer same-day registration, allowing citizens to register and vote on Election Day, often right at their polling places. Despite all this outreach, the US Census Bureau estimates that 21 percent of eligible citizens were not registered to vote in 2014. [3] A 2017 survey of eligible voters conducted by the Pew Charitable Trust revealed the following: Of those eligible citizens who were not registered, 44 percent said they didn't want to vote, 27 percent said they wanted to but didn't get around to it, and 25 percent said there wasn't a candidate who inspired them to register. [4] Combine this data with the historical average of 50-60 percent voter turnout for presidential elections and 35-50 percent average for midterm elections, and it paints a picture of a pretty apathetic electorate. It seems only logical that if we require citizens to register in order to vote, we should also require ID to actually vote. You need to show ID to travel on airplanes, receive government benefits, drive a car, stay at a hotel. For goodness sakes, if you're an American citizen who has a problem with showing ID for something as fundamental as voting, then there must be some other motive at work. And, if you don't vote, stop complaining about the government.

New Amendment – Federal Government Debt as Share of GDP Can't Exceed 120%

This proposal is a recognition that there are benefits to the Hamiltonian vision but that there are also limits and we are at those limits now. There have been many proposals for a balanced budget amendment, all having some version of requiring the federal government to balance its budget each year where spending cannot exceed revenue, except in wartime, major catastrophes, or by legislation passed by a supermajority of Congress. After all, 49 out of 50 states and several countries have balanced-budget requirements in their constitutions. Why can't we do this on the federal level?

While I agree with the intent of trying to compel fiscal responsibility, there are some important negative repercussions to consider. First, compelling Congress to balance the budget each year would be hard to enforce. Congress can certainly pass a budget (though that has recently been rare), but it's impossible to know the timing of tax receipts, which depend largely on economic activity. Second, politicians are experts at financial tinkering and would certainly find ways to defer spending to make the budget appear to be balanced while liabilities for future spending accumulate. Finally, we wouldn't want to hamstring the ability of Congress to respond to wars, catastrophes, or economic crises. Even though most existing balance budget proposals contain language providing for this, Congress could unilaterally declare a constant state of emergency to justify massive deficit spending. Don't laugh. This is a real possibility.

As if the political difficulty of maintaining a debt ceiling weren't enough, there is a growing crop of economists who now tell us that debt levels don't matter. They say that as long as the growth rate of government debt is less than the GDP growth rate, countries can issue nearly an infinite amount of debt. These economists point to research like the IMF, showing that since 1960, GDP grew between 1.7 percent and .8 percent faster than the debt service growth rate. They stipulate that there were periods of volatility when debt grew faster than GDP but overall the trend is in favor of GDP growth being faster. These Modern Monetary Theorists (MMT) rationalize that the conventional wisdom of governments needing to run surpluses to pay down debt is faulty, because "responsible" nations don't pay off debt but rather simply roll over existing debt into new debt. So long as interest payments can be comfortably paid and the debt can be refinanced, nations can issue as much debt as they like with no economic consequences. This is a wonderful theory until creditors wake up one day and decide they want to be paid back.

Sound crazy? That's because it is. We only need to look at countries like Venezuela, Argentina, Zimbabwe, and Greece, where decades of profligate government spending racked up debts that couldn't be refinanced even at much higher interest rates. Apparently, people who lend money care about being paid back. When debt couldn't be refinanced, they took to printing money, or defaulted, or, in the case of Greece, threatening to withdraw from the EU common currency so they could print money. The rampant inflation that results from these actions brings an economy to its knees.

The MMT crowd justifies its theory by using IMF data from six "responsible" governments, including the US, which can issue debt in their own currencies so they can simply print the money to service their debt if the growth rate of debt service as a percentage of GDP is less than GDP annual growth rate. But how long will these countries remain responsible as their debt-servicing costs continue consuming an increasing share of GDP as it is in the US?

The CBO projects that interest on our national debt will rise from about seven percent of GDP in 2019 to 25 percent in 2050, driven by entitlement spending. That represents an average annual increase of 11.5 percent for the all-important debt service to GDP ratio that MMT uses. To my knowledge, there has never been a 30-year period in the US (or any country) where the economy grew by more than 11.5 percent rate every year. [5] You don't need an advanced degree in economics to understand how wrong MMT advocates are.

When discussing government debt, Locally Grown Government considers state and local obligations to be as important as federal debt because, ultimately, the US government would never let a wave of states, important agencies, or municipalities default. I believe the Federal Reserve would step in and buy the defaulting obligations, trying to prevent widespread catastrophe. The Fed already showed the willingness to do this in the 2008 financial crisis with their various quantitative easing programs and strong-arming of financial institutions. I remember years ago when politicians and executives at government-sponsored organizations (GSO) Fannie Mae and Freddie Mac firmly denied there was an explicit federal guarantee for the investor-held mortgage bonds of these companies. That lie was exposed in broad daylight in 2008. According to USspending.com, all government-issued and guaranteed debt including state, local, agencies like Fannie and Freddie, student loans, and total government debt was $33.5 trillion or 170 percent of GDP in 2018.[6] This level is higher than all countries except Japan, whose economy hasn't grown meaningfully in decades because public debt is crowding out private investment.

In a recent interview at the SALT Conference, a global thought leadership forum, Carlyle Group Co-Executive Chairman David Rubinstein expressed his concerns over the national debt. The Carlyle Group is one of the largest investment firms on the planet, and David is representative of what the "smart money" thinks about the macro economy. He believes that US federal government debt at $22 trillion, with a $1-plus trillion per year deficit, is completely unsustainable and that a day of reckoning is closer than people think. [7] In his view, most voters don't care about the issue and politicians are all too happy to encourage their apathy. He says it will take a bad crisis where global capital markets will enforce discipline, and it won't be pretty.

When considering a constitutional amendment that can be practically enforced, it would be unwieldy to establish a debt-GDP cap that includes implicit debt guarantees like Fannie Mae and Freddie Mac. In my opinion, the federal government has no business guaranteeing the mortgages of 46 percent of the US housing market.[8] It's well outside its constitutional scope, represents over $6 trillion in corporate welfare, and creates a toxic brew of moral hazard for lenders and borrowers alike. Managing credit risk is the job of banks, not government.

It's also probably unconstitutional to limit the borrowing abilities of states and municipalities. For these reasons, I'm proposing an amendment for a very generous hard limit of 120 percent of GDP for direct federal obligations. I recognize the need to not hamstring government in times of national emergencies, so this cap could be overridden by two-thirds of both houses of Congress and signed by the president. This cap is not far from our current 105 percent federal debt-GDP ratio, but it provides time for political consensus to develop to make the important and hard decisions to curb the growth of government spending. It also eliminates the political circus that is the annual Congressional authorization to raise the debt ceiling. As Locally Grown Government is implemented, the federal government will be block granting much of its social budget to the states. The fixed, rather than open-ended, grants will stem the automatic growth of these programs.

New Amendment – Inclusive of all Types of Taxes, the Federal Rate of Taxation Can't Exceed 40 Percent of a Citizen's or Company's Gross Annual Income

We have just discussed how we curtail the growth of government with a constitutional amendment limiting how much it can borrow. We now must try to curtail its power to tax the productivity of its citizens as a source of funding. The reality is that every dollar the federal government spends must be either taxed or borrowed from the private sector. And the more resources the government takes from the private sector, the less job creation occurs. Even the commonly held view that increased government spending stimulates the economy in economic downturns has limited effects. The St. Louis Federal Reserve Bank concurs:

> "In the short and intermediate run, there are only small employment effects of government spending in both high and low-unemployment times. In the longer run (e.g. seven or eight years), we also found almost no effect on employment from government spending. The estimated effects are not statistically different from zero." [9]

If the Keynesian view that government spending is at least as efficient as private sector spending, why would we need a private sector? The government could just borrow infinitely and spend infinitely. But then who would lend government the money since the private sector would have disappeared? You also would have nobody to tax as all the formerly productive citizens would have made the rational decision to reduce or stop working because of confiscatory taxation.

In *Atlas Shrugged*, Ayn Rand describes a plausible, if not dystopian future where government fiscal responsibility leaves the building. [10]

Table 24 from USGovernmentSpending.com shows that, in the last 118 years, federal, state, and local government annual spending has grown to more than 37 percent of our entire GDP.

Table 24 – Growth of All Government Spending

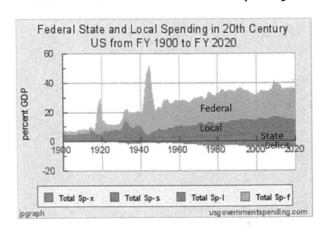

It's true that the US economy has performed remarkably well despite increasing levels of government spending. So, what's the big deal? To get an idea of what things might look like if we ignore the trends, let's look at another mature semi-democratic republic, France, which believes in a more expansive role for government. Table 25 compares key economic performance metrics for the USA and France. Like most European countries, they have expansive social spending that includes free college and healthcare, shorter work weeks, lots more vacation, and lots more regulation of business. Also like most European countries, they don't spend much on their military and instead depend on the United States to defend them.

Without the US military, their fiscal condition would be worse. In order to pay for their society, the French government borrows slightly less but taxes its citizens about 70 percent more than the USA. French government spending represents nearly half of the entire economy. As a result, French unemployment is more than double that of the United States. For those French citizens lucky enough to have a job, they earn 38 percent less than their American counterparts. For those French workers who can save money, the interest rate they earn is nearly four times lower than their American counterparts. If they instead choose to invest their savings in the French stock market (CAC 40), they earn less than one-third the annual return than Americans investing their savings in the US stock market (S&P 500).

Table 25 – United States versus France

Key Metrics (source: OECD)	USA	France
GDP ($US trillions) 2017	$ 21.50	$ 2.78
Govt Debt ($US trillions) 2017	$ 29.46	$ 3.36
GDP Growth Rate 2012-2018	2.39%	1.12%
Government Spending as % of GDP 2017	37.70%	56.5%
Government Debt % GDP	137%	121%
Govt 10 yr Bond Yield % Dec 2018	2.68%	0.70%
Debt Carrying Cost % GDP	3.7%	0.8%
GDP per Capita 2017	$ 59,945	$38,476
Average Wages 2017	$ 60,600	$43,755
Unemployment Rate 2017	3.9%	9.10%
Taxes as % of GDP 2017	27.10%	46.20%
CAC 40 12/31/1998-3/16/2019		38.1%
S&P 500 return 12/31/1998-3/16/2019	130%	

Maybe the French people have gotten use to less opportunity in a less vibrant, more centrally controlled economy. But as of this writing, French citizens are rising up in the worst riots in decades over the government plans to increase taxes yet again. *Vive les gilets jaunes!* The lyric to one of my favorite tunes from Pink Floyd, "Wish You Were Here," comes to mind:

Did they get you to trade
your heroes for ghosts?
Hot ashes for trees?
Hot air for a cool breeze?
Cold comfort for change?

Did you exchange
a walk on part in the war
for a lead role in a cage?

The lesson here is that high tax rates diminish innovation and productivity to the detriment of the common good. Steadily, government needs to consume more to keep its redistribution promises, and most other functions get crowded out. Then things start to go exponential as the interest-carrying cost is added and rising debt crowds out private investment in the economy. We are starting to see this now even in America in our 50 state laboratories. Governments in the states of IL, CT, NJ, CA, RI, and NY cannot raise taxes enough to fill their budget gaps and, as a result, many of their most productive citizens and businesses are moving in droves to lower-tax states. For the moment, America's three-tier model of bottom-up government provides a firewall against this unsustainability virus from spreading. However, there is a growing number of politicians and citizens who want the French model for America.

The truth is that funding an efficient, sustainable government that encourages its citizens to be productive and provides for the common good is a balance of taxation and spending. There are many important functions the federal government must and should perform like defense, environmental protection, justice system, food and drug regulation, and plenty of others. However, 50 percent (and growing) of federal government spending is just redistribution of money from one group of citizens to another plus interest on the money borrowed for that redistribution. [11]

Our constitutional amendment proposal of capping federal taxation means that no citizen or business will pay more than 40 percent of their income after all the IRS tax code tinkering. It means ALL taxes including payroll, income, capital gains. We are talking major tax code reform and simplification here. Considering that a top-earning US citizen residing in California with its 13.3 percent top rate will pay more than 50 percent of their income to government. I think this is simply unfair. No person should have to pay more than half their income to the government. Government should have more than enough funds to do what it needs without choking the goose that lays the golden eggs. I expect there will be those folks who say there will still be some income inequality and they might be right. In a society that rewards hard and smart work and risk taking, there will always be those who have better financial outcomes. There will also be those who are happy and comfortable with less risk-taking. America was never about equality of outcomes but rather freedom and opportunity, and history has proven this freedom-biased approach to be better at raising all boats then any others.

CHAPTER 10

Locally Grown in Action

*Government budgets
must grow slower than GDP.
The new golden rule.*

I agree with most of the current roles played by our government but disagree with some of how that authority is distributed between the federal, state, and local levels. My measuring tape for where the separation ought to be is the federal enumerated powers in our Constitution, which are basically the following:

- Defense
- Foreign policy and trade
- Immigration
- Establish and regulate a national currency
- Post office system including roads
- Establish and manage a federal court system underneath the Supreme Court

- System of intellectual property protection
- Protect against piracy on the high seas
- Regulate interstate commerce (this includes a lot of things like the FDA and other agencies)

These enumerated federal powers represent about one-quarter of the $4.4 trillion federal budget for 2019, with defense about two-thirds of that amount. That means 75 percent of ALL federal spend¬ing falls under the nebulous "promotion of general welfare" clause in the preamble of the Constitution. Before the 1930s New Deal era of Franklin Roosevelt, the general welfare clause was interpreted as having at least some limits.

In "Federalist No. 41," James Madison stated that any taxing and spending must be at least somewhat related to one of the enumerated powers.[1] Alexander Hamilton had a broader interpretation, which held that Congress could enact any laws and raise taxes to assist national needs like agriculture and education as long as the federal spending doesn't favor any parts of the country over other parts.

Prior to 1937, US Supreme Court rulings supported federal taxing and spending only as it relates to federal enumerated powers, pretty much holding to the Madisonian view. That all changed in 1937 when SCOTUS ruled in *Helvering v. Davis* that Social Security was constitutional as an exercise of the power to spend for the general welfare.[2] In my view, this ruling effectively eliminated any limits on federal power. Hamilton won in the end. As a result, over the decades the political class has expanded government so that now spending on just one undefined power, promoting the general welfare, is crowding out the ability to perform the other nine defined federal responsibilities.

Reforming Social Security, Medicare, Medicaid, and Welfare

Despite the wishful thinking of some politicians, Social Security, Medicare, and Medicaid aren't legal entitlements. In addition to the

1937 Helvering decision that ruled Social Security was a constitutional federal power, the 1960 Supreme Court *Flemming v. Nestor* decision ruled that citizens have no right to collect a retirement even though they theoretically "paid into it" with a specific tax over their working lives. Social Security is just a tax, and any Congress can reduce or eliminate those benefits at any time it feels it's necessary. The problem, of course, is political, and any Congress attempting this might be voted out. Hence, the moniker of Social Security as the "third rail" of politics. The same can be said of Medicare, Medicaid, and welfare. This is the problem with inventing entitlements. They form a slippery slope that, once promised, are nearly impossible to reverse because people believe they have a right to them. Manipulating voters becomes child's play for politicians who provide their Hobson's Choice: *Vote for us* and your benefits will continue to flow. *Vote for them* and they will stop.

But citizens must understand there is no free lunch. 2018 became the first year since 1982 that Social Security expenses exceeded their earmarked payroll tax revenue, and government trustees project this deficit to get worse each year until the so-called "surplus" is totally exhausted in 2032. To make the program sustainable, the choices are raising taxes, reducing benefits, raising the retirement age, or a combination of all three. Some politicians propose raising the current $128,700 income limit, against which the 6.2 percent tax is applied. Keep in mind that the employer matches the employee taxes, so the total FICA tax rate is 12.4 percent of earnings. This means that raising the income limit affects both the employer and employee. From the perspective of a business, raising payroll taxes incentivizes companies to reduce full-time hires and replace them with contract workers or invest in automation instead. The cumulative negative effects become profound on the economy, and citizens must understand the important tradeoffs when they vote for more benefits.

Raising taxes with no reduction in benefits could mean trading government retirement income for maybe having a poor job or no job at all, like in some European countries. Combine this with other employer mandates like providing healthcare, family leave, and minimum wage and you effectively have additional taxes on labor that will hasten the already unsettling trend of machines replacing humans. The better machines become at substituting for human labor, the bigger negative effect any tax or mandate will have on employment. We are watching this happen now in states like California and New Jersey, where tax rates and mandates are so onerous, people and businesses are moving out, which further exacerbates the economic dilemma in those states. This will happen at a national scale if we do nothing.

So how do we save still important safety net programs without severely hampering the economic activity that funds them? There are lots of practical ideas out there already, ranging from mean-testing Social Security and eliminating the $128,700 income cap to which the FICA tax applies. Both of these solutions simply confirm what has always been true, that Social Security is not a guaranteed benefit but just another tax with redistribution that can be changed at any time. The net effect will be to encourage companies to automate jobs instead of hiring employees, which will make any fiscal benefits short-term.

Ironically, one of the most practical solutions to fix our social security problem comes from Sweden, a country that many politicians on the American left cite as the model for "successful socialism." In an August 24, 2019 Wall St. Journal article titled "Why Bernie Sanders Is Wrong About Sweden", Johan Norberg, a Swedish author and historian, points out that for a century between 1860 and 1960 Sweden was one of the world's fastest growing economies when "classical liberals" were in power. They preserved property rights, protected religious and press freedoms and promoted free trade. Then in the early 1960s, Sweden began its socialist experiment by doubling the size of government as a percentage of GDP to fund a massive social safety net. The results were predictable: less work, flight of the entrepreneurial class out of the country, and a stagnating economy for twenty years. Then in 1991, moderate politicians rose to power to cut taxes and regulations, expanded school vouchers and reformed the social safety net. The results were also predictable: faster growing GDP, higher employment, an *efficient locally run healthcare system* and an overall better lifestyle for its citizens. Norberg points out that Sweden's "dirty little secret" for maintaining its still large social safety net is a substantial "non-progressive" taxation. This means, everyone pays much higher taxes, not just the rich. His advice for making the US Social Security system sustainable, is to follow Sweden's example: change the system from defined benefits to *defined contribution* and *reduce Social Security payments when the economy is doing worse.* I think these are brilliant reforms that should be strongly considered in this country.[3]

Disability Income (SSDI) is also part of the overall Social Security program, and it provides income for people between the ages of 18 and 64 who are unable to work. The program was started in 1955 and was designed to help workers who couldn't perform a job because of a medically diagnosed physical condition. In 1985 the rules were expanded, and the program predictably began to grow quickly. According to the CBO, from 1970 to 2014, the share of working-age people who receive SSDI benefits more than tripled from 1.3 percent to 4.5 percent. In 2015, over 11 million citizens received benefits representing a total of $143 billion and, when Medicare is included, the total was $228 billion or 1.3 percent of GDP.[4] Growth of this entitlement is a combination of more expansive government policy, changing characteristics of the workforce, and fraud.

Reducing SSDI fraud can be hard to pin down but is a good place to start. Social Security ranks third among all government agencies in terms of identified fraudulent payments, which totaled $7.4 billion in 2015.[5] This is still a relatively small amount in relation to the program, but the federal government is undermanned in its efforts to police fraud, and many believe the rate of fraud to be much higher. I know some people who work as disability program auditors and they estimate fraud at 8-10 percent, including overstating disabilities and under-reporting income. The US Office of Inspector General reports some amazing cases like the man who received $175,000 in DI benefits. He claimed he was blind but was found driving speedboats and running two business. Then there is the man who received $150,000 in benefits. He claimed he couldn't work because of back pain but was found digging graves and was paid under the table.

According to the CBO, the SSDI program is projected to go bust by 2022 unless Congress changes the current law. [6] This is the definition of unsustainability. Unfortunately, it is nearly impossible to effectively police a large welfare program with 11 million recipients. This is a perfect opportunity for Locally Grown Government to make a difference. With one in 30 citizens receiving these benefits, it's likely most of us know somebody receiving benefits. If the SSDI was block granted to states and municipalities with incentives for people to report fraud, I believe the results would be much more effective than the current undermanned federal policing. There are already well-established federal statutes that reward whistleblowers. We should expand and modernize their usage.

SSDI is just one example of safety net programs that need serious fixing. However, any attempts at reform are met with massive political resistance. In my opinion, the only way to stop this rendezvous with catastrophe is through a constitutional amendment that explicitly limits federal taxing and spending. A "balanced budget amendment." This would force the Feds to prioritize limited resources: More social spending and less on national defense, schools, and infrastructure? America's unique characteristic as being the de-facto global reserve currency (i.e., 60 percent of all global trade is done in $US) gives it "an exorbitant privilege" where our federal debt is viewed essentially as a riskless asset. The US government will always pay interest and principle on its debt. No matter that the United States gross government debt (at all levels) is 137 percent of its GDP as of 2017, according to the OECD. Only Portugal, Greece, Italy, and Japan have worse ratios. [7] This amount doesn't count the borrowing from federally backed programs like Fannie Mae and Freddie Mac that come with implicit guarantees from the federal government. We saw in the 2008 financial crisis that those guarantees are actually explicit. When you count those amounts with the current account deficit, the debt-to-GDP ratio is a whopping 172 percent. No worries, though, since the US Federal Reserve can simply print more money, according to the Modern Monetary Policy proponents. We cannot count on our elected representatives to reduce spending because we know what really motivates them. When the catastrophe hits, many will be happy to declare a national emergency to capture more of our inherent power.

If this sounds like a Ponzi scheme, it's because it is. With a constitutional amendment we can stop the madness. What's needed is a frank discussion with the American people. I'm optimistic that if that discussion is fact-based, bipartisan, and civil, the American people in their collective wisdom will understand what needs to be done.

Transfer 45% of Federal Budget to the State and Local Level

Do you think local governments having more money and control over, say, healthcare and caring for the poor and elderly could do a better job than Washington, DC? Do you think folks managing these programs would be more accountable and citizens more interested in policy if a lot more money was at stake in their own backyards? I think that re-casting of most of our social safety net delivery system as "federally funded - locally delivered", would usher in a renaissance of problem-solving innovation. Thousands of local laboratories working on the same issues would have a much better chance at creating cost-effective solutions to serving its citizens than bureaucrats in Washington. Here's my roadmap to getting there.

- Reduce federal government spending by 10 percent across the board, including entitlements. Also reduce state and local spending baselines by five percent and one percent, respectively.

- Increase current level of transfers to states from the Feds by 230 percent. Transfers change to fixed block grants rather than "pay as you go." The vast majority of transfer increases are from entitlements and welfare.
- Cap combined federal, state, and local government spending to 33 percent of GDP.
- Increase combined government taxes as a percent of GDP from 32.9 percent to 34.9.
- Use the resulting modest federal surpluses to reduce government debt outstanding.
- Amend our constitution either through heavy pressure on Congress or directly through a state-organized constitutional convention.
- Deploy the Locally Grown Government Voting Platform, starting in local governments.

I analyzed government financial data to create the chart in Table 26. [8] It shows a profit and loss statement for all three levels of government. You can see from the "Transfer" columns the amount of money the federal government currently transfers to the states. For example, the "Education" expense category shows that $59.5 billion (54.9 percent) of the $108.3 billion federal Education budget is sent to the states to support local public education. The State and Local columns show the respective finances for those levels of government. You can see that states spend $329.5 billion and local governments spend $708.4 billion. The transfers from the federal government are reflected in the state and local numbers. The Total column combines income, expense, and debt categories across all three levels of government, and the %GDP and %Budget columns are calculated based on the total government spend. So, government education spending at all levels equals 5.4 percent of GDP and 14.2 percent of the combined budgets. You can see that seven of 10 spending categories already involve some level of transfers to the state and local levels.

Table 26 – All Government P&L with Transfers

Source: USGovernmentSpending.com

Function ($US Billions) FY 2018	Fed	Transf. %	Transfer$	State	Local	Total	% GDP	% Budget
GDP						$20,029.3	17.5%	
GDP Growth Rate								
Revenue								
Income Taxes	$2,191.0			$441.2	$45.8	$2,678.0	13.4%	
Social Insurance Taxes	$1,224.3			$221.3	$21.8	$1,467.4	7.3%	
Ad Valorem Taxes	$223.9			$542.4	$723.1	$1,489.4	7.4%	
Fees and Charges	$0.0			$225.3	$310.8	$536.1	2.7%	
Business and Other Revenue	$70.1			$171.0	$234.8	$475.9	2.4%	
Transfers	-$55.0			$0.0	$0.0	-$55.0	-0.3%	
Total Direct Revenue	$3,654.3			$1,601.2	$1,336.3	$6,591.8	32.91%	38.94%
Expenses		$2,535.8						
Pensions	$1,061.8	0.0	$0.0	$268.5	$58.4	$1,388.7	6.9%	18.1%
Health Care	$1,120.5	-38.5%	-$431.3	$692.9	$182.6	$1,564.7	7.8%	20.4%
Education	$108.3	-54.9%	-$59.5	$329.5	$708.4	$1,086.7	5.4%	14.2%
Defense	$710.0	0.0%	$0.0	$1.5	$0.0	$711.5	3.6%	9.3%
Welfare	$353.5	-34.9%	-$123.2	$122.3	$94.1	$446.7	2.2%	5.8%
Protection (Fire, Police)	$41.5	-23.9%	-$9.9	$75.8	$191.0	$298.4	1.5%	3.9%
Transportation	$91.8	-70.0%	-$64.3	$134.0	$157.2	$318.7	1.6%	4.2%
General Government	$52.4	-6.7%	-$3.5	$59.2	$85.2	$193.3	1.0%	2.5%
Other Spending	$63.9	-50.4%	-$32.2	$83.5	$386.1	$501.3	2.5%	6.6%
Interest	$314.9	0.0%	$0.0	$44.9	$59.7	$419.5	2.1%	5.5%
Total Spending	$3,918.6	-18.5%	-$723.9	$1,812.1	$1,922.7	$7,653.4	38.2%	
Govt Operating Incomes	-$264.3	% GDP	$0.0	-$210.9	-$586.4	-$1,061.6	-5.3%	
Gross Public Debt	-$21,093.3	-105.3%	$0.0	-$1,195.2	-$1,862.2	-$24,150.7	120.6%	
Other Borrowing	-$298.7	-1.5%	$0.0	$0.0	$0.0	-$298.7		
Agency/GSE Debt	-$8,875.9	-44.3%	$0.0	$0.0	$0.0	-$8,875.9		
Total Govt Liabilities	-$30,532.2	-152.4%	$0.0	-$1,406.1	-$2,448.6	-$34,386.9	171.7%	

Increase Block Grant to States from the Feds

Locally Grown Government means more bottom-up government with local autonomy for a wide range of government functions. Ideally, we'd love to see taxation done at the level of government where the actual services are delivered. However, it will be challenging enough to convince voters to block grant huge federal programs to the states more than what happens now. Transferring the taxation for these programs from federal to state and local levels could only come after several years of demonstrated success of the block grant process. It is much easier to convince voters and their representatives to simply increase the flow of the block grants already in place. This is simply an act of Congress to increase transfer funding to the programs and provide more autonomy on how it's spent. No constitutional issues here at all given that SCOTUS confirmed the federal government has the power to grant and take away spending as it wishes.

I propose increasing the overall level of federal transfers 230 percent, 200 percent of which is with Medicare, Medicaid, SSDI, and welfare. For example, Medicaid, the federal healthcare program for poor citizens, is currently funded with federal tax dollars in the form of open-ended subsidies to states that range from 50-75 percent of each state's cost of administering the federally mandated program. In my proposal, we start by answering the question: "What percentage of the federal budget are we comfortable allocating to Medicaid?" In my proposal, the 2018 federal cost of Medicaid was $350 billion. After, the Locally Grown across-the-board 10 percent cut, this fixed amount is now $315 billion. That's the maximum the Feds would have contributed in 2018. The states also spent $210 billion on their share of Medicaid so in total, there would still be $535 billion versus $560 billion spent on Medicaid.

The major difference introduced here is budget discipline. States will have a fixed contribution from Uncle Sam and that's it. We already do this with Medicaid in US non-state territories. States need to become more efficient in using the funding. With 10-20 percent waste, fraud, and abuse in the system, it shouldn't be too difficult to serve the same low-income constituency more efficiently. This is in contrast to the open-ended federal commitment to subsidize 50-70 percent of whatever the state administration costs are. There is much less incentive to reduce costly waste, fraud, and abuse when you know the Feds are matching at least every dollar the states put in. In exchange for accepting a fixed amount for a federally mandated program, the states should get new rules that make it easier to experiment with creative ways to deliver lower-cost but higher-value healthcare. In addition to funding at least half of the costs, the Feds will improve its oversight and best practices sharing it gathers from all state and local governments. Just as a big consulting company like McKinsey or Bain would come in to improve operations, so would the Feds become a true partner in improving the performance of an important common good safety net.

However, there are social safety net needs that still only the government can provide because it can shift resources to places that need it most, as with natural disasters and areas of the country with economic challenges. Keep in mind that this "federal role" is core to the national social contract that unifies our republic. This is normal and appropriate for any civilized society. In my view, that's the point of becoming "a union of states": directing group resources to address the common good. However, this argument isn't a license to randomly usurp inherent power. Striking a proper balance between inherent power and the common good is the main purpose of a constitution.

Difficult changes are often best introduced slowly to avoid shocks to the system. For this reason, working within the existing block grant construct to increase transfers to states is a great first step in executing government from the bottom up. In the chart below, I've added a "Proposed Transfer %" column that shows the overall level of block grants from federal to state in Table 27. Currently, seven of the 10 major categories of spending already involve transfers from federal to state. This is great because there is already a mechanism in place that transfers federal funds to states. Locally Grown Government would cause little or no bureaucratic disruption, so all that is needed is legislation that increases the block grants to a level that retains a much smaller federal percentage for program administration.

Table 27 – Locally Grown P&L with More Federal Transfers

Function ($US billions)	Fed Net	Current Transf. %	Proposed Transf. %	Proposed Transfer$	Fed Net	State	Transf. %	Transfer$	State Net	Local	Total	% GDP
GDP											$20,029.3	
		Tax increase			*Tax increase*				*Tax increase*			
Revenue	*Rev increase*	7.0%				5.0%				1.0%		
Income Taxes	$2,344.4					$463.3				$46.3	$2,853.9	
Social Insurance Taxes	$1,310.0					$232.4				$22.0	$1,564.4	
Ad valorem Taxes	$239.6					$569.5				$730.3	$1,539.4	
Fees and Charges	$0.0					$236.6				$313.9	$550.5	
Business and Other Re	$75.0					$179.6				$237.1	$491.7	
Transfers				-$151.4	-$151.4	$151.4		-$676.9	-$676.9	$676.9	$0.0	
Total Direct Revenue	$3,969.0	*Budget Cuts*		-$1,668.4	$2,149.1	$3,501.1		-$1,979.8	$844.4	$4,006.4	$6,999.9	34.9%
Expenses	*Reduce Cost*	10.0%					*Budget Cuts*	$0.1		*Budget Cuts*	$0.0	
Pensions	$955.62	0.0%	-15.0%	-$143.3	$812.3	$391.3	-$0.1	-$47.0	$344.3	$104.3	$1,260.9	
Health Care	$1,008.5	-38.5%	-98.0%	-$988.3	$20.2	$1,209.0	-$1.0	-$1,148.5	$60.4	$1,317.8	$1,398.4	
Education	$97.5	-54.9%	-98.0%	-$95.5	$1.9	$350.2	-$1.0	-$332.7	$17.5	$1,030.7	$1,050.2	
Defense	$797.3	0.0%	0.0%	$0.0	$797.3	$1.4	$0.0	$0.0	$1.4	$0.0	$798.7	
Welfare	$318.2	-34.9%	-95.0%	-$302.2	$15.9	$292.4	-$1.0	-$277.8	$14.6	$368.2	$398.7	
Protection (Fire, Police	$37.4	-23.9%	-50.0%	-$18.7	$18.7	$80.8	-$0.7	-$56.6	$24.3	$245.1	$288.0	
Transportation	$82.6	-70.0%	-90.0%	-$74.4	$8.3	$140.1	-$0.3	-$42.0	$98.0	$197.2	$303.5	
General Government	$47.2	-6.7%	0.0%	$0.0	$47.2	$53.1	$0.0	$0.0	$53.1	$84.3	$184.6	
Other Spending	$57.5	-50.4%	-80.0%	-$46.0	$11.5	$94.1	-$0.8	-$75.2	$18.8	$456.7	$487.0	
Interest	$314.9	0.0%	0.0%	$0.0	$314.9	$42.7	$0.0	$0.0	$42.7	$59.1	$416.7	
Total Spending	$3,716.5	-44.9%		-$1,668.4	$2,048.1	$2,655.0		-$1,979.8	$675.2	$3,863.5	$6,586.8	32.9%
Govt Operating Income	$252.4		230.5%	$0.0	$101.0	$846.1			$169.2	$142.9	$413.1	2.1%
Gross Public Debt	-$21,093.3		198.1%	$0.0	-$20,992.3	-$1,195.2				-$1,862.2	-$24,150.7	
Other Borrowing	-$298.7		85.9%	$0.0	-$298.7	$0.0				$0.0	-$298.7	
Agency/GSE Debt	-$8,875.9			$0.0	-$8,875.9	$0.0				$0.0	-$8,875.9	
Total Govt Liabilities	-$30,015.5			$0.0	-$30,066.0	-$349.1				-$1,719.3	-$32,912.2	164.3%

For example, with Healthcare, Locally Grown Government proposes transferring 98 percent of its budget to the states to fund all federally mandated healthcare services. This would leave two percent or over $20 billion to handle what should remain of the federal bureaucracy to manage its newly limited role of compliance and gathering data on the effectiveness of the program across states. I believe we need a major infrastructure project to modernize and integrate the operating infrastructure across all three levels of government so that we can measure and share outcomes. For example, why do we need 50 different state computer systems to manage Medicaid? The federal government should contract to have a single modern system that it provides to the states for free. This guarantees that data from lower levels of government can be efficiently and quickly collected and analyzed by the federal government, and best practices shared.

To illustrate the point that we are leaving plenty of money for federal administration, $20 billion in annual revenue to manage federal healthcare would rank number 150 among the Fortune 500 companies. At $20 billion, this is bigger than the non-accounting revenue of PricewaterhouseCoopers, the largest accounting firm in the country. If you assume that every one of the federal healthcare administrative employees was a certified public accountant with a median salary of $62,410 (we are being generous here), you'd have a company with over 300,000 employees.[9] This agency would land within the Top 15 in the Fortune 500 by employee headcount. You could cut the budget by 50 percent and the federal health agency would still be among the Top 300 of the Fortune 500 companies in terms of revenue. It seems reasonable that retaining two percent of the federal healthcare budget for overhead is more than adequate to execute a robust federal management and auditing function, especially with incentives from better use of whistleblower laws.

We have made some broad assumptions about the percentage of transfers for the various major functions that are related to their mission. This means some functions retain a larger share for administration. Still, with management that is close to the average of its private sector peers, we think the federal process of capped block grants would yield great efficiencies that would free up even more funds to be transferred to the states for their ultimate purpose of helping citizens. I'm confident that we can arrive at more accurate transfer percentages with a few folks in the room who are smarter than me, but hopefully I've offered a reasonable starting point for that discussion.

There are still three major functions where there is no budget transfer to states. They are tied to the enumerated federal powers in the Constitution. The federal government must provide for the common defense. We cannot outsource this, and, in fact, we need to upgrade our capabilities to meet the challenges of a more complex and dangerous world than we've seen in a long time. Defense should continue to be a national priority for all of us, without which nothing else would be possible over the long term. I think too many people in this country undervalue our armed forces, which is now funded at about 4.2% of GDP, the lowest level since 2003.[10] Like cyber security and insurance, the military is something nobody pays attention to until they need it. Then, it becomes THE most important thing. However, this doesn't mean that defense is immune from the same budget cutting and efficiency efforts as other federal agencies. To the contrary, defense should also be cut to a sustainable level and modernized so that it still meets our security needs. I propose a 10 percent cut just like all other federal departments!

Next, we must pay interest on our national debt. After all, the US is the indispensable guarantor of world trade with the $US as the reserve currency and theoretically "risk free" asset. Finally, the "General Government" spending category covers all those important functions the Feds need to provide to make the rest of the government work. This includes the administrative costs to run our three main branches of government: the judicial, legislative, and executive branches. Social Security for retirement income would still be administered federally but we would block grant most of the disability income program to the states, which represents 15 percent of the overall Social Security budget. This program needs reform such as raising the retirement age and fraud reduction. And yes, we should follow the example of countries like Sweden who have made sustainable government pension reforms like switching from defined benefit to defined contribution and temporarily reducing payments when the economy is in bad shape. However, from an operational perspective, the old-age pension program is managed reasonably well. After all, the Feds are just sending out Social Security checks until people die. Not difficult. Plus, the burden would be too great if administration were transferred to the state and local level, in my opinion. Oh, and anyone who touches it will be toast!

Locally Grown Government proposes shifting a significant percentage of the 2.1 million federal civilian non-postal jobs to become state or local employees as states and municipalities.[11] This shouldn't represent massive disruption since most federal workers are already spread out across the country. Only 15 percent currently reside in the Washington, DC, area.[12] In fact, every state has its share of federal employees roughly on a pro-rata basis to their populations. What the exact percentage is of federal employees that would transfer to state and municipal workers would depend on the job functions and the local characteristics. For example, most workers who support healthcare or welfare functions would become state workers while national parks would retain all of their federal workers. I would anticipate smaller population states to absorb federal workers at the state level, which is where the majority of those functions are performed now.

There is a size threshold where it doesn't make sense for small towns to have their own safety net administrative functions. For smaller towns, the transferred government functions would be more efficiently administered at the state level. By the same token, large metropolitan areas that contain millions of people would absorb many federal workers at the municipal level. For example, Los Angeles County generates over $700 billion in GDP, more than all but six US states.[13] Again, the workforce distribution is consistent where these federal workers are living and working already. We are simply changing the accountability from federal to state or municipal so each can explore different solution to deliver government services more effectively.

Once workers have transferred to lower level government authority, they become subject to that authority. With incentives in place to hit key performance metrics like reducing waste fraud and abuse, there is an enormous amount of money on the table to create more accountable and sustainable government. In 2018, for example, the US Department of Justice recovered $2.8 billion in fraudulent payments, 75 percent of which was represented by Medicare and Medicaid fraud. It also paid $310 million to individual whistleblowers in accordance with federal False Claims Act. This represented 14.8 percent of recoveries, a pretty good payday for those that called foul.[14]

Now contrast that with the amount of waste, fraud, and abuse that actually exists. A 2012 study, "Eliminating Waste in US Health Care", authored by the RAND Corp. and Donald Berwick, the head of the Centers of Medicare and Medicaid Services (CMS) in the Obama administration, estimated that fraud represented 6-10 percent of all Medicare and Medicaid payments.[15] In 2017, our country spent $1.138 trillion on these two programs, of which up to $113 billion was fraudulent. The same study found roughly the same amount represented waste and other lesser forms of abuse like improper billing by doctors and hospitals. Together that represents a staggering $227 billion or 20% in waste, fraud, and abuse in our federally mandated healthcare entitlements.

Now this is where I put my business hat on and start to ask questions, like how do private sector businesses manage fraud? Well, according to the Federal Reserve, credit card transactions totaled nearly $6 trillion in 2016 [16] and had a fraud rate of about .05 percent. [17] It boggles my mind how an industry whose transaction volume is over six times larger than the federal healthcare entitlement function performs fraud management 160 times more efficiently. Think about this deeply and you get a sense of why our country is facing such a fiscal crisis. Clearly operating efficiency isn't a priority in the federal government or they tolerate this level of incompetence by design. I tend to think it's a combination of both reasons.

So, here's some thoughts how Locally Grown Government can tackle this problem. The federal government already pays 14.8

percent of fraud recoveries to whistleblowers. Let's expand this reward to include employees who work to uncover the $227 billion of waste, fraud, and abuse. In the private sector, we pay people handsomely who are effective at making business more efficient and profitable. This means that there is potentially over $33 billion (14.8 percent of $227 billion) available to pay a combination of private sector whistleblowers and government employees to root out waste, fraud, and abuse. When you include the roughly 71,000 state employees who work in social insurance administration with the 6,000 federal CMS healthcare administration workers, that represents over $434,000 for each one of those 77,000 combined workers. [18] A potential bonus equal to many times your average annual salary is a lot of incentive to fix a problem. And the best part is that there is another potential $200 billion annually to shore up our social safety net *after* those bonuses are paid. Focus on the right problems, create adequate incentives for employees to fix those problems, and hire enough employees at the local level to do the work. That's Locally Grown Government in action. There are many other areas of federal government besides healthcare entitlements that would also benefit from this approach.

Reduce Government Spending (Federal, State, Local) as a Percent of GDP to 33 Percent or Less

The Locally Grown Government path to sustainability includes a cap on total government spending of 33 percent of GDP. This is another new limit on the Hamiltonian view of unlimited government power. Getting there will require real tax increases and real spending cuts. Spending cuts doesn't mean cutting the rate of growth as some politicians define it, but rather the actual baseline. This doesn't mean that the programs will not grow over the long run, but they can no longer grow faster than GDP or inflation as has been the case for decades. The US has made these kinds of spending cuts several times in its past, including after major wars and most recently in 1986, when Congress introduced the concept of budget sequestration with the Gramm-Rudman-Hollings Deficit Reduction Act of 1985, which set hard caps on federal spending. Not long thereafter, the hard caps were abandoned because they were, well, hard. It's hard to cut spending when the country has become addicted to federal largesse. The sequestration concept was reintroduced in the Budget Control Act of 2011. In exchange for authorizing an increase in the federal debt ceiling, Congress committed itself to $2.4 trillion of deficit reduction over 10 years. If Congress couldn't agree on where the spending reductions were to happen, it triggered an across-the-board cut for all government agencies. Of course, Congress couldn't agree, and automatic cuts were triggered, and the legislation worked as planned for a while. However, the sequestration was predictably watered down as Congress couldn't agree on cuts to entitlement spending and tax increases.

To summarize: Table 29 in previous pages shows that getting to 33 percent of GDP requires across-the-board spending cuts for all three levels of government; 10 percent at the federal level, five percent state, and one percent local. Block grants then occur downstream from this reduced baseline.

The Locally Grown Government plan includes a constitutional amendment for a balanced budget to close loopholes Congress might employ to circumvent the hard spending caps. Of course, there would be great political clamor claiming the budget is being balanced on the backs of the poor and elderly and that national defense will collapse. Nothing could be further from the truth. We outlined a plan to reduce waste, fraud, and abuse in our largest entitlement program by up to 20 percent. That more than covers the proposed 10 percent reduction in the baseline of that program. In fact, a proper functioning government more biased to local management will allow more vulnerable citizens to be helped because local officials will have a better sense of local need. A core mission of Locally Grown Government is to reduce the dangerous dependence on government and replace it with economic opportunity.

Increase Taxes as Percent of GDP from 32.9 to 34.9 Percent

Yes, we need to raise taxes. Our nation's fiscal problems are large enough that spending cuts alone won't close the budget gap. Governments at all levels need to raise more revenue. Locally Grown Government proposes to raise federal taxes by 7 percent across the board for both individuals and corporations. For an individual in the 25 percent federal income tax bracket, their new tax rate would be 26.75 percent. For an individual in the 20 percent bracket for capital gains, the new rate would be 21.4 percent. For corporations, the flat 21 percent federal rate would increase to 22.47 percent. This means that *all* federal tax rates would increase by 7 percent, including payroll taxes. Also, I propose a five percent state and one percent local tax increase with the same across-the-board structure as federal, but each state and local government would have to make this decision itself.

The Locally Grown tax increase also means that the 15 percent of low-income Americans who receive income tax credits (i.e., refunds of any and all taxes they might have paid) will see their credits reduced. Some would argue that's it's not fair to have citizens on the lower end of the income scale share in the burden of tax increases. My answer to that is that a 7 percent reduction of the $3,191 average Earned Income Tax Credit (EITC) represents a very modest $223 per year. These folks are still getting a refund of nearly all their payroll taxes, which means they still receive their federal benefits almost for free. Fixing a problem as big as our fiscal mess requires all hands-on deck and, excluding segments of the citizenry from participating in the solution, deprives them of the dignity of belonging and doing their part. Everyone doing their part, no matter how small, is a critical first step in healing the bitterness and political division in our country. My proposal does nothing to change our already quite progressive federal tax code where rates rise as income rises and 65 percent of all taxes are paid by the top 20 percent of households. Wealthier citizens will be shouldering the large majority of this tax increase.[19]

The historical practice of shielding lower income brackets from tax increases only further narrows an already shrinking tax base. It is unsustainable to continue to penalize work and productivity. If we are ever to find common ground, all citizens must contribute so there is a sense of shared sacrifice. The last time we had this was WWII, where everyone contributed. Rich and poor families alike sent their sons and daughters to fight. Industry was reconfigured to support the war effort, and civilians stood in lines because certain food was rationed. "Rosie the Riveter" was the star of a campaign to get female workers into factories to replace the male workers who went off to fight. When I hear calls from politicians calling for a WWII level of effort to combat climate change, I struggle to see how a country currently so divided could come together again to produce that level of effort. No, the number one priority is making our government sustainable because, without that, there is no money to address climate change, income inequality, and any other social problems.

Slowly Pay Down Our Debt

Kati and I were big fans of the popular HBO series *Game of Thrones*. It was a mandatory Sunday night formation for the past eight years. In the story, the central ruling family, House Lannister, has a tag line that everyone in the kingdom knows: "A Lannister always pay his debts." This proved to be an invaluable tool to all members of the Lannister clan when they had no money and needed to bribe their way out of trouble.

So, it is with the United States. As the "reserve currency" that has facilitated global commerce since WWII, not paying our debt would cause untold destruction to the global financial order. Nobody would be spared except those who owned lots of gold and maybe Bitcoin. As of 2018, US government debt at all levels exceeds $34 trillion. That equals $104,615 for every man, woman, and child in our country. Do you have a spare $104,615 lying around to help Uncle Sam? And this debt is growing rapidly at a rate of more than *$73 billion per day,* which is 36 percent faster than the entire economy that is supposed to generate the tax revenue to pay that debt. [20]

Remembering that the US is the indispensable country, with its reserve currency considered as a theoretically risk-free asset; we are spending at a rate that exceeds our income. If you were lending the US money, how long would it be before you'd start to question its credit worthiness? After all, the total government debt outstanding is much larger than our entire economy. As Table 28 illustrates, a combination of a 7 percent tax increase and a 10 percent decrease in spending generates a modest surplus, enabling us to reverse the momentum and slowly reduce our outstanding debt. The positive ripple effects of changing this momentum would be incredible for the global economy.

Table 28 – Locally Grown Government Fiscal Sustainability Over Time

	Start	1	2	3	4	5	6	7	8	9	10
GDP	$ 20,029	$20,230	$ 20,432	$ 20,636	$ 21,049	$21,470	$21,899	$22,337	$ 22,784	$23,240	$23,705
GDP Growth		1.00%	1.00%	1.00%	2.00%	2.00%	2.00%	2.00%	2.00%	2.00%	2.00%
Rev/GDP	32.9%	34.9%	34.9%	34.9%	34.9%	34.9%	34.9%	34.9%	34.9%	34.9%	34.9%
Revenue	$6,592	$7,070	$7,141	$7,212	$7,356	$7,503	$7,653	$7,806	$7,963	$8,122	$8,284
Spending/GDP	38.2%	32.9%	32.7%	32.5%	32.3%	32.0%	31.8%	31.6%	31.5%	31.5%	31.5%
Spending	-$7,653	-$6,653	-$6,681	-$6,707	-$6,799	-$6,870	-$6,964	-$7,059	-$7,177	-$7,321	-$7,467
Surplus-Deficit	-$1,062	$417	$459	$505	$557	$633	$689	$748	$786	$801	$817
Debt	-$34,387	-$33,970	-$33,510	-$33,005	-$32,448	-$31,815	-$31,125	-$30,377	-$29,592	-$28,790	-$27,973
Debt/GDP	172%	168%	164%	160%	154%	148%	142%	136%	130%	124%	118%

As you can see from Table 28, there is nothing draconian about the budget I am proposing. Government revenue is increasing, with the wealthy continuing to shoulder the majority of the tax burden while we are reducing spending baselines for everything. In fact, government revenue as a share of GDP remains stable while spending as a share of GDP is slowly decreasing. The modest surpluses are used to slowly reduce our debt or at least stop it from growing. The irony is that we still have a BIG government, but it is just more distributed. I believe this formula, along with pushing more functions down to state and local, will keep our economy thriving with a more robust and accountable public safety net. Now let's get into more detail about how things can work better at the local levels of government.

CHAPTER 11

Locally Grown Education

Children must be taught
how to think, not what to think.
Don't brainwash our kids.
– Adapted from Margaret Mead

Education is one of the most important aspects of the common good because it invests in the future generation. Appropriately, it is the third highest 2018 spending category at about one trillion dollars across all levels of government, with 88 percent of that funded and spent at the local level. According to the latest data from the OECD, the US ranks fourth in annual public K-12 spending per student and first in college spending per student.[1] And yet the US is about middle of the pack for K-12 science, math, and reading.[2] Since 70 percent of US kids attend college,[3] it makes sense that we have the most expensive education system in the world but being middle of the pack with outcomes is unacceptable. Why is this? Reforming our public education system is the Marshall Plan of our time. If we don't get it right, we all suffer. But when we dive deep to uncover root causes, some uncomfortable facts emerge. Effective solutions should recognize these facts.

Stop Indoctrinating and Start Teaching

The goal of education must be to help students develop critical thinking skills required to become productive self-sustaining citizens. However, many of our nation's traditional public schools have deviated from this mission and now focus on indoctrinating students with alternative versions of history to suit political agendas nd "dumbed-down" curriculum that inflates grades to give the appearance of meeting minimum standards. This system forces teaching to the middle and enforcement of conformity. Government aid also comes with political agendas that are often at odds with the values of the parents. The result is dissatisfaction and frustration among parents and teachers and underachievement by students. It is vital that education in this country be restructured and that it be done on the local level. Parents must be involved, and local communities must have the freedom to develop education in the way that works best for them. As H. L. Mencken famously stated, "The aim of public education is not to spread enlightenment; it is to reduce as many individuals as possible to the same safe level, to breed a standard citizenry, to put down dissent and originality."

Student and Parent Interests Are More Important Than Teachers' Interests

Unfortunately, there is often a fundamental divergence between the interests of teachers and students in our public schools. The power of teachers' unions to collectively bargain for more salary, more retirement benefits, less teaching time, and less accountability is at odds with student and parent interests. When combined with the political influence of teachers' unions, the challenge is often too much for parents and communities to overcome. Despite the claims from supporters of the status quo, teachers are not underpaid when considering their generous benefits. Public school teacher's pension costs are crowding our local school budgets everywhere. A 2011 study, *Assessing the Compensation of Public-School Teachers* by Jason Richwine, Ph.D., and Andrew G. Biggs, Ph.D., concluded that public school teacher total compensation is 52 percent greater than the equivalent private sector job with comparable education and skills requirements. [4] Although salaries are comparable to the private sector, generous pension and healthcare benefits along with much higher job security make public school teaching a well-paid profession. This disparity costs taxpayers more than $120 billion more each year than they should pay.

The public school system is the largest expenditure by far on most local government budgets, and funding is often a dominant election issue. In 13 states, teachers who are unhappy with their contracts are allowed to strike, an option not available to police and firefighters. Public sector accounting practices hide the true cost of teacher compensation by allowing lower employer contributions to benefit plans than their private sector counterparts. The federal Bureau of Labor Statistics similarly lowballs teacher compensation by excluding retiree healthcare contributions.

According to the US Census, local school districts have $437 billion in outstanding debt as of 2016, mostly driven by rising retiree costs that deprive resources each year from school operating budgets. [5] This shell game protects most public sector employees, not just teachers. As I have discussed, after a certain point government takes on a life of its own with interests that diverge from the citizens it is supposed to serve.

I am hating myself as I write this because my dad spent 20 years as a teacher and contract negotiator for the local union. I am a product of good public schools. We desperately need them to succeed. I would love teachers to be extremely well-paid if they deliver the high-quality educations our children deserve. Many charter schools are very successful with this economic bargain. However, non-charter public school teacher compensation is out of line for the outcomes they currently deliver. Unfortunately, people who recognize this and call it out are decried as heartless skinflints who are depriving children of the resources they need to succeed. A typical Hobson's Choice from the typical sources.

Fix Immigration, Fix Public Education

The second major driver of underperformance of our public schools is our loose immigration laws. Immigrant families are flooding into many large metropolitan areas, and the language and culture barriers are putting great pressure on the public schools. Here are some sobering statistics from a 2017 study by the Center for Immigration Studies:

- 23 percent of public school students in the United States came from an immigrant household in 2015, compared to 11 percent in 1990 and seven percent in 1980. About one-third of those public school students from immigrant households came from illegal immigrant households.
- In 2015, 23 percent of American public school students spoke a language other than English at home. This compares to 14 percent in 1990 and 9 percent in 1980.
- Immigration has added disproportionately to the number of low-income students in public schools. In 2015, 28 percent of public school students from immigrant households lived in poverty and they accounted for 30 percent of all students living below the poverty line.
- Local schools struggle to deal with teaching in multiple foreign languages, which creates enormous challenges. In 315 Census areas (combined enrollment 6.7 million), 10 or more foreign languages are spoken by public school students.
- There are over 700 Census areas in the country where the public schools contain at least half of their students from immigrant households. Examples include:

- 93 percent in Northeast Dade County, North Central Hialeah City, FL
- 91 percent in Jackson Heights and North Corona, New York City
- 85 percent in Westpark Tollway between Loop I-610 & Beltway, Houston, TX
- 83 percent in El Monte and South El Monte Cities, CA
- 78 percent in Annandale & West Falls Church, VA [6]

The children of illegal immigrants attend our public schools, which usually means that those schools need to make provisions for teaching in other languages besides English. Algebra is hard enough to learn without a language barrier. This dynamic also affects kids who are citizens who suffer from resources and curriculum being diluted in order to meet the needs of an increasing non-English speaking immigrant population. With this kind of challenge, we should not be surprised at the diminishing performance of our public schools. We cannot solve the problem of underperforming public schools in the long run without also reforming our immigration laws. I am certain there are a few billion people on the planet who would move to America if they could, especially if they could receive most of the public benefits citizens enjoy. Unfortunately, America would cease to exist if this were to occur. As our Constitution explicitly provides, solving our immigration challenge is solely the duty of the federal government. It is one the few enumerated powers outlined by our Founders.

Charter Schools Are a BIG Part of the Solution

When we talk of K-12 education reform, we mean public education. Private schools are doing just fine with their student enrollment largely from upper-income families, but they only represent about 8.8 percent of all students in our country. The vast majority of K-12 students are educated in public schools. Table 29, compiled from data from the National Center for Education Data Statistics, illustrates the breakdown. [7]

Table 29 – K-12 Enrollment

School Type	Fall 2018 K-12 National	Pct
Public	56,600,000.00	86.0%
Public Charter	3,396,000	5.2%
Private	5,800,000	8.8%
Totals	65,796,000	100.0%

As you can see, there are two different flavors of public schools that are structured and funded in very different ways and generate very different student outcomes. Traditional district schools represent about 86 percent of public enrollment while charter schools represent about 5.2 percent but growing quickly. Both are publicly funded schools, but charters are organized by specific state laws and are exempt from some state and local laws. In exchange for the flexibility and autonomy, charter schools must meet the certain accountability criteria as well as abide by the same rules as public schools. These include being open to all children, not requiring entrance exams, not charging tuition, and participating in state testing and federal accountability programs.

One of the big advantages for charters is that they are not obliged to hire only teachers who are members of the union. They can hire anyone they want and create teacher performance criteria and work rules that aren't governed by collective bargaining agreements. Also, at $7,131 average per student, charters received significantly less public funding than their district counterparts at $12,136. [8] The majority of this cost gap is due to the disparity in teacher compensation. Charters have other handicaps mostly due to the clout teachers' unions wield with politicians. In many localities, charters are not permitted to use public buildings and must find commercial properties to rent or build on their own, which represents a significant portion of their budgets. Some cities like NYC are openly hostile to charters and create other barriers to their expansion like providing less information about city charters in relation to their district school counters in their online open enrollment process. This is society at its worst when politically motivated adults choose their financial interests over the interest of children.

Despite the structural handicaps of charters schools, they are growing rapidly with waiting lists averaging 220 students nationally and in the thousands in many larger cities. The demographics show charter schools overwhelmingly serve disadvantaged families of color in communities where the traditional district schools are viewed as substandard or even dangerous. Table 30 illustrates:

Table 30 – Racial Demographics of US Public Schools

Race / Ethnicity	Charter Schools	Non-Charter Public Schools
White	34.9%	51.1%
Black	27.1%	15.0%
Hispanic	30.0%	24.6%
Asian	4.1%	5.2%

While performance can vary greatly by geography, a 2017 study by Stanford University's Center for Research on Education Outcomes titles found that all charter schools showed statistically significant better outcomes than their district school peers on a national basis. Furthermore, the study showed that large charter school networks—such as Achievement First, Basis Schools, and KIPP—generate extraordinary outcomes compared to their non-charter counterparts. Some of these charters achieve student results equivalent to an additional 125 days of learning in math and 57 days in reading. These are incredible outcomes, which explain why there is such high demand for charter schools, especially in lower-income communities. [9]

I think this is powerful evidence that educational outcomes

are not as much a function of money as school choice opponents contend. It's about methodology, accountability, and empowering teachers. Kids are sponges and will emulate good or bad examples in society. Parents are the first role models, and millions of low-income minority families are showing the courage to vote with their feet and enroll their children in charter schools to increase the odds of success. On the other hand, if kids see teachers constrained by poor curriculum and work rules that prioritize teacher interests over a student's interests, they will be less motivated to do their best work. Great teachers are inspiring and can change lives. I have witnessed this several times with my own kids. But there is more than ample room to raise the bar for all our teachers. The unfortunate result is that many underperforming kids in public schools are simply passed on to the next grade, where they will be another teacher's problem. I've witnessed this more frequently than the life-changing teachers. Competition makes us all better, including schools.

I realize that there are still many great district public schools and plenty of underperforming charter schools. We need to share and learn best practices for great education no matter where they come from. There is no more important common good in the US than improving our public schools. There are so many societal problems that get fixed by simply reforming our public secondary education system.

Improving K-12 Education

Here are some double bottom-line suggestions for improving public secondary education:

- Cut the current federal education budget of $97 billion federal education budget by 10 percent (Locally Grown Government budget cuts), then increase the federal transfer from 55 to 98 percent. The additional 43 percent of the federal budget going to public school districts ($41 billion), would mean an average of $416,000 extra money for the 98,700 school districts in the

US. The twist is that two-thirds of this extra money will go to public nonprofit charter schools to increase competition and quality. The additional money would come with new rules that would prohibit local school districts from unfairly obstructing the growth of charter schools. I would also encourage state and local governments to orient their school budgets to provide more support for charter schools with a bias toward proven successful charter networks.

- Allocate some of the federal education transfer to support online learning organizations such as Khan Academies, Coursera, and Udacity. These massive open online course (MOOC) organizations take some of the brightest college professors and put them online so their teaching can reach tens of thousands of students instead of just those lucky enough to be in their classroom. This is a great example of using technology to improve quality and access and bend the cost curve in higher education.

- Build more vocational and trade high schools. In a 2017 paper by the Brookings Institution, author Brian Jacob cites research of a 12 to 17-year-old national cohort of students that tracked education outcomes over time. The research suggests that "CTE (vocational school) participation is associated with higher wages, with the increase driven entirely by upper-level coursework...in more technical fields." Other findings suggest than CTE students are more engaged with their coursework that they otherwise would have been attending a traditional public high school.

Colleges and Universities

Our American colleges and universities have traditionally been the envy of the world. Today, the United States remains the country of choice for the largest number of international students, hosting about 25 percent of the 4.6 million enrolled worldwide in 2017. [10] The growth of foreign college students in the US has gone from 1.5

percent in 1975 to about 5.2 percent of US college enrollment in 2017. It's well known that having a college degree has become, for better or worse, the most important variable in career earnings prospects. It has become nearly a necessity, with nearly 70 percent of all high school graduates attending a two- or four-year college, albeit at a lower graduation rate than it should be. [11] Like healthcare, education is a "must have" for students, and parents go to extraordinary lengths to get their kids into what they consider "the best schools." Sometimes those efforts turn into criminal behavior as demonstrated by the 2019 college admission scandal where a consulting company arranged fake college profiles for students of wealthy parents. This included bribing college coaches to grant athletic scholarships to students who never played the sports and falsifying standard testing scores. This scandal has reached into the halls of the most elite schools in this country, and it is probably just the tip of the iceberg. [12] And for decades, the private sector has also been a key driver of demand by increasingly requiring a college degree as basic table stakes for many jobs that probably don't really require it.

What do you think happens to a product that is considered a necessity and there is an immense amount of government subsidy available? If you answered "price increases" you'd be correct. Healthcare is another product with similar characteristics. Do you know which product in America whose cost has increased faster than healthcare? If you answered "college education" you'd be right. The cost of attending a four-year college has increased eight times faster than the rate of inflation since 1986. [13] At $1.5 trillion, student loans represent the largest chunk of non-housing debt in America. [14] By the way, over 20 percent of student loans are delinquent as of 2018, up from 10.4 percent in 2014. Keep in mind that, in 2009, the federal government shut down the private student loan industry and now guarantees most student loans. These and other "agency obligations" are excluded from the official $22 trillion in federal debt outstanding.

We know that anything that becomes a necessity risks creating monopolies, and I fear that's what the university education establishment is becoming. However, there are some signs of hope. Former Indiana governor and current Purdue University president Mitch Daniels has implemented effective innovations in his short tenure. With his deep experience as a private and public sector executive, he asked a basic question: "Why can't we make the cost of our product fit the budgets of our customers rather than the other way around?" He found an answer to the questions, and the result is that he has controlled costs to the point where Purdue tuition has not increased in constant dollars since 2012. [15]

Even more impressive, Daniels implemented an income-sharing program as a way of financing student costs. Students who exhaust federal loans can pay the balance of tuition with an agreement to pay between three and five percent of their income for up to 10 years after they graduate. Repayments are capped at 2.5 times initial costs. In a September 2018 interview with Forbes magazine, Daniels said, "If you want indentured servitude, it's the student-loan program. With Income Sharing Agreements, the risk shifts entirely to the lender, since grads who don't find work pay nothing." American universities could use more Mitch Daniel types. [16]

And who decided all American kids needed a college education anyway? When I was growing up, we had vocational high schools for kids who knew they weren't going to attend college for one reason or another and they learned a trade instead. Policy wonks refer to vocational training as career and technical education (CTE), and it has been declining for decades as states began mandating increases in core curriculum of math, science, language, and social studies. Not that there is anything wrong with everyone learning more core curriculum, but education is not one size fits all. We currently have over seven million unfilled job openings in an economy with the lowest unemployment rate since December 1969 (3.6 percent as of July 2019). [17] Most of those jobs don't require a college degree. Do you think those jobs are attractive to a kid who just graduated from college with $75,000 in student debt? As a society, we have raised our kids to think they are a failure without a college degree, and there is certainly plenty of evidence showing a significant advantage in average lifetime earnings for those with a college degree. But life is not lived on the average, and the supply and demand for college-educated labor varies greatly depending on the field of study. Nothing is immune from the laws of supply and demand. The educational priorities over the past couple decades have misallocated human resources and need to be rebalanced.

Let me provide a little illustration of career math. According to the website Tradingeconomics.com, the median hourly wage for manufacturing is about $22 per hour. [18] This equates to $45,760 annually. According to the National Center for Education Statistics, the median annual wage for someone with a bachelor's degree is $46,900. [19] A bachelor's degree student graduates with an average of $30,100 in student debt. The $1,140 annual earnings advantage for the college graduate disappears over a 40-year working career because, discounted for inflation, the college degree job is only $26,763, not enough to pay back the student debt. Obviously, there are plenty of jobs not requiring a college degree that pay far less than the manufacturing wage, just as there are many jobs that require a college degree that pay much more than the $46,900 average. However, the point is that young citizens need to think more seriously about what they want to do for work and weigh the costs/benefits of attending college. With the astronomical rise in costs, the old credo of "Just get a college education and all will be well" no longer applies automatically.

Reducing the Cost of College

The US college and university system is a natural resource just like our national parks. Students from around the world beat the doors down to attend American universities, and those universities generally have quotas about how many foreign students are accepted. However, the percentage of foreign students has climbed rapidly so that they represent over five percent of total graduate and undergraduate enrollment. This number has doubled since 1980. Some of the top schools in the US have over 10 percent foreign students. About 35 percent of these students are from China, by far the largest country in the mix. China's government is an adversary that doesn't respect human rights, cheats on international trade rules, steals intellectual property, and seeks to undermine US interests. The bottom line is that the influx of foreign students has made it more difficult and expensive for American kids to attend college and is a big contributor to rapidly rising college costs. [20] This is simply an issue of a fixed supply of university seats being chased by an increasing number of students. If schools are accepting more rich foreign students that don't receive financial aid, it follows that there are fewer seats for American citizens. Basic math.

By providing nonprofit status to universities, we expect the priority to be educating American citizens, especially given the huge endowments many of the schools have. There are over 100 universities with endowments exceeding $1 billion. Harvard tops the list with $36 billion followed by Yale and the Texas University system at $27 billion each. [21] Total endowments at American universities were over $537 billion as of 2015. [22] That's a lot of money. According to the 2018 *U.S. News & World Report* annual college and university ranking, 27 percent of the 512 schools on their list have foreign student populations greater than 10 percent with some as high as 40 percent. [23] Fewer foreign students at elite schools would both open opportunity for more American kids and put downward pressure on tuition costs. There's plenty of fat that can and should be cut at these institutions of higher learning.

So, I recommend that there be reasonable limits to the number of foreign students (10 percent feels about right), with far less accepted from adversarial countries like China. The nonprofit status of universities that violate these limits should be subject to revocation.

Invest in Youth Public Service, Reduce College Costs, Strengthen Our Military

I propose modifying and expanding the post-9/11 GI Bill signed into law in 2008 that pays for college costs for active-duty service members and honorably discharged veterans. The law provides three years of education benefits for attending accredited colleges, including 100 percent tuition and fees for public in-state institutions and up to $22,805 for private/foreign institutions, a monthly living/housing stipend, up to $1,000 a year for books and supplies, and more. The eligibility requirements start at 100 percent for three or more years of service to 40 percent for six months of service. [24] Currently, over 30 percent of the 2.1 million active-duty and reserve military personnel are enrolled in the program. [25] However, 20 percent of those enrolled don't complete their degree, mostly because they were attending two-year degree programs and weren't strong high school students to begin with. [26] The government still pays for the school costs even though they don't complete the coursework. This amounts to $2.9 billion in essentially wasted taxpayer funds on unachieved educational goals. The major portion of the 20 percent of GIs who don't complete their degrees are from for-profit institutions. I'm not a supporter of the for-profit educational model because the outcomes are often substandard. Still, the GI program is beneficial because it produces active, engaged citizens who understand the value of the freedom they are defending, which just increases the number of young adults with a better chance of moving up the economic ladder. Here is a short list of proposed GI Bill changes that I think can achieve better outcomes including a larger, more stable, better educated military and a steady supply of skilled young leaders in our society:

- Change eligibility requirements that start after at least two years of service rather than the six-month level now. This requires more "skin in the game" from service members, which would make them less likely to drop out.
- Eliminate for-profit institutions. The dropout data is significantly higher than nonprofit. Only nonprofit public and private institutions are eligible.
- Raise the maximum years of benefits from three to four. GIs serving two years get two years of college, three years of service

gets three years of college, four or more years of service gets four years of college.

- GIs accepting benefits would not be ineligible for any other federal education aid programs such as Pell grants. No double dipping.
- 21.6 percent of GIs already have college degrees, with the vast majority of those officers graduating from college ROTC programs or service academies. Any GI who enters service would also be eligible to have their out-of-pocket college costs reimbursed based on the same two- and four-year service requirements. The additional cost for this (net of service academy grads) would be about $747 million annually. Pocket change.
- American universities must use this $747 million reimbursement (i.e., not add to endowment) of college expenses for graduates who enter military service. Universities must adhere to this policy or forfeit their nonprofit status.
- Allocate 2-3 percent of the remaining $1.9 billion in Department of Education budget (after Locally Grown Government changes) in marketing this fantastic educational opportunity to American youth. The financial comparisons are too compelling to ignore.

So, let's review our new GI bill. A new high school graduate who serves four years earning an average of $34,750 over that four years and lives in free military base housing should be able to save at least 8 percent of his (or her) income and have $11,000 saved at separation in year four. This veteran now earns a degree with minimal out-of-pocket costs worth over $88,000 while his non-GI buddy starts his post-college career with $88,000 in student debt that must be paid back over 10 years. The GI starts his post-grad career four years later than his civilian counterpart now saving at the same five percent rate of net income, but without the $11,417 annual debt service cost. This represents 28 percent more savings than his civilian buddy with the same degree and post-graduate job. This math must be explained to young adults so they can understand the opportunity before them.

Investment in education is an investment in our future. Thankfully, at $1.7 trillion annually, the money our nation spends on education reflects its importance. Table 31 outlines national spending for K-12 schools and colleges.

Table 31 – Total National Educational Spending

Private K-12 Spending 2015-16 *	$ 62,292,000,000
Fed, State Local K-12 Spending 2018 **	$ 1,086,700,000,000
Postsecondary Spending 2015-16 ***	$ 559,000,000,000
Total Education Spending USA	**$ 1,707,992,000,000**
* Council for American Private Education	
** US GovernmentSpending.com ***	
National Center for Education Statistics	

Between government and private sector out-of-pocket costs, the US spends 8.5 percent of its GDP on education. That's second to only Luxembourg among OECD countries. Federal, state, and local government account for more than 64 percent of the total. There is no question that there is plenty of money sloshing around in the halls of our schools to achieve better outcomes than we get now. The problem isn't not enough money. The problem is that we are paying too much for the quality we receive. Either we demand better quality for what we pay now, or we cut costs to be in line with the work product. It's that simple. So, the next you hear that we are underinvesting in our schools in this country, tell that person to read my book!

CHAPTER 12

Locally Grown Social Safety Net

Hard work beats talent
when talent doesn't work hard.
A natural law.
– Adapted from Tim Notke and Kevin Durant

As my dad tells it, his Italian father imparted to his children his three secrets of success in America. Like millions of immigrants, he came to America with little money but a ton of desire. His first secret was to learn the English language. If you can't speak the language, how can you work or go to school? Although Italian was sometimes spoken in his household, Giovanni Fini insisted on English. I remember Nonno and Nonna's English was pretty sketchy even after living 65 years in this country. However, my dad and most of his 10 siblings took this lesson to heart and changed their given Italian names as soon as they were old enough. My father, Umberto, became Herbert; Francesco became Frank; Assunta became Sue; and so on.

Nonno's second secret was to save money. No matter how much or little you earned, you can always put away something for a rainy day, he said. Always live below your means. That lesson was drilled into me and my siblings growing up. My savings allowed me to start businesses and take advantage of opportunities that changed my life. Giovanni's third secret was to own property. In Nonno's view, when you owned property, you were somebody. You started the process of building wealth while also giving yourself a place to live. That was the American Dream. Nonno understood double bottom line. Hard to argue with his formula for success.

Let's Measure Income Inequality Accurately

In his 2015 book, *The Economics of Inequality*, French economist Thomas Piketty describes how persistent income inequality creates long-term damage to societies and ultimately becomes unsustainable. While I agree with his premise, the research he presents contains some glaring defects that other economists have pointed out. [1] Most importantly, Piketty only measures before-tax income and doesn't include government redistribution to the lower levels of the economic ladder. According to an August 2018 paper by the US Treasury and the Congressional Joint Committee on Taxation, "Income Inequality in the United States: Using Tax Data to Measure Long-term Trends", when these uncounted forms of real income are included, about 80 percent of Piketty's income disparity disappears. [2] This is what happens when scientists and other experts conduct research with an agenda in mind. This phenomenon is called "confirmation bias", and it can compromise scientific research that society depends on to make informed decisions.

Even with a recalibration of Piketty's work, I recognize that there are still forces at work that continue to concentrate wealth and power. The best freedom and capitalism can do is promise opportunity, not outcomes. It rewards those who work hard and rewards more to those who work smarter. There are plenty of people who work hard but don't seem to make the progress they desire. In my experience, when you're not achieving your goals, you need to try something different. It might be changing jobs, getting training or education, finding a mentor, taking some risks. As humans, we all possess the capacity to learn from experience, and those who learn to repeat successful behaviors become successful. It takes discipline and sacrifice to achieve long-term goals. We must resist the temptation to blame others and demonize success since society greatly benefits from that success, first with the innovation that enhances our lifestyle and second by the taxes that are paid to fund the common good done by government. The good news is that, for folks who are having a harder time changing their trajectory, I believe there will be more jobs and better jobs in the Locally Grown world, and the public safety net will operate more effectively to help people rise to a newly productive and prosperous life.

Welfare Spending in America

The US spent $442 billion in non-housing welfare benefits in 2018. The federal government accounted for 79 percent of that total and then transferred $123 billion of it to the states in the form of Supplemental Nutritional Assistance Program (SNAP) or food stamps and the special child nutritional assistance programs. The balance of transfers goes mostly to unemployment benefits. Still, that leaves 52 percent of the $442 billion with the federal government that goes toward direct cash payments to families through a myriad of programs. [3]

According to the 2016 US Census, 52 percent of people under 18 lived in a household where at least one family member received benefits from a means-tested government program. This compares to 37 percent in 1998. [4] Think about that for a moment. More than half of our next generation of Americans are dependent on government for some portion of their subsistence, and the rate is growing. A 2014 research paper entitled "Family Welfare Cultures," by the National Bureau of Economic Research, found that children living in a household that receives public assistance are more likely to receive public assistance when they become adults. Here is a good summary of their conclusions:

> "If parents become welfare dependents, the likelihood of their children eventually becoming welfare recipients also increases. Specifically, when parents are awarded Disability Insurance (DI), the likelihood that one of their adult children will participate in DI rises by 5 percent over the next five years, and 11 percent over the next decade. These findings suggest that a more stringent screening policy for DI benefits would not only reduce payouts to current applicants but would also reduce participation rates and program costs. The results underscore how important accounting for intergenerational effects can be when making projections of how participation rates and program costs may be affected by program reforms." [5]

I hope we can all agree that our common good safety net is designed to be temporary, not a lifestyle choice. It was designed to be a hand-up, not a hand-out. The data suggests that the latter outcome is often the reality, and by any measure, this is financially and morally unsustainable. Having a large and growing multi-generational segment of the population dependent on government is corrosive and divisive for our country.

It wasn't always this way. In 1996, President Clinton signed the Temporary Assistance of Needy Families (TANF) program, promising to "end welfare as we know it." With TANF, most recipients are required to work up to 30 hours per week. It also included a generous five-year period where citizens could receive benefits. The program was delivered as a block grant transfer to states that had flexibility in how it could be spent as long as it met one of four goals: helping poor families; promoting work and marriage; reducing out-of-wedlock pregnancy; and increasing two-parent families. Who can argue with these goals for society, especially when it comes to children? At the time, critics forecasted a catastrophe. Instead, TANF accomplished its mission of getting people back to work, in a big way.

A 2016 study, "Poverty After Welfare Reform," by Scott Winship of the Manhattan Institute, analyzed data on over 2.3 million children over 46 years and found that child poverty overall fell between 1996 and 2014 after including non-cash government benefits to the lowest point since 1979. This includes the small portion of citizens in "deep poverty" (50 percent or less than the official poverty line). The study also found that poverty among the children of single parents was at an all-time low in 2014 after including refundable tax credits and noncash benefits. Mr. Winship's data shows that rolling back the 1996 TANF welfare reform would likely reverse the gains among families with dependent children. [6]

Some might point to 52 percent of people receiving public benefits as just more evidence of rampant income inequality in the US. However, a little more research reveals that all these benefits hinge on the concept of "means testing." In other words, if you pass the means test, you must need the benefits. But what if means-testing rules are intentionally loosened or ignored so that lots of folks collect benefits who wouldn't have qualified previously? This would be kind of a form of political bribery, right? For example, Obamacare's expansion of Medicaid eligibility to 138% of the federal poverty level moved the goal posts of what constitutes "need." There is no mandatory verification process, allowing people simply to declare their income and start receiving benefits. A 2013 brief from the Centers for Medicare and Medicaid Services states that "Eligibility will be verified primarily through self-attestation."

To see how these "loosened" eligibility requirements show up in practice, we can look to a 2017 report from Louisiana's state auditor, Daryl Purpera, who took a random sample of 100 Medicaid recipients and found that 82 shouldn't have qualified for all the benefits they received. Most were underreporting income by gaming the "self-reported income" rule. Ten of those getting benefits even had incomes higher than Louisiana's median household income. [7] This kind of waste, fraud, and abuse tolerated in benefit programs erodes the trust of citizens in the sustainability of the public safety net and cheats the vast majority of deserving recipients.

Habitat for Humanity

A great example for how local government can help its poor citizens out of poverty is Habitat for Humanity. It was founded in 1976 by Millard and Linda Fuller in Americus, Georgia. Habitat has built or restored over 800,000 homes, providing 13 million people with the American dream of home ownership. Former president Jimmy Carter and his wife, Rosalyn, have been tremendous supporters of Habitat for decades. It is a great example of real, sustainable results from the private sector and a model that should be considered by government for providing affordable housing.

Habitat is a kind of chaordic organization in that it has no real central authority and is a self-organizing entity. Each local chapter is responsible for its own fundraising, staffing, and project management. It is consistent with several of our Locally Grown Government principles including the bias toward work by requiring Habitat recipients to participate in the building of the home alongside volunteers. Recipients also have to save $2,000 for a down payment, just like my grandfather would have advised. After the home is completed, the recipient must also pay a monthly mortgage that they can afford, which is much less than the cost of the home and typically much less than the recipients pay in rent. This savings is like a substantial pay raise for these working families, which they can use to continue their upward economic rise in our society.

The Habitat founders knew that people with "skin in the game" act differently than people who just get something for free. Work and accomplishment are the foundation of self-esteem, which is essential in helping people rise out of poverty. At my former company Enservio, we sponsored Habitat homes in Massachusetts. Kati and I participated with our kids when they were in elementary school to give them their first volunteer experience. With billions more in Locally Grown federal transfer funding hitting the state and local levels, I would encourage some of the 20,000 cities and towns to experiment with grants to Habitat and similar organizations that have proven results in reducing poverty and creating a basis for accumulating wealth for low-income citizens.

As with most categories of government spending under the Locally Grown Government plan, TANF would remain in place and states would be given even more money and flexibility through the block grant process to find more sustainable solutions to meet the needs of their citizen residents. The program is not perfect and could probably use some tweaking, but it's hard to argue with the results. I propose block granting 95 percent of all federal welfare spending to the states, leaving a reasonable five percent for administration. I'm sure critics who favor big government will warn of catastrophe again, and I expect once the data are in, they will be proven wrong again. Table 32 illustrates the impact a public-private partnership with Habitat could make.

Table 32 – Habitat for Humanity is a Better Model for Public Housing

Total Welfare Spending all Government *	$ 446,700,000,000
Allocation to Habitat Program	10%
Allocation to Habitat Program	$ 44,670,000,000
Median Cost of Habitat home **	$ 100,000
Cost of Home Paid by Donees	20%
Cost of Home Defrayed by Volunteers	20%
Net out of Pocket Cost per Home for Government	$ 60,000
Number of Additional Homes that can be Built Annually	744,500
2018 New Homes Built by Habitat in the US **	18,180
*USGovernmentSpending.com **Habitat for Humanity*	

If we allocated 10 percent of our total welfare spending to building Habitat homes to help poor Americans build wealth, we could build 744,000 homes per year. Think of the massive dent that would put in income inequality not to mention a fiscal stimulus that would create thousands of great middle-class construction jobs. Instead of having to spend more than 30 percent of their income on rent, that money goes to mortgage payments that build equity. The mortgages would be highly subsidized via 20 percent of labor cost performed by volunteers including the government picking up the tab on 60 percent of the remaining cost, and the Habitat recipient paying a mortgage based on 20 percent of the cost of the home. This approach to reducing income inequality is way more effective that subsidizing rent in crappy homes, or food stamps and other expensive subsidies that tend to create permanent dependency. This method gives people wealth. A much different proposition.

Welfare Recipients Should be Required to Work

About 40 million people received SNAP benefits (food stamps) in 2017 and the total government spending on food supplement programs was $98 billion in 2018, according to USGovernmentSpending.com. [8] The SNAP program contains work requirements, which is good, but there is significant non-compliance through state-requested waivers, as well as loopholes in the complex work rules. Of the 40 million SNAP recipients, 3.5 million were non-disabled adults without children, and nearly 70 percent of those folks were not working or enrolled in a qualifying training program. The Factcheck.org article tells the story of a Minnesota millionaire who received SNAP benefits for 19 months to expose loopholes in the system. He purposely took no income during the period to illustrate there wasn't an asset test on receiving benefits. Let's hope Congress closes that loophole. Politicians like to defend or criticize program non-compliance data, depending on which side of the political aisle they reside. However, my analysis of the data shows that there is meaningful waste, fraud, and abuse in our system of public benefits.

I strongly advocate making our public safety net delivery as local as possible by introducing a modernized version of the poor farms that were common in the US in the 19th and early 20th century before Social Security. I know what you're thinking. Poor farms, really? Before you start accusing me of being an inhuman wretch, hear me out. These facilities would be a combination work training center, food pantry, agricultural and temporary work coordinator, day care, drug and alcohol counseling, and healthcare clinic. This approach addresses the problems of needy citizens more holistically. This facility would also be a public-private partnership by integrating local charitable organizations and businesses. For a single mom who can't attend job training currently, she would be able to go to a local facility to attend digital classes while her kids were being cared for. Some of those folks caring for those kids would themselves be aid recipients, learning a new skill while providing value to society and raising self-esteem. From drivers to caregivers to food service, a significant portion of the staff at this facility would be current or former aid recipients. These new community facilities can also provide temporary shelter to the rising number of homeless folks in America while they get some of the mental health and other services they need. Besides the obvious help with physical needs, Locally Grown community centers most importantly start to build the self-esteem and dignity that comes with meaningful work with others.

Better Coordination Between Government and Non-Profits

Our family volunteers and supports a nonprofit focused on mentoring and tutoring at-risk kids where we live. Indian River County is blessed to contain a lot of wealthy, generous residents, and it is awash with millions in annual charitable giving at the local level. There are at least a dozen charities that address the community we are focused on, most of them with similar mission statements. The county has a population of about 154,000 and receives about $10 million in federal support from the Department of Housing and Urban Development.

Seems like there is a substantial amount of money available to address the most pressing needs where we live, especially with a poverty rate well below the national average at about 10.6 percent. [9] However, despite the best efforts of all the volunteers and donors, there is so much overlap in mission with charities and government programs that the ecosystem is rife with inefficiency. We see citizens regularly falling through the cracks in both the government and

charitable structures designed to help. It often starts with eligibility rules that are outdated and even unfair. I was listening to HUD
Cabinet Secretary Ben Carson recently in an interview where he
discussed the reforms he's made over the past two years. Initially, he
was frustrated with the bureaucracy that seemed more interested in
rules than outcomes. He pointed out that his first move when he was
appointed was to hire a CFO, a position that was vacant during most
of the previous administration. As a businessman, I cannot imagine
an organization with a $50 billion budget without a CFO. Carson
said he finally has visibility and accountability for where the money
is being spent. He also said he is updating their information systems
to support that accountability.

I see a huge opportunity to harmonize the efforts of federal, state,
local, and charitable institutions in order to better serve the needy
where they live. HUD could explore outsourcing a portion of its
budget to supporting highly effective organizations like Habitat for
Humanity to deliver more affordable housing and provide needy
citizens with their first opportunity to build wealth. As a condition
of partnership, HUD could require charitable partners to use the
same tech platform so that data can be easily consolidated to better
measure outcomes. And the outcome that matters most is reducing the ranks of welfare recipients as they become full self-sustaining families.

Case Study for HUD Partnering with Habitat for Humanity

The New York City Housing Authority is the largest public housing
agency in the United States. It manages about 174,000 apartments for nearly 400,000 income folks across the five boroughs. If
NYCHA were a city, it would be in the top 50 largest cities in the
United States. [10] When I lived in Manhattan in the 1980s, I drove
past many of these skyscraper apartments in the Bronx on my way
back to Boston for family visits. They reminded me of buildings in
the Soviet-era eastern-bloc cities, which is to say quite unappeal-
ing. And that's from the outside. Inside, it is well known that much

of this housing is infested with vermin, crime-ridden, and poorly maintained by both the City of New York and the housing authority residents.

I believe a Habitat for Humanity-type solution would work great here. Is see an achievable double-bottom line outcome that gives poor residents *immediate wealth* in the form of home equity by transferring ownership of the units as condominiums. A consortium of local, state, and federal government would act as "the bank" to finance the purchase by the residents. Like Habitat, residents will be required to save a small down payment (maybe $2,000), and work on their home (these units need lots of maintenance) and pay a mortgage (mortgage principal is about 35 percent of the cost of home). Currently, the US Dept of Housing and Urban Development pays NYCHA $1.5 billion each year to maintain these 170,000 units. According to a 2017 NYCHA report, these units require $31.8 billion of maintenance over 20 years or $1.59 billion per year. [11] This amount is ironically 98% of the $1.5 billion annual amount HUD sends to NYCHA. I'm betting that the "maintenance requirements" have more to do with making sure NYCHA spends all the federal money than it has to do with the actual repair costs. The 2017 NYCHA report also states that, over the next 20 years, the aging public housing stock will require $45 billion to replace things like lead pipes, faulty appliances, and fixtures.

So, NYCHA states that the total costs to bring its public housing stock up to date is about $77 billion. My proposal would reduce that amount by 20% to account for the waste, fraud, and abuse that the evidence shows exists in most government spending. Using this reduced capital amount ($61.6 billion) as a proxy for the value of the 177,000 housing units equates to an average value of each unit of about $348,000. Now let's give 65 percent of that value to the low-income residents. That's over $226,000 in real wealth created instantly for 170,000 low-income families in New York City. *The government would still invest 65 percent of the total adjusted cost ($40 billion) for repairs and upgrades.* However, staying true to the Habitat model, these families would have to buy the remaining 35 percent of equity in the form of a 30-year government-guaranteed fixed mort-gage at a below market (three percent) interest rate, which equals a $514 per month mortgage payment. This mortgage payment, which builds further equity, is less than the average $533 rent paid by NYCHA residents, which builds no wealth. [12]

So, what have we accomplished here? We have reduced a federal, state, and local joint annual obligation of $3.08 billion by 35 percent and created instant wealth for 400,000 low-income citizens by giving them access to the American dream of home ownership. The best part is that these mortgage-paying residents pay less than their rent. They have the pride of home ownership and become part of the normal economy that most citizens enjoy. The federal, state, and local government cost to maintain these housing units ends imme-diately. Rather than spending money, the governments receive $32.7 billion in new revenue over 30 years in the form of mortgage repay-ments. Win-win. Double-bottom line.

Privatize Social Security

The concept of Social Security is a good one: Force workers to save, in the form of a wage tax paid by workers and their employers, and then provide them with a pension in retirement. The problem is in the implementation. Our nation's demographics have changed greatly from when Social Security was created. We are living longer and having fewer and smaller families to replenish the new genera-tions of workers who pay the benefits for the retired generations. As we have explained, Social Security is not a right. But perception is reality and politicians have promised citizens that it is a right and the federal government must make good on the promise lest the "peasants with pitchforks" come for them. We've shown the unsus-tainable math for Social Security and that the first fix will be denying some Americans their promised benefits under the mantle of fair-ness. This will not be near enough to close the actuarial gap, and the next fix will be to reduce benefits for everyone else and raise taxes for all. Still, in theory, it's not a bad plan and was a good faith attempt to support "the general welfare," albeit far outside the original constitutional scope of our federal government.

So, starting with the assumption that Social Security must remain in some form, how do we reform it using Locally Grown Government principles? I see another double-bottom line opportunity similar to our welfare solution where we reduce government obligations and provide more wealth to the average citizen. The idea of privatizing Social Security has been around a while. During the 1990s, policy wonks began talking about private investment accounts as an option to prevent the projected insolvency of Social Security. In 2000, one of the things President George W. Bush ran on was letting younger citizens invest a portion of their payroll taxes in retirement accounts. It never succeeded because politicians from both parties were afraid of "the third rail of politics." Also, there were many big government politicians who saw any privatization of Social Security as diminishing the power that keeps them in business.

Recently, in response to political calls for government to do something to narrow the income inequality gap, economist Stephen Moore dusted off and modified the earlier Bush proposal in way that seems to be grounded in Locally Grown principles. Like my example for NYCHA, it reduces government obligations, immediately increases the personal wealth of citizens who need it most and supports the inherent power of the people. Not that it would be difficult for a market-based approach to beat the meager annual returns of Social Security. In a July 25, 2019 article in the *Wall Street Journal* titled "Counter Inequality with Private Social Security Accounts," Mr. Moore says that Social Security has returned 1% annually over the past 40 years, while stocks have returned 6% annually. Moore states in the *WSJ* article:

> "Over a career of saving, the difference amounts to a literal lifetime's worth of additional income. A recent study commissioned by the Committee to Unleash Prosperity found that the average American who retired in 2016 after 40 to 45 years of work could have saved more than $1 million in balanced index

accounts, and many middle-class families could have accumu-
lated closer to $2 million." [13]

Even if a conservatively managed fund only returned 3.5 percent
over that time period, Social Security would now be completely
solvent, and citizens would have much more retirement income.
This double-bottom line solution seems so obvious to me. I think
voters would listen to reason and see the benefits if politicians had
the courage to solve problems instead of waging ideological warfare
meant to divide the nation. Instead, Social Security is about keeping
political and economic power in the hands of the few who seek to
be our overlords.

CHAPTER 13

Locally Grown Healthcare

Real tort reform.
Reduce drug company ads.
Bend the health cost curve.

I n 2018, US healthcare insurers booked $938 billion in revenue, a 4.3 percent increase over the previous year. [1] The industry profitability was 13 percent or about $122 billion. [2] That's a lot of money. Insurers receive about 60 percent of their revenue from government via programs like Medicare, Medicaid, and the Affordable Care Act exchanges. I've always had a basic rule that if a company collects more than 50 percent of its revenue from the government, it starts to become an appendage of government. Taken as an industry – government, pharma companies, hospitals, dentists, device manufacturers, suppliers, etc. – healthcare spending in the US is about $3.5 trillion, growing at a 3.9 percent annual rate. [3] That represents 17.9 percent of our GDP, far and away the largest industry in our economy. Increasingly, healthcare is becoming more regulated and funded by government. There are some politicians who are fighting for the government to take over the entire industry and become the "single payer" of all healthcare services. Half of the current candidates for president support some version of "Medicare for All" where private insurance would be all but outlawed as all healthcare runs through Washington DC. They view healthcare, along with education, food, shelter, and other areas of life, as basic human rights that must be guaranteed by government. As of this writing, 106 House members support a new Medicare for All proposal that claims "a moral imperative" to get rid of all profit from private healthcare providers. This would force a majority of doctor practices, nursing homes, home care agencies, and specialty clinical providers to reorganize as nonprofits or find another line of work. Some of these single-payer proposals would even revoke the patents for drug manufacturers who didn't agree to some government-established price. I'm no fan of the sometimes-rapacious drug companies, but this move would destroy the innovation that makes US a global leader in healthcare innovation. Medicare for All supporters think a government takeover of 17.9 percent of the economy will result in a better-quality and less expensive system than what we have now. Despite the clear unsustainability, we are told it is the only moral choice. It's really just another Hobson's Choice.

Why Medicare for All Is a Bad Idea

For years, 2020 presidential candidate Senator Bernie Sanders has been clamoring for single-payer government-run healthcare. Some version of his Medicare for All idea has been endorsed by several of his fellow presidential candidates. Let's take a look at his plan, which you can find at his Senate website. Bernie's plan claims that by forcing all healthcare to be paid through the federal government, the United States will cover all people within its borders (including undocumented immigrants) at a cost that is about the same as the $3.5 trillion we pay now. His plan tries to accomplish this mainly by forcing healthcare providers and pharmaceutical companies to be reimbursed at the same rate as Medicare, which is 42 percent less than private sector insurance reimbursement rates. His plan also claims that administrative costs would be reduced by a third. In exchange for eliminating all healthcare premiums, he would introduce a slew of new taxes (some of which he calls "premiums") that would collectively be over $1.6 trillion annually. Over 78 percent of those new taxes would be paid by corporations and families that earn more than $250,000 per year. [4]

For now, let's just stick with basic math. Bernie's plan states: "About 65 percent of [current] funding, over $2 trillion, is spent on publicly financed health care programs such as Medicare, Medicaid, and other programs." According to the Center for Medicare and Medicaid Services (CMS), the United States spends $3.5 trillion on healthcare and only 44 percent of it came from all levels of government, 47 percent from private health insurance, and 10 percent from individuals out-of-pocket. [5] That means that 57 percent (47+10) of health spending comes from the private sector. Bernie's plan significantly overstates the amount of existing government spending at 65 percent to make it appear that absorbing the remaining 35 percent that is now private won't be a big deal. Being wrong by that much isn't an accident. Besides, if our healthcare system is as broken as single-payer supporters say and our government effectively runs almost two-thirds of the system now, why in seven hells would anyone agree to let the government run all of it?

Sticking with the math, we are going to use the CMS figure for total national healthcare spending ($3.5 trillion), which is 8.4% higher than Bernie's number. CMS is a more reliable source in my view. This also means we should increase by 8.4 percent the new taxes Bernie would raise because I am sure he'd want to maintain his ability to tout that his plan can be done for about the same annual health costs as we spend now. Finally, I annualize Bernie's numbers to make it easier to compare with how CMS reports. Table 33 below shows the math:

Table 33 – Bernie Sanders Medicare for All Economic Model

2017 Healthcare Economics	($ Trillions)
Healthcare Spend (CMS)	$ 3.50
Less: Bernie's New Taxes	$ 1.76
Plus: Individual Out-of-Pocket Exp.	$ 0.35
Net Govt Spending after New Taxes	$ 2.09
Current All-Gov Health Spend (CMS)	$ 1.51
Bernie's Plan Additional Spend $	$ 0.59
Bernie's Plan Additional Spend %	39%

Bernie is telling folks that deductibles and co-pays disappear from his plan, which means that that Uncle Same picks up that tab. From Table 33, you'll see that Bernie's plan requires $2.09 trillion Net Government Spending after New Taxes. From this, we subtract the Current Government Health Care Spend, which shows that Bernie's plan will cost taxpayers 39 percent more than now, an additional $590 billion annually. I wouldn't call that "about the same cost."

If it weren't bad enough that Medicare for All adds another $590 billion to an already unsustainable government budget, Bernie then raises taxes by 48 percent on an already shrinking tax base. In fact, Bernie's plan would raise taxes to nearly 42 percent of GDP from the current level of 33 percent. You'll recall from the earlier study I cited from Christina Romer, former head of President Obama's Council of Economic Advisers, found that "each 1 percent increase in taxes as a percentage of GDP lowers real GDP by about 3 percent after two years." Well, Bernie Sanders would increase taxes as a percentage of GDP by a whopping nine percent, meaning that our GDP would be reduced by 27 percent (9x3) two years after implementation of his plan. This would introduce "The Great Depression Act II."

We aren't done yet. Bernie's plan would outlaw private insurance companies. Doctors and hospitals would be paid the Medicare rate for their services, which is 42 percent less than what private sector insurance pays. [6] In fact, former Maryland congressman John

Delaney said the following at the July 30, 2019, Democratic presidential debate: "I've been going around rural America and I ask rural hospital administrators one question: 'If all your bills were paid at the Medicare rate last year, what would happen?' And they all look at me and say, 'We would close.'"

In 2015 in Bernie's home state of Vermont, governed entirely by Democrats at the time, the state rejected a proposal for single-payer healthcare when people found out it would double the state budget. Residents would have had to pay an 11.5 percent payroll tax and a nine-point increase in the state income tax. [7] In 2016, 79 percent of Colorado voters also rejected a single-payer plan for the same reason; it would have doubled their state budget. [8] And in California in 2017, where Democrats control all branches of government, the legislature killed its own Healthy California single-payer healthcare plan because it would have tripled their state budget. [9]

Here is an interesting irony. The US is the fifth largest exporter of medicines in the world with (6.3 percent at $21.6 billion sales), behind France, Belgium, Switzerland, and global leader Germany (15.9 percent at $54 billion sales). [10] The US also has by far the largest medicine trade deficit in the world at $44 billion. This means we import $98 billion in medicines, and US consumers spend about three times as much on drugs as those in Europe. According to a January 2018 report by the Brookings Institution, "U.S. consumers account for about 64 to 78 percent of total pharmaceutical profits, despite accounting for only 27 percent of global income.... American patients use newer drugs and face higher prices than patients in other countries." [11] European single-payer systems get huge discounts while we pay exorbitantly more because we can afford it. In effect, Americans are subsidizing the lion's share of global pharma R&D. If Europeans and other countries paid their fair share, it would meaningfully bend the cost curve. For those who think healthcare is better in Europe, I'd ask, "What would Euro Care look like if America wasn't subsidizing their drug costs?" Between subsidizing their government healthcare and national defense, the United States spends a great deal of money propping up the Eurozone.

The Medicare for All crowd also ignores the fact that the vast majority of citizens are already covered by good healthcare insurance. They are trying to solve a problem of 8.8 percent of the population without health insurance by completely disrupting the system that is working for everyone else. This makes no sense. Segregate the 8.8 percent into a common pool and deal with it separately. The Property & Casualty Insurance industry, where I spent a large part of my career, has had effective mechanisms for decades to deal with this problem. For example, high-risk people who do not qualify for standard auto insurance can still get insured through high-risk pools that all insurance companies contribute to. The same situation exists with homeowner's insurance through state-sponsored insurance plans. These solutions allow for a robust and effective private insurance market that serves the vast majority of citizens while segregating the much smaller population of high-risk individuals into special plans.

Foreigners from single-payer countries with serious health problems who can afford it often come to the US for treatment because there are long waits for many procedures in their home countries. Waiting lists are a form of healthcare rationing that comes with the territory for single-payer systems. Take the UK for instance. A March 2019 report from the Royal College of Surgeons "shows there were 227,569 patients waiting over six months, and 36,857 patients waiting over nine months, to start planned National Health Service (NHS) treatment in January 2019." The same study reports that only 84 percent of patients waiting for emergency room care were treated within the four-hour goal of 95 percent. In fact, the 95 percent goal hasn't been reached since 2015 but, instead of cutting wait times, the NHS is looking to scrap the goal instead. [12] A classic "move the goal posts" technique. But according to a survey of more than 20,000 global citizens from 80 countries by *U.S. News & World Report*, Britain ranks in the Top 10 of nations where people are most satisfied with their healthcare system. The United States is 19th. [13] The Brits famously love their NHS, but I'm guessing it's because they think it's free and not the poor service. Single payer promises months- or years-long waits for services that Americans currently get with an appointment in a few days. I guess "free and crappy for all" is a form of equality.

Because we have 50 state laboratories, there is domestic evidence we can analyze to test the Medicare for all proposal. In a March 2018 article in the *Wall Street Journal*, author Bill Hammond describes the experience of New York State where regulation has caused 100 percent of its hospitals to become nonprofit over 10 years. Here are some key statistics for NY healthcare from the article:

- Second worst operating margins and highest debt load in the country
- Last place in quality in the federal Hospital Compare report card
- 33 percent below national average on percentage of revenues donated to charity

Despite such poor performance, apparently the state allows plenty of hospital executives to earn more than $1 million per year. As Hammond points out, "If banning profit is an effective way to improve healthcare, there's no evidence to be found in New York." [14]

I am trying to imagine what America would be like with a government takeover of nearly 18% of the economy. I cannot imagine why many healthcare providers wouldn't quit if they were forced to accept 42 percent less for their services across the board. The destruction of massive amounts of capital in an industry that is the world leader in healthcare quality is a grand experiment with massive downside risk if it doesn't work out like it didn't in Sweden and other Nordic countries admired as heroes by American socialists. Hopefully, I've presented enough evidence to convince you that single-payer healthcare, Medicare for All, whatever you want to call it, is a very bad idea.

Locally Grown Healthcare Reforms

In my opinion, healthcare insurance is not a natural right to be guaranteed by the government. It is not an enumerated constitutional power of the federal government, and the resources required to create a fully government-run healthcare system on top of our already unsustainable federal government will bankrupt our country. It is far beyond even the Hamiltonian view of "the general welfare."

Still, there are some recent healthcare reforms that I fully support like mandatory coverage for preexisting conditions, but overall, people should be responsible for their own health. If you choose to smoke, take drugs, eat fast food every day, and get no exercise, why is it someone else's responsibility to pay for the health consequences of those choices? According to the Center for Disease Control (CDC), nearly 40 percent of Americans are obese, which accounts for $147 billion in healthcare spending. [15] Why should American taxpayers be responsible for paying for this behavior?

Certainly, our common good safety net should include some kind of healthcare for those less fortunate, but the question is always "Who picks up the tab?" None of this should be construed that our American healthcare system is perfect. At $10,224 in 2017, the US spends more per capita than any other country on earth. Quality costs money, but there are still many things that can be done to "bend the cost curve" in healthcare, starting with better eating habits and more exercise.

During our time in Jackson, Wyoming, we became friends with the Friess family. We helped boot up a new school with our neighbors Polly and Steve Friess because we found the limited choices of public and private schools were not a good fit for our kids. Through Polly and Steve, we met Steve's dad, Foster Friess, who, in addition to being very smart and successful, is the most generous guy we know. Foster is also active in politics with a foundation and think tank tackling some of the more vexing public policy problems. In a 2017 policy paper, "When Hospitals Resist Change," he shares some great suggestions on how to make healthcare sustainable while providing a robust public safety net for those who need it. We've incorporated a few of Foster's suggestions in our list of good ideas. [16]

Stop Practicing Defensive Medicine

A huge cost savings could be realized if we reduced the practice of physicians ordering medically unnecessary tests, procedures, and medications due to fear of malpractice lawsuits. According to a report by Thomson-Reuters, defensive medicine costs our economy $250-325 billion annually. Of that, almost half impacts federal and state taxpayers, as money is wasted on defensive medicine by doctors who see Medicare and Medicaid patients. [17]

These defensive medicine costs are driven by lawsuits from trial lawyers who become very wealthy suing healthcare providers. Given the massive amount of industry revenue provided by government, you can easily see how trial lawyers are one of the biggest political lobbyist groups in the US. Trial lawyers don't want tort law reform and vigorously lobby our federal government accordingly.

Eliminate Waste, Fraud, and Abuse

As we outlined earlier, according to a 2012 study by Donald Berwick, a former head of the Centers for Medicare and Medicaid Services (CMS), and Andrew Hackbarth of the RAND Corporation, fraud comprises about 10 percent of annual Medicare and Medicaid spending. In 2018, that represents over $227 billion in potential savings for US taxpayers. [18] While trial lawyers perform an important accountability function, they are not immune to abusive tactics. How about redirecting some of the efforts of trial attorneys toward eradicating true fraud and abuse rather than suing doctors who may have made honest judgment errors while giving best efforts to serve their patients?

Now here I go contradicting myself. My home state of Florida seems to be the medical fraud capital of the world. Our local papers regularly expose medical scams that prey on the elderly, some perpetrated by doctors that are bad apples. It's a great sin for someone in a revered profession to betray the public trust. It's immoral and costly and must be stopped, and I am glad to have trial lawyers policing this. Doctors, teachers, and lawyers are more duty-bound than most professions to uphold the public trust. The vast majority are good ones and need to do a better job policing their own. We need them.

Restructure Medicaid and Medicare

As our Locally Grown Government budget transfer expansion lays out, most federal Medicaid and Medicare dollars will be transferred downstream to the state and local level. As we outlined earlier, this will provide lots of resources for experimentation and accountability. If private companies can provide health services equal to or better than Medicare and Medicaid and meet the requirements, then they should be permitted to offer plans in that market and be reimbursed accordingly through government funds. In poor communities with lots of Medicaid recipients, it would make sense to locate more hospitals and clinics to reduce the transportation costs for people.

Competition Between Healthcare Providers Is More Important Than with Insurance Companies.

As Foster Friess mentions in his policy paper, "That trend is going the opposite way as hospitals gobble up orthopedic, cardiac and anesthetist groups and skin doctors. Medicare pays a cardiologist $200 for a cardiogram done in his office. When a hospital buys his practice, they are allowed to attach a "facilities fee" of $700. How can we stop such increases?" [19]

Veterans Hospitals

Our vets defend our liberty and there isn't a government role that is more important than that. However, neither the Defense Department nor the Veterans Administration are immune to waste, fraud, and abuse and we see many stories on all these fronts. Veteran's healthcare is administered mostly in veterans hospitals under the Veterans Administration, which is under the Department of Defense. The VA is the second largest federal agency with over 300,000 employees and a $200 billion budget. Veteran's healthcare represented over $70 billion in 2018, increasing annually at about the rate of Medicare. [20]

Also, about 80 percent of vets carry private insurance or Medicare, creating a duplication of coverage that encourages lots of "double dipping." [21] When vets choose to get care *not related* to their service disabilities through the VA, the VA should serve as their secondary payer for care not covered by their primary provider. In 2016, the CBO projected this change could save about $200 million over 10 years. Overall, reducing waste, fraud, and abuse in the Veterans Administration would save $5-7 billion annually.

Expand Use of Association Health Plans

There are currently many choices to obtain healthcare insurance at discounted rates through affinity groups like AARP, Small Business Association (SBA), Nation Association of the Self-Employed, Knights of Columbus, and many more. People in any organization with sufficient members should be able to negotiate lower premiums for their members. I welcome any market-based solution to reduce healthcare costs. I would support loosening of rules for people to organize in any fashion they want to negotiate lower premiums and improve quality. I'd like to take things even further by advocating that those member organizations negotiate actual provider costs. For example, someone may survey their zip code for all elderly people who need knee replacements and start an organization just for that purpose. I imagine conversations with local orthopedic surgeons like: "My name is Joe and I am president of the Needy Knees Club. We have 200 members who need knee replacements next year. What price can you commit to if our organization makes you the exclusive provider for procedure?" It's like doing the insurance company's job for them. All members might be required to have healthcare coverage that pays for the procedure, but by negotiating a much lower rate than the insurance company has to pay, we will reduce premiums over time since those knee replacements are all done at a lower cost.

Make Healthcare Prices a Transparent Marketplace

Years ago, my father gave me copy of the local Leominster, Massachusetts, *Enterprise* newspaper from 1950, in which doctors were advertising their prices for childbirth, tonsillectomies, flu shots, and other procedures. I was dumbfounded that this actually happened. I advocate going "back to the future" by allowing healthcare providers to compete on price. There are some hopeful signs of this starting to happen. On June 24, 2019, President Trump signed an executive order directing the Health and Human Services agency (HHS) to draft new rules that would require hospitals to disclose the prices that patients and insurers actually pay in an easy-to-read, patient-friendly format.

A 2016 study by McKinsey & Company, "The next imperatives for US healthcare", finds that improving price transparency and productivity in our healthcare system could reduce costs from $284-532 billion, making healthcare costs growth comparable with the rest of the economy. The study suggests that transparent pricing allows patients to shop for value and that higher prices will tend to be associated with better outcomes, as is the case in the rest of the economy. [22]

I have a recent personal experience that supports price transparency and consumer choice. After years of pounding my knees playing tennis and skiing, I needed arthroscopic surgery to repair a torn meniscus. During my pre-op meeting, my orthopedist asked where I'd like to have the surgery done. My choices were Indian River Medical Center or a local outpatient surgery center. I asked him what the difference was, and he answered, "The outpatient surgery center is much less expensive than the hospital." Given that I viewed his expertise as the most important part of the procedure, I opted for the outpatient surgery center. I probably saved over $2,000 with that decision and my knee feels as good as new.

Of course, true competition isn't just on price but also on quality, timeliness of delivery, and other factors. In this digital age, a company like Health Grades could extend its business model from just grading doctor performance using patient input and other factors to include posting prices for common procedures or desired outcomes. In conjunction with our previous suggestion of group benefits negotiation, this could be a powerful agent for innovation. I think real solutions cannot come from government but from the marketplace by shrinking the economic distance between providers and patients.

Tax-Advantaged Income for Doctors

It is expensive to become a doctor. Between medical school average tuition of $250,000 and the lost-opportunity cost of the four years of medical school plus a three-year residency, the total investment to become a physician averages $750,000. [23] That's a huge investment of time and money, and it takes a lot of years of after-tax income to recoup that. So, it shouldn't be a surprise that doctors are paid a lot compared to other professions. However, because the rising cost of healthcare is such a huge societal problem and the government is the biggest stakeholder, part of "bending the cost curve" means doctors getting paid less. Less pay means less incentive to attract new doctors to the profession. Already there is a scarcity of primary care physicians, arguably the most important part of the service provider food chain. According to a 2018 report by the Association of American Medical Colleges, the United States could see a shortage of up to 120,000 physicians by 2030, impacting patient care across the nation. [24] Are you starting to see how government takeover of healthcare will work? Primary care also carries the lowest average compensation for physicians. According to the *2015 Medscape Physician Compensation Report*, primary care physicians and family physicians earn an average of $195,000 annually, compared with $284,000 for physicians in other specialties. [25] One solution to the growing shortage of primary care doctors is using the New GI Bill I proposed earlier. The military already can pay for four years of medical school in exchange for a four-year commitment to active duty. We should double down on this program.

We need smart, motivated doctors to be the backbone of our healthcare system, and we require them to invest a huge sum and take big risks to become doctors, but we want to regulate their compensation when they achieve their goal. Still, we demand the world's best care, requiring the latest treatments be available to all people regardless of their ability to pay. There are too many logical inconsistencies here to mention. But hey, that's what we want, and we are told it is our right. Here's an idea. How about we allow doctors to offer patient financing for the out-of-pocket portion of major medical procedures? The interest income from that financing could be taxed at a lower rate. Certain loans could be guaranteed by the government, making this a relatively low-risk opportunity for physicians. Kind of a guaranteed source of long-term income. Some of this could be rolled into their retirement plans. The insurance companies and government programs could spread their payments over time, therefore reducing current expenditures.

Leverage Life Insurance to Pay for Healthcare

As soon as someone gets seriously ill, the interests of that person and their healthcare insurer diverge. The person wants the best possible treatment to get well and so does the life insurer, who wants to delay paying the death benefit as long as possible. In contrast, the health insurance company wants to meet its contractual obligations in the least costly way possible, and if you die before you get expensive treatments, well, that's unfortunate for you and good for them. This divergence of interests is a big reason why most people don't trust the healthcare industry and why Medicare for All has gained traction. A person is paying a significant portion of their income in premiums for a product they hope they don't have to use, but when they need to use it, the provider often does the minimum required. Actually, it's not just health insurers that are subject to this dynamic. All insurance is. During my career, I saw plenty of property insurance companies take the least expensive route to adjust property claims that was still compliant with the insurance policy. When friends and family would ask me who I recommended for homeowner's insurance, I had a well-informed opinion about who was good and who wasn't.

Now imagine a situation where two different insurance companies are competing against each other, each with different interests in your health, and the net result benefits you. Such is the subject of a March 20, 2018 op-ed in the *Wall Street Journal*, "Healthcare's Killer App: Life Insurance." Authors Dana P. Goldman and Darius Lakdawalla describe the early innings of just this. Imagine that a person diagnosed with cancer has a $250,000 life insurance policy. The life insurance company has an interest in keeping you alive as long as possible, paying premiums, and delaying the payout of the $250,000 death benefit. There are a growing number of immunotherapies with excellent survivability results, like Yervoy for metastatic skin cancer. For Medicare patients, the therapy costs $96,000 and the out-of-pocket cost would be $24,000. If the life insurance company covered the out-of-pocket costs, it could generate about $28,000 in additional value for them. The article describes researchers who have calculated that the longer lives resulting from new immunotherapies could save life insurance companies over $6 billion per year. To make this approach work at scale, life insurance companies would need access to more health data from its policyholders. Care providers and case managers could identify opportunities for appropriate treatment that could be financed by a patient's life insurance policy. How about that for double-bottom line? [26]

Re-architect Treatment Codes to Be Based on Outcomes

The American Medical Association publishes all billing codes for medical procedures. It is considered the standard for both private and public reimbursement of healthcare providers. And there are about 10,000 CPT (Current Procedural Terminology) codes currently in use. [27] This means that our entire healthcare system pays providers based on procedures done and drugs taken whether those treatments are successful or not. The idea of "I get paid whether it works or not" doesn't pass the common-sense test and it certainly creates a moral hazard that contributes to fraud and abuse in the industry. Thankfully, others see the illogic of this approach as certain large health insurers are now beginning to include outcomes as part of the compensation mix for doctors. However, these efforts are still in their infancy and need to be sped up, especially since the majority of healthcare spending is through government institutions, which are traditionally resistant to change.

Another benefit of this suggestion is that it supports our Locally Grown double bottom-line principal by killing two birds with one stone. The great social benefit of less expensive healthcare is also good business for those doctors who get the expected outcomes. The healthier people get, the less costly our system becomes as the continuous improvement cycle gathers momentum.

Expand the Scope of Services Offered by Healthcare Professionals Other Than Physicians

For example, in Europe, midwives assist more than 70 percent of natural births. [28] In 2014, midwives delivered only 8.3 percent of American babies. [29] Midwives see these women from the beginning of their pregnancies onward, at a far lower cost than doctors. There is also a wide disparity in cost for delivering a new baby across OECD countries, from a low of about $1000 in Argentina to about $11,000 in the US.

A 2009 study by United Healthcare, our country's largest health insurer, recognized that using nurse practitioners (NP) to control costs for older adults leads them to recommend using NPs to manage nursing home patients. Keeping in mind that competition makes us all better, having NPs doing some things competently that have been jealously guarded by doctors, is a good thing. The study states this extended usage of NPs alone could result in $166 billion healthcare savings.

Increase Patient Adherence to Doctor-Prescribed Treatment

Many people argue that healthcare is a right. However, according to a 2014 study by the National Institute of Health (NIH), as much as 30 percent of health-care costs are due to failure of patients to follow their doctor's instructions regarding medication and unhealthy lifestyle choices. [30] If government is responsible for citizens' health, what do you do when the citizens refuse to help themselves? Conflicts between individual rights and privileges are inevitable. Will government have the right to outlaw large sugary drinks as NYC has tried to do, or Big Macs and motorcycles? If it's responsible for our health costs, why shouldn't the government have the authority to then regulate everything that could impact our health? Hopefully, you see the slippery slope here that accompanies the invention of new rights that fundamentally changes the relationship between the citizen, who is supposedly free to make risk-reward decisions, and the government.

Expand Home Care

Japan is a window into a potential future for the US. Its generous entitlements state combined with horrible demographics where 28 percent of the population is over 65 (nearly double that of the US) have ballooned the national debt to 250 percent of GDP (more than double the US). Debt service consumes 25 percent of the Japanese national budget. One wonders how they remain solvent. Now the Japanese are scrambling to find ways to reduce their public healthcare costs, and one of the promising areas is local home care. This means

doctors making old-fashioned house calls rather than patients incur-
ring the cost of hospital stays. Doctors are even paid more for these
visits than office visits. They are also significantly raising co-pays and
deductibles for elder care, and the elderly are okay with this. On
the whole, Japanese prefer to receive care at home. Only 13 percent
of Japanese die at home but most want to. This is what "healthcare
rationing" looks like in a socialist country. The Japanese can get
away with this because they are an extremely homogenous society
ethnically and culturally. Some of these sensible solutions would
attract no shortage of criticism in a huge ethnically and culturally
diverse country like America. Still, on our current course, healthcare
rationing is certainly in our future and the Japanese experiment is
worth noting.

Increase Funding for Mental Health and Addiction Treatment

The Substance Abuse and Mental Health Services Administration
(SAMHSA) is the primary agency coordinating federal funding
for states to implement proven and effective services for individuals with substance use or mental health conditions. These programs
reduce expensive hospitalizations, emergency department usage,
and involvement with the criminal justice system. Access to behavioral health services is key to improving Americans' health and con-
taining US healthcare costs.

Disaster relief efforts around the world have been a proving ground
for the practice of "psychological first aid" where taxi drivers, teachers, and waitresses are taught to notice people in distress in order to
provide ad-hoc emotional support. It has been shown to be effective
in preventing post-traumatic stress disorder. In places like Jordan,
Haiti, and Zimbabwe, where psychologists are few and far between,
non-specialists are trained by agencies like UN Health Services to
treat mild to moderate anxiety and depression, which affect 15-20
percent of the population. These symptoms are often brought on by

the stress of daily challenges like finding housing and food, so the priority is to provide them with simple techniques to relieve symptoms like slow, calm breathing. Some of these counselors can even dispense medication.

I think these and other techniques can be applied in the US not only in the poor geographies but everywhere. Teaching people how to be an empathetic helper without needing long and expensive training can significantly broaden the resources available to victims of trauma, drug addiction, social media addiction, depression. Not that folks trained to be empathetic can treat serious psychological issues but recognizing symptoms and being a good listener can create the environment where victims can be convinced to seek treatment.

Reduce Unnecessary Paperwork (i.e., Electronic Healthcare Record)

According to a 2009 study by the National Center for Biotechnology Information (NCBI), the medical prior authorization process costs over $80,000 per year, per medical practice.

The cost for all this time wasted is between $23 billion to $31 billion each year. This study indicated that physicians are spending two-thirds of their time doing paperwork and data entry. The elusive "single patient record" seems like a no-brainer. Everyone knows the lunacy of having to complete the same medical history for each new doctor they see. And these are paper records that must then be transcribed into digital format. Our Locally Grown Government blockchain platform can be extended to include a single patient healthcare record that can permit patients to securely and easily grant access to authorized service providers.

Switch from Disposable to Reusable Instruments

The US is also wasting billions of healthcare dollars on disposable tools, even though sterilized, reusable tools work just as well and at considerable savings. Another NCBI study calculated that the instrument cost per procedure of a full disposable set is between seven to 27 times higher than the cost of the same procedure with reusables. [31] When you consider that there were 51 million surgical inpatient procedures performed in the US in 2010, we can see that a simple switch to reusable tools would save a huge amount. [32]

Better Management of Surgical Supplies

According to a 2016 study by researchers at the University of California-San Francisco, "Operating room waste: disposable supply utilization in neurosurgical procedures", $48 billion per year could be saved if operating rooms cut down on surgical waste. Unused medical supplies represent 13 percent of total surgical supply costs, or approximately $968 of waste per case. According to the study, this amounts to "$242,968 in operating room waste per month. The most expensive item wasted was the Surgifoam absorbable gelatin sponge (Ethicon US), which is used to stop bleeding. One sponge can cost close to $4,000," reports Managed Care. "Nearly $1,000 per procedure is being wasted," wrote Dr. Michael Lawton in the study. Extrapolated across the 51 million surgical inpatient procedures performed in the US in 2010, eliminating this waste would result in savings of approximately $48 billion. Operating room costs could also be slashed by establishing an efficient procedure for surgeons to identify the list of instruments they might need in a given procedure. [33]

So, using the above suggestions where a credible savings number has been cited, my math shows that over $1 trillion can be saved in our healthcare system by deploying these suggestions. That's nearly one-third of the entire annual spend on healthcare in this country! Even if this number is inflated by 50 percent, $500 billion in savings is a HUGE number, which makes it worth summarizing below:

Stop practicing defensive medicine	$300,000,000,000
Transparent pricing	$284,000,000,000
Waste, fraud, and abuse	$194,000,000,000
Expand usage of healthcare professionals other than MDs	$166,000,000,000
Better management of surgical supplies	$48,000,000,000
Reduce unnecessary paperwork	$31,000,000,000
Leverage life insurance to pay for healthcare	$6,000,000,000

CHAPTER 14

Locally Grown Elections

*When 60 percent
voter turnout is lauded,
we are in trouble.*

How We Vote Now

always vote. I consider it a basic duty of every American. In my humble opinion, if you don't vote, you forfeit your right to bitch about government. Being in the middle of writing a book on revitalizing our republic, I took the 2018 midterms elections a bit more seriously than the past. One thing I noticed is that most of the workers are older than me and I'm not young anymore. I asked lots of questions, many of which were answered with a shrug. At my location there was a man wearing what looked like a bright orange road crew vest. He was an election observer. This is the first I've seen of this as I imagined them to be associated with corrupt third world countries. I asked the man in the jacket if there were folks like him at all the polling stations and he said, "No." I had to present my driver's license as ID, which was then scanned by the new election software that Indian River County had purchased just the previous year for $1 million. Again, I asked if you needed to present an ID at every polling station and the clerk answered, "No."

According to the National Conference of State Legislatures, there are only nine states that require a government-issued ID to vote. There are 25 states that request an ID but don't require it, and 16 states where no document is required to vote. [1] We require photo IDs for driver's licenses, receiving government benefits, and checking into hotel rooms but the majority of states don't require it for the most important function in a democracy. In fact, there are well-organized activist groups supported by politicians who resist any form of legislation trying to require ID for voting. Their position is that there is little evidence of voter fraud and it unduly restricts the right to vote while imposing unnecessary administrative costs. However, a 2012 Pew Research study, "Evidence That America's Voter Registration System Needs an Upgrade", shows that our voting system is so antiquated in many areas of the country that we don't have the capability to detect voter fraud reliably if we wanted to. The study also shows that the main ingredients for cooking up voter fraud, inaccurate voter rolls, is present in abundance. Federal law requires that municipal polling stations keep their voter rolls accurate, but many places can't or won't do this. Here are some of the disturbing lowlights from the Pew study:

- One of every eight voter registrations in the United States are no longer valid or are significantly inaccurate.
- More than 1.8 million deceased individuals are listed as voters.
- Approximately 2.75 million people have registrations in more than one state.
- In Los Angeles County, there are *1.7 million more voters on file than there are citizens of voting age.*
- More than 24 percent of eligible voters are not registered.
- In Oregon in 2008, taxpayers spent $4.11 per active voter to

process registrations and maintain a voter list. In contrast, Canada, which uses modern technology to register people, spends less than $0.35 per voter to process registrations, and 93 percent of its eligible population is registered. [2]

In an era where our country is so divided, many state and federal elections are very close. Senate and House seats and even presidential elections can turn on a few hundred votes. In 2000, George W. Bush beat Al Gore by 537 votes out of nearly 6 million cast. It doesn't take much voter fraud to move the needle in US elections.

Some equate voter ID as a form of racial discrimination. We know from our history that mechanisms like the poll tax in southern states were efforts to prevent African Americans from voting in the Reconstruction era. Bad stuff to be sure because each citizen has the right to vote, but we are 50 years past the civil rights legislation that corrected these defects.

Still, we witnessed what seems like an act of voter suppression in the 2018 Georgia gubernatorial election. Republican candidate Brian Kemp was also the secretary of state. He presided over the blocking of 53,000 voter registrations – 70 percent African American – because the name in the registration didn't exactly match a public record in other state databases such as driver's licenses. This means that if you have a hyphen missing in your name, or if you use "Joe" on one form and "Joseph" on another, your registration would be blocked by the state of Georgia. Although these citizens could still vote by showing up at the polling place with their ID, the letters informing them of the need to correct information seemed to confuse some into thinking this meant they were ineligible to vote at all. This matching process had long been legally approved by the state legislature but is still unfair. In a very close election that Kemp won over Democratic candidate Stacey Abrams by 55,000 votes, this process could have had an impact. Georgia is a great state that must do better than this. This example, and others we will discuss here, shows that we need to be concerned about the integrity of our election system. Proof of citizenship is not a race issue but an effort to protect our system from attacks on our society by hackers, corrupt politicians, and those looking to subvert our republic. Once again, it seems like the lack of consistency in our election process is a feature, not a bug, in our system.

Back to my 2018 voting experience. After checking in with the election volunteers, I was ready to put pen to paper like tens of millions of my fellow citizens across the country. The first 20 percent of the 30 decisions I had to make were the high-profile candidates for Congress and executive state offices. I felt as though I was reasonably informed about each of those decisions given the amount of political advertisements I'd seen on TV, talking to others, and doing my own research. The next 15 percent were state legislature elections I knew less about but still knew enough information to make a reasonably informed decision. The remaining 15 percent on the front page were county and local positions with no party affiliation. There were two judges where the question was to retain them or not, so at least I knew they were incumbents. All the rest were just names. No delineation of party or incumbency.

The second page of my ballot included proposals to amend the state Constitution. These proved to be the most fascinating part of the ballot. I could use my experience to make a reasonably informed decision for each. What made some of the proposed amendments interesting is that they mashed up several different issues, some seemingly unrelated. For example, Amendment Nine was a prohibition of offshore drilling of gas and oil "bundled" with prohibition of vaping in enclosed indoor workspaces. What a combination!

These ballot question mashups were curated and delivered by the Florida Constitution Revision Commission, which convenes every 20 years. The last ballot with this number of amendment questions came in 1998, the last time the commission met. They chose 20 proposals from among the public input for this year's ballot but decided to "group" distinct proposals together into eight amendments, meaning that in some cases voters must approve or reject multiple proposals in batches. This bundling technique has been used before and is controversial. Critics have charged that the way ideas were linked was politically motivated, to "log roll" less popular ideas so more favorable ones succeeded. But the chair of the commission's Style and Drafting Committee argued that the groupings make it easier for voters to read and save time. I agree with him. Good politics is the art of compromise, something that is sorely missed in our country now.

There are some things to like about this approach from a Locally Grown Government point of view. First, it was an effort to simplify things for voters. Second, it seemed like a negotiated solution by both Democrat and Republican appointees of the commission. Third, the idea of a regularly scheduled commission to collect and curate ideas to amend the state constitution is in keeping with our belief of the continuous improvement model to achieve sustainability.

As has become usual recently in Florida, two marquee races were extremely close. The race for US Senate between an 18-year incumbent and the former Florida governor had the challenger winning on election night by approximately 57,000 votes, about a 0.5 percent margin. This narrow margin automatically triggered a recount. Three days after the election in Broward County, which mysteriously hadn't finished counting early voting as required by statute, the winning spread had narrowed to only 15,000 votes. Election officials in Broward were releasing extra votes in overnight hours while refusing to disclose how many ballots were remaining. Broward County became infamous for the "hanging chads" controversy in the 2000 recount of the Bush vs. Gore presidential election. The official overseeing the election process in Broward County is a woman named Brenda Snipes, whom the state courts ruled had destroyed ballots in 2016. Snipes was being sued for failure to disclose required information like how many people voted, how many ballots had been counted, and how many remained to be counted. A Broward County judge again ruled against Ms. Snipes for failure to disclose, which underscores the illegality of her actions. In January 2019, Ms. Snipes retired with a life-long government pension of over $130,000 per year for her time as a schoolteacher and election supervisor. [3]

So here I am, writing a book about revitalizing the American political system starting at the local level, and I am ill-prepared to cast an informed vote for a chunk of the people running for office. I can only imagine what the vast majority of people who aren't political junkies are doing. Surely, we can design a better way to inform voters, both at the ballot box and prior to elections, about who and what is on the ballot. We live in a country where social media and digital life was invented. I'm sure many would say "as a citizen it's your responsibility to dig for information" and they would be correct. Still, as a simplification junky and technology guy, I know that we can do better without compromising the process or disenfranchising any citizens.

Whether for president of the US or town council or as a shareholder in a corporation, voting is what makes an organization work. And it is critical that citizens trust the integrity of their elections. It's sad to see how voting is regularly corrupted in developing countries where blatant election rigging is often the rule, not the exception. In the United States, we have largely avoided this outcome, although over the last two decades federal elections seem to have regularly become much closer and more contested. This makes the stakes much higher for getting it right. We all remember the 2000 election between Bush and Gore. The entire election came down to Florida recounts for president that ultimately went to the Supreme Court, which had to decide on the meaning of "hanging chad." Still we accept the results of an election even if we don't like it. That's what enables orderly transitions of delegated power. However, as I discussed earlier in my description of the 2018 midterms, there seems to be no standard procedure from one polling station to another and from one state to another. That level of inconsistency simply invites the possibility for corruption in the process, especially as votes get closer and the stakes higher in a divided country already losing trust in its institutions. We must be better than this.

I believe technology can be a critical enabler for Locally Grown Government principles to thrive and proliferate. It's apparent to me how rickety our current voting process is, and there are some interesting voting platforms out there that could help with this. But the change we seek isn't just about how we vote. It's about the power of local government supplanting and optimizing a chunk of what the federal government does now. That's a big, hairy, audacious goal that requires serious infrastructure. This means the Locally Grown Government architecture must be flexible enough to grow beyond voting into the other critical government functions like registry of deeds, business licensing, inspections, healthcare, and welfare management. This local infrastructure should also easily connect both laterally (with other municipal governments) and upwards (county, state, and federal). It should be open source and transparent to use. And most importantly, it should be designed to increase inherent power rather than centralized power.

Locally Grown Elections

We now have the means to guarantee fair and incorruptible elections. There are an increasing number of companies focused on developing a new class of election software to address the shortcomings of our current voting system. New technology can reliably authenticate voter ID with biometrics (e.g., fingerprints, retina scans) that tie back to other government data records during the voter registration process. This means no more debacles like 2018 in Georgia and Florida. Thankfully, there are those at the federal level that are already leading the charge like the US Election Assistance Commission. They recently announced that Votem would participate in its voting system testing and certification program. Votem is partnered with the Blockchain Research Institute and the National Association of Secretaries of State and already testing its election software platform with state and local jurisdictions around the country. Then there is the nonprofit Democracy Earth Foundation, which focuses on the "liquid democracy" paradigm where a person can delegate their vote on certain issues to a trusted person, much like proxy voting in corporate shareholder elections. This approach permits citizens to delegate a friend who is educated and passionate about climate change to vote on those relevant issues on your behalf. Now this wouldn't pass constitutional muster for federal and some state elections but there is nothing preventing their use in local elections and private organizations. Liquid democracy would be a narrow delegation of the inherent power of the individual that is informed and discretionary for that individual.

Other companies like Clear Ballot, Smartmatic, and Intelivote are successfully deploying modern voting platform technology in many locations around the globe. Some more recent entrants like Democracy Now, Agora, and Votem are on the blockchain and I'll reference some of their features and framework to further describe our vision of secure voting.

Delegative Democracy

The concept of "delegative democracy"(also known as liquid democracy) goes as far back as Lewis Carroll of *Alice in Wonderland* fame. He wrote about political candidates being able to delegate their votes to others running for Parliament. In the decades following, several others like William U'Ren, Gordon Tulloch, and James Miller built on the idea of a more representative voting process where citizens could delegate their votes to others who would elect politicians directly without a political intermediary.

In 2002, Professor Bryan Ford, of the Swiss Federal Institute of Technology in Lausanne, authored a paper called "Delegative Democracy," which coalesced and improved these ideas into a structure that could actually be implemented. [4] We see seedlings of this approach being implemented now with some of the blockchain voting startups with the "ranked choice" voting movement. Our current system of representative democracy laid out in the Constitution defines how citizens vote to delegate some of their inherent power to elected representatives. These delegates are paid to represent our interests in local, state, and federal government. This form of government is vastly more practical than "direct democracy" where all citizens vote on every issue directly. Who has the dedication, time, and knowledge to make informed choices on all the issues facing our society? As Dr. Ford explains it, pure democracy is neither feasible nor desirable because there is such a "wide variance of knowledge, interests and abilities" in a society, that if each citizen has the exact same influence (i.e., one person, one vote), then the wisdom of the group may be no better than the average wisdom of the citizenry. He says the results can actually be worse than average because the random "aggregation of multiple sensible but conflicting policies can easily result in a completely nonsensical collective policy."

According to Dr. Ford, there are still key defects in the American form of representative democracy, including the size and the geographical limitations of the representative bodies. Too small and the threat of concentration of power and corruption looms. Too large and there are too many cooks in the kitchen following the recipe of gridlock. In the US, we have 435 congressional districts and 100 senators and one president and one vice president for a total of 537 federally elected officials. This works out to about 609,000 people per representative. It is impossible for each of the federal reps to have met, much less personally know, any but a fraction of their constituents so our system relies on the public media to inform citizens of at least who they are and what they stand for. Dr Ford describes the key features of delegative democracy as voter choice of delegates being as "broad and unrestricted and based on a personal trust relationship." I'm guessing he wouldn't agree that 537 federal officials representing 327 million people meets that standard, but that is our current constitutional constraint, at least at the federal level.

But what would the "citizen-representative" ratio look like if we included all the elected officials at every level of government? The only trusted source I could find on the topic was a 1992 report by the US Census, stating there are about 513,000 elected officials in every dimension of government from president to state governors to local school committee, with the vast majority being local reps. [5] Adding these people to the mix yields a ratio of 637 citizens per rep and a much higher probability of personal relationships existing between the people and their delegates. Pretty good, but what if we further extended our pool of potential delegates to include government workers? These folks are typically full-time employees, paid by tax dollars and theoretically knowledgeable about their domain of control.

According to the Bureau of Labor Statistics, in 2018 there were 22,700,000 federal, state, and local employees. [6] This yields a ratio of 14.3 people per rep, suggesting there's a high degree of probability that you will know or have met one at least one of these people. This isn't to suggest that in a delegative or liquid democracy, the pool of delegates should be limited to only those currently employed by the government. Every citizen should have the right to become a delegate. I think the idea of a delegative democracy aligns well with Locally Grown Government principles starting with the fact that it represents true "bottom-up" governance. It provides the maximum degree of inherent power without unduly burdening citizens who are either unable or unwilling to wade through the details of governance.

An important constraint of delegative democracy is that it be constitutionally bounded. I am not trying to upend 243 years of successful self-governance with something completely new, but rather provide infrastructure that increases citizen participation and therefore their inherent power. Therefore, a US citizen cannot delegate someone else to cast their vote in federal elections and probably most state elections. However, I see no reason why liquid democracy cannot be deployed in most local elections. That said, the Locally Grown Government platform can at least use a polling and survey tool to provide much better guidance to federal and state elected officials and candidates. By having incorruptible detailed analytics hosted on the blockchain, of who supports what and providing access to political campaigns and office holders, we have the tools to create a more responsive democracy. Each voter will know exactly how their delegates voted and, as the ecosystem self-organizes, the politicians will seek out powerful delegates and influencers to get their input.

This basic construct is already in place with our federal Electoral College, which consists of 538 electors with a majority of 270 electoral votes being required to elect the president. A state's allotment of electors equals the number of members in its Congressional delegation: one for each member in the House of Representatives plus two for the senators. The total number of electoral seats are apportioned using Census data, and the individuals are chosen by the political parties according to those state or party rules. By the way, you can see here how loose immigration policy directly affects our republic as Electoral College delegates in each state are apportioned using Census data, which counts people living here illegally.

Each party chooses its slate of electors either by citizen vote or the party central committee and the candidates. Whichever party's candidate wins the popular vote in a presidential election, the number of electors for that party in that state typically cast their votes in line with the popular vote, though they are not bound by the Constitution to do so. It is very rare that electors don't vote in line with the popular vote.

The Electoral College was a brilliant mechanism added to the Constitution precisely to "slow down" democracy. Some are agitating for eliminating it. This is a horrible idea. First, it would require repealing and replacing the 12th Amendment because we are a representative republic, not a pure democracy. Second, getting rid of the Electoral College would shift power to a few large population states and large urban areas and by inference to the wealthy influencers in those areas. Candidates would never visit Wyoming or North Dakota because there just aren't many people there.

It's worth remembering that in 1860, an Electoral College majority elected Abraham Lincoln out of four candidates, none of whom had a majority of the popular vote. I think without the Electoral College, there would have been a high likelihood that the South would have seceded from the Union and slavery might have persisted for decades longer. Eliminating the Electoral College is simply a crazy idea espoused by people with an interest in further centralizing power and reducing inherent freedom, and I would hope voters reject this idea.

Since there are no constitutional requirements for how electors are chosen and there is a patchwork of different processes across the nation, Locally Grown Government could provide the perfect opportunity to standardize this process for choosing electors and make it more transparent and accountable to the people. Even though each citizen would still need to cast their vote directly for candidates, they could vote for electors, and in that way Locally Grown Government makes an impact at the federal level.

Another important way that Locally Grown Government can improve our current system is by creating better informed citizens. I discussed earlier my shameful lack of awareness of several of the candidates on my 2018 midterm election ballot. Armed with the data on how every Locally Grown Government delegate voted on every issue and the actual election ballot a few months in advance (candidates and referenda), we can deploy artificial intelligence to cull the right candidates that match the profile of each voter. Voters can get a mock ballot sent to them via email about how their votes on each office and ballot position is optimally matched to their unique desires and beliefs. Voters can review this information, do a bit more research on their own, including reaching out to their delegates, and finalize their choices before they walk into the voting booth. Imagine that. Active, informed citizens at the touch of a button!

Organization and Constitutional Smart Contracts

Labor unions, civic organizations, corporations, private clubs, and religious organizations are all part of the fabric of society just like government. Like governments with their constitutions and body of laws private organizations have bylaws that govern how they operate. In the blockchain world, these rules of the road are called smart contracts. Instead of words on paper they are built from computer code. In running a business or government, there is a hierarchy of interrelated rules that govern transactions like buying and selling a product, paying employees, registering a real estate deed, and collecting property taxes. Smart contracts have two or more parties in a transaction, and when each party satisfies the terms of the contract, the transaction is automatically executed across the decentralized blockchain network, anonymously, securely, and without the need for a central authority, legal system, or external enforcement mechanism. A copy of this transaction now exists on hundreds or thousands of computer servers in the network, and they are traceable, transparent, and irreversible. Encryption and the distributed nature of the transaction make it next to impossible for nefarious actors to mess with it. It's way more secure than your credit card data that's stored and regularly hacked across all the ecommerce sites you buy things at.

Here's our list of what our Locally Grown Government constitutional bylaws might include:

- Require Proof of Identity (POI).
- Have a method of re-verifying a POI over time.
- Establish conditions for invalidating a verified identity (e.g., identity fraud).
- Establish voting rules (e.g., rank choice, one vote per issue, delegate voting).
- Have a method of allocating voting tokens to each verified citizen; the tokens could even be worth money as they could be bought and sold on cryptocurrency exchanges that are available now.
- Determine which citizens are allowed to participate in the system (e.g., all ci-tizens, only certain delegates on certain issues).
- Outline codes of conduct and rules for banning citizen participation for a period of time and rules to expel citizens from the Locally Grown voting system entirely.
- Outline criteria to amend the Constitutional Smart Contract (e.g., a two-thirds majority of all verified citizens).

Locally Grown Example: Smallville, FL

Smallville is a quiet, fictious city of 25,000 residents on the east coast of Florida. It is part of Manatee County. The county installed the Locally Grown Government blockchain software platform to handle its elections and other functions like deed registration and tax collection. Dennis is a full-time resident of Smallville, and he just received a letter sent to all residents from the county supervisor of elections explaining some of the new features of the election and survey functionality of the newly installed system. He loves the super-strong security aspect of the system and the fact that he will be able to receive emails and text messages from various county offices instead of snail mail. The letter says the new voter registration requires a one-time visit to the county offices for Proof of Identification, where he will simply present his driver's license, passport, or other government-issued ID. The county does a biometric scan of his fingerprints, and when he shows up at the polling station to vote, he just does a thumb scan. He can still register online prior to elections just like he does now, just more securely.

Dennis really likes the feature where he can view online reports in advance of elections showing all the candidates, their party affiliation, incumbency, positions, and votes on key issues, and how much campaign money they've raised. He also gets to see some ballot questions in advance and blogs linked to them so he can learn more before he votes.

But the new survey tool and vote delegation process is really what's fascinating. For elections of local officials, he can choose to vote directly for each official like he does now, or he can delegate someone else he trusts with more knowledge on a ballot question or slate of candidates to cast votes for him. And all of this can be done securely in his regular polling center where he reviews his electronic ballot in the voting booth. If he chooses to delegate on a particular local candidate or ballot question, he simply begins typing the name of his delegate into the text box next to the candidate or question, and the system works like a web browser type-ahead search to narrow results as he types. Once Dennis finds the right delegate, he chooses them. Of course, he can also cast his vote directly just as he does now. Behind the scenes, the Locally Grown Government system aggregates Dennis' and others' delegations and records votes on his behalf, according to how his delegate votes. When he is done voting, the system gives him a printed copy of his ballot, and when the election is complete, he can log in to his online account and see his full ballot, including what his delegates voted for on his behalf. He can print this or save a copy to his computer if he wants. The election officials also get a printed copy of Dennis' ballot, which provides an important audit trail.

Dennis was excited and decided to organize a lunch with his friends who also lived in the county to discuss this new election system. Sally, one of his friends expressed some reservation with the vote delegation process, worrying that the 40 percent of residents in the county who don't normally vote might be susceptible to being paid by delegates and candidates for their votes. Dennis and his friends initially thought this would be a bad thing until his friend Kalie piped up and said that the only way that would work is if the people who don't normally vote actually go to the polls and vote. They would then have to go through the process of delegating. Wouldn't it be a good thing to get people to the polls who didn't normally vote, even if somebody paid them a little?

At this point, Dennis could see the lightbulbs going on in the heads of the lunch crew. Jen spoke up, saying that buying votes has been around since there were elections. Don't some politicians buy votes by promising things for their constituents and supporters? It's not as overt, but wasn't it the same thing? Paolo added that he remembered his father's stories about local ward bosses knocking on doors in the neighborhood and handing out cash for those who got to the polls. Everyone agreed that delegation could provide great benefits by outsourcing certain votes to trusted people with more expertise in a particular area. By the time dessert and coffee rolled around, the group agreed that the benefits of vote delegation appeared to outweigh the risks and that they would reconvene the newly coined Smallville "Lunch Club" to further discuss this intriguing new form of governance.

A couple days later, the Lunch Club was back at it at the Wagon Wheel Cafe. Dennis started things off by saying how much he liked the idea of online surveys, which could be a way to provide real-time visibility for elected officials of the public sentiment on big issues. Dennis was concerned that a new shopping mall proposal to build on swamp land might have negative environmental impact, but he also wanted the new jobs it would bring to the county. He said he would prefer to outsource decisions like this to his friends: Joe, who was a civil engineer, and Sally, who was a real estate broker. The conversation turned to how people would delegate votes on surveys and elections. Of course, all state and federal elections were limited to the traditional "one person-vote" method, but this new option was viewed as a great way to get more efficient responsive government. Everyone agreed that the stakes were much higher now that local revenues and expenses were going to be much greater due to the new federal policy of increasing block grants to states that Congress passed the year before.

That evening after the Lunch Club meeting, Dennis started mapping out how he would delegate his future voting on some issues and candidates. The rest of the group resolved to do the same and bring their "delegation maps" to the next meeting. Dennis got information on a regular basis, like news feeds, to inform him on the issues he cares about. For example, Dennis decided to delegate certain decisions on climate change to Jen and all other issues equally between Joe and Sally, who both delegated their proxies to Emma. Dennis delegated any votes on education like local school committee to Kalie and Jen, while any state-level issues went to Paolo and federal-level issues like local HUD funding to Sally. He could choose to retain voting on any of these issues himself as well. Of course, Dennis could not delegate his right to vote for official elected representatives, which he did himself. That didn't preclude Dennis from using the Locally Grown Government survey capabilities to poll his network for insight into the local, state, and federal candidates. The beauty is that Dennis got information from, and delegates proxy voting to, a network of people he knew and trusted. Table 34 illustrates his delegation map:

Table 34 – Locally Grown Election Platform Vote Delegation

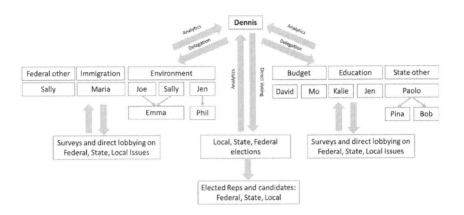

During the lunch the following week, Dennis' friend David presented the group with some research on the new Locally Grown Government system and found that there was an option to deploy this feature called blockchain tokens that could be used to compensate citizens who participate in the county's democratic process. This included participating in surveys, voting, volunteering, or anything the county residents believed was helpful to the common good. It took a little while for David to explain how blockchain tokens worked, but at the end of the day, the group understood that the tokens could be used to pay for property taxes and county fees, so they were worth real money. The county had not chosen to deploy this feature yet, but the group resolved to create an open "issue" on the Locally Grown Government system to create awareness among residents and garner support through the survey and polling feature, with the ultimate goal of an official county vote on deployment of tokens. After hearing this, the group was buzzing. Separate animated conversations broke out, like crossfire at the OK Corral. If the waitress was listening, she would have heard things like "think of the possibilities," "imagine how this could unlock volunteering," "we can change education in the county." After 10 minutes of group scrum, David whistled the group to reconvene so he could present a chart diagramming how this new Locally Grown Government system worked. Table 35 is a rendition of David's chart.

Table 35 – Locally Grown Election Platform Flowchart

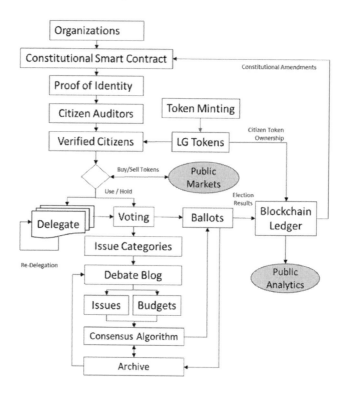

I am sure after reading my little story, you have tons of questions. My goal is not to design a system that considers every potential use case, but rather to provide enough detail to spark your imagination of what is possible. All human accomplishments start with ideas, and I have thrown one on the table for everyone to consider. My hope is to make an election system like this a reality and welcome any of you who are interested in learning more about this to contact me. Maybe you can start your own "Lunch Club" with trusted friends to explore the possibilities!

CHAPTER 15

Incentivizing the Good Behavior

Think of incentives
nobody else has thought of.
Meet them and you win.
– Adapted from Eli Broad

Changing the Nature of Civil Debate

In some ways, an organization is a collection of issues. What's the right tax rate? What should the school budget be? Should we do the Christmas bake sale this year? Issues are debated and decided upon and action taken if warranted. Civil debate is as important as voting in any democracy. Part of my proposed blockchain-enabled Locally Grown platform is a debate forum that would use the familiar threaded conversation format found in popular social media sites like Reddit, Facebook, and Twitter. I envision an online version of the "Smallville Lunch Club" where any citizen can ask questions and post issues into the forum. Each issue is tagged with a category (e.g., Education, Property Taxes). Multiple members can also author and sign a proposal or issue. Citizens can choose to ignore an issue, agree with the issue, or disagree with an issue.

However, what makes the Locally Grown Government approach different than traditional social media is citizens can only express support or non-support by voting. They can spend some of the Locally Grown tokens that might be allocated to them periodically in the form of votes. The token would have actual value as it trades on cryptocurrency exchanges like Coinbase. That means a vote is like spending a little cash. This mechanism creates real impact for the voting process compared to the infinite amount of "likes" or "re-tweets" used in other social media. This makes debate more frequent, rewards good arguments, and reduces "trolling" without the need of human curators or moderators.

Most of the user engagement on the internet is a form of voting. Each time a user "likes," "hearts," "upvotes," "re-tweets," or "links" content they are showing a preference. This preference becomes a feedback loop that produces more personalized content and recommendations. It can be valuable to users in that it better customizes the experience to match their interests. The "like" data are certainly valuable to the social network companies because it monetizes those votes with advertisers. But social media "likes" are essentially worthless as they can be infinitely inflated since there's no limit to how often users can hit the "like" button. The network effect turns this engagement into a measurement of the influence of certain ideas or celebrity or brands within the crowd, but the financial and political benefits of these transactions are kept entirely by the owners of the network (e.g., Google, Facebook).

Within the Locally Grown Government platform, issues take the form of surveys or polls and are voted on. Some issues are short-term or tactical and others are long-term or strategic. Short-term issues typically have a fixed timespan to which they apply. A local government example might be "which company to award the trash removal contract to for a particular year." The decision may need to be made within a few months because the contract for the prior company is expiring. In this case, an issue to be voted on would have a specific date when the polling would close. As long as the poll is open, votes can be rescinded by the citizen or their delegate, but once the poll is closed votes are counted.

For long-term or strategic issues, polls may stay open until specific criteria are met. An example of this is voting on new citizen applicants that might require at least 50.1 percent of citizens to vote for their approval. Another example might be a poll on building a new school playground or affordable housing units. Maybe the smart contract for this issue requires a two-thirds majority of citizens. The Locally Grown Government platform would handle both these types of surveys or polls.

Reaching Consensus

The Locally Grown Government platform is not just for elections; it can be used for surveys and polling on any issue or area of consumer or public research. In this way, it can be a powerful ecosystem where citizens can express their will in a way that guarantees trust and fairness. It contains a mechanism for compensating people and incentivizing good and important behavior that builds community and fosters value of citizenship and the common good. Of course, I am under no illusion that any of this will happen overnight, but I believe my suggestions are starting points. As Locally Grown Government grows, the correlation between consensus and how politicians vote grows.

Voting is a blunt form of reaching consensus on any issue. However, defining what the issues are and putting them into language that everyone understands is not an easy trick, especially since obfuscation and inefficiency are often features, not bugs with government. One of the great benefits of the Locally Grown Government platform is the amount of data that quickly accumulates that can be used to improve the network, not just the balance sheets of big tech companies. This data can feed algorithms that analyze and extract patterns that represent consensus. Game Theory is a branch of mathematics focused on strategies for dealing with competitive situations where the outcome of one participant depends on the actions of other participants. It has been applied in war, business, biology, and, of course, video games. Game Theory can also be applied to politics where there are multiple competing priorities within and between political parties.

Within the field of Game Theory is an important math construct called the Nash equilibrium. Named after the late mathematician John Forbes Nash Jr., it is a proposed solution of a competitive game with two or more players where each player is assumed to know what the others want. This knowledge is referred to as the "equilibrium strategies" of the other players (i.e., point where they will make a bargain). It provides a way of predicting what will happen if several people or several institutions are making decisions at the same time, and if the outcome for each of them depends on the decisions of the others. The simple insight is that one can't predict the result of the choices of other decision makers if one analyzes those decisions in isolation. Instead, we need to ask what the others player would do. [1] Politics is the ultimate multi-dimensional game that can benefit from the Nash equilibrium.

A strategy is considered to be in Nash equilibrium if no player can do better by changing their strategy. To see what this means, imagine each player is told the strategies of the others. Suppose then that each player asks themselves: "If I knew the strategies of the other participants, would I change my strategy?" If anyone can answer "Yes," then those strategies are not at Nash equilibrium. But if every player doesn't want to switch, then the strategy is in Nash equilibrium. I think of it as the best possible deal that can be made at the time.

As an illustration of the Nash equilibrium as a negotiation tool, let's look at a hypothetical list of priorities of our two major political parties. Table 36 shows a list of issues comparing Democrats and Republicans and how the priorities for each side might stack up:

Table 36 – Nash Equilibrium for Political Priorities

	Issue	Democrats	Weight	Republicans	Weight	Total Wt.	Cum Wt.
1	Overall Reduction In Federal Spending	0	19	1	20	39	39
2	Free Single-Payer Healthcare	1	20	0	18	38	77
3	Expansion Of Federal Entitlements	1	18	0	16	34	111
4	Liberal Immigration Policy Including Sanctuary Cities	1	14	0	17	31	142
5	Higher Taxes On Wealthy Citizens	1	17	0	11	28	170
6	Legal And Tax Payer Funded Abortion Thru Planned Parenthood	1	13	0	12	25	195
7	Expansion Of Collective Bargaining Right And Unions Within Governme	1	12	0	13	25	220
8	Reducing Choice With Public School Options (E.G. Anti-Charter)	1	11	0	14	25	245
9	Expanded Gun Control Laws	1	10	0	15	25	270
10	Tort Reform For Medical Malpractice	0	15	1	9	24	294
11	Protecting Rights Of Religious Liberty Within The Workplace	0	16	1	7	23	317
12	Balanced Budget Amendment	0	2	1	19	21	338
13	Federal Government Should Be In The Business Of Originating Student	1	9	0	6	15	353
14	Consitutional Amendment Term Limits	0	6	1	8	14	367
15	Increased Military Spending	0	3	1	10	13	380
16	Requirement For Voter Id	0	7	1	5	12	392
17	Expanded Regulation Of Fossil Fuels	1	8	0	1	9	401
18	Usa Retaining Control Of Root Internet Domains	0	4	1	3	7	408
19	Eliminate Net Neutrality	0	5	1	2	7	415
20	Federal Reserve Audit	0	1	1	4	5	420
	Total		**210**		**210**	**420**	

The "Issue" column in the chart describes the issue, the next column shows whether Democrats generally support the issue (1 = Yes, 0 = No), the "Weight" column shows the relative weight of the issue to Democrats (larger = more important). The fourth and fifth columns show the same data for Republicans. The sixth column adds the weights of both parties, and the last columns shows the cumulative weight of all the issues.

The last Cumulative Weight column shows that more than 50 percent of the value of all priorities are covered in the top seven items on the list. This indicates a potential starting bucket of priorities that could be negotiated as a group. However, they are probably the most contentious issues, which would make it difficult to reach consensus. Instead, the Nash equilibrium list might include a few top priorities and a few lower priorities to reach a point where each party feels like it's a fair deal. Neither side gets everything they want, but both get something. This approach can be embedded in a computer algorithm that can analyze the data accumulating on the Locally Grown Government platform to suggest possible different combinations of issues that could be successfully negotiated as a bundle by legislators.

Data Privacy

You are probably aware that everything you do or have ever done on the internet has been captured and stored on at least one computer server somewhere. More likely it exists on many servers, and even likelier that that activity has been mashed up with your name and address, age, marital status, credit data, credit card data, homes and cars you own, how you vote...and the list goes on and on. Our country has some privacy laws, but for the most part, you sign away the right to privacy when you click through the Terms & Conditions while registering for the websites and apps you use. That data is also being bought and sold on the internet because you give the likes of Google, Facebook, Amazon, Macys.com, Walmart.com etc., the right to use your information for any legal reason they see fit.

That's a scary thought, especially for a privacy advocate like me. What is even scarier is that your data sitting on all those servers in all those companies you have interacted with has probably already been hacked. Bad people probably already know who you are, and it's their job to add bits and pieces to your "personal profile" on the dark web when they can find them. The list of companies that have been hacked are a "Who's Who" of global business and new hacks are happening all the time. In September 2017, Equifax announced the largest data breach of all-time with data from 147 million customers being stolen by hackers. Keep in mind that Equifax is a major credit bureau that contains immense amounts of sensitive customer credit data. In July 2019, Capital One announced that over 100 million customer credit card accounts were hacked. Who can you trust with your data anymore? I'm a Capital One customer who promptly can-celled our family card after this breach of trust. I will pay for things with Bitcoin from now on. Only kidding!

What makes matters worse is that companies that are hacked hate to admit it because it deservedly damages their reputations. The black hat hackers might not actually do something nefarious with your data right away, but they consider you an asset on their balance sheet to be used when they want for things like identity theft or

Social Security fraud. In contrast, stealing your data on the block-chain requires that a hacker would first have to gain access to the blockchain and convince a majority of the server nodes that they are you. Then a hacker would need to perform another near impossible task of breaking into your data that rests in an encrypted state. Even then, they would find no personally identifiable data since, as part of the POI process, you are assigned a public hash ID that makes you just an anonymous number that points to all your encrypted transaction data elsewhere on the network. There is no way to tie it to your identity unless you authorize it. However, there could still be a lot of benefit to permitting companies to know something about you because they may have products that you're interested in. You should be able to choose who can access your data and be compensated by those allowed to access it, say for advertising to you. There are several cryptos that specialize in personal ID protection as a repository that can be safely shared with others.

Like Facebook, the Locally Grown Government platform would capture all your activity in its database, but unlike Facebook it is cryptographically secure, and only you would be in control of it. Citizens can remain completely anonymous to the extent they are legally able to so in the United States. Citizens could also decide for what purpose they would share information and how much they would be compensated for doing so. However, anonymous voting data is something that would be collected and shared among all citizens. Nobody would know the identities of who voted, but the aggregated voting data would be part of the data archive for the purpose of feeding analytics back to citizens. Many citizens might want to see reports of voting sorted and filtered by gender, geography, and other anonymous demographic information that can feed the Locally Grown Consensus Algorithm to help generate actionable negotiated lists of priorities that are likely to appeal to diverse groups. After all, finding consensus on the common good is one of our core principles.

In addition to voting data, the US Constitution, the Federal Registry of Laws, and state and local laws can also be part of the data archive. This is in keeping with our core principle of being constitutionally bounded. One of the features of the Locally Grown Consensus Algorithm can be checking whether an issue being voted on is constitutional either on the federal or state level or if a similar law already exists. The issue of not being constitutional doesn't prevent it from being voted on but tags it as something that might require a constitutional amendment. I imagine there could be a broad effort in collecting citizen priorities for a much-needed Constitutional Convention of States.

Other cryptos, like Steem, are social networks that reverse the "Facebook takes all" economic model that has powered social media until now. They actually pay the content producers on the network, with cryptocurrency of course. In similar fashion, Locally Grown Government participants could earn crypto income from participating in preferred behavior like voting, volunteering, or taking surveys. They could convert their tokens to fiat money and spend it or save the tokens as they increase in value. Tokens could also be spent directly for taxes and fees related to their local government. I can see the emergence of diverse local economic subsystems based on a form of "local currency" rewarding virtuous behavior that promotes the "general welfare."

CHAPTER 16

Q & A with the Author

Q: What prompted you to write this book?

A: I have been an observer of politics and government for decades and I am dismayed by what we have allowed to happen: exploding debt and unsustainable government that steps further into the lives of its citizens. I think many Americans share my dismay, but the problem is easier to see than the solution. One side of the political aisle believes federal government is the solution to most problems and the other side believes government *is* the problem. The middle layers of our two major parties are disappearing fast and we are left with parties that are more extreme. My book is an attempt to reestablish the political middle ground where most American citizens actually live. My book is a plan for what happens next. A solution rather than just yelling at the problem. It is an equitable solution that raises taxes, cuts expenses, and redistributes some federal power to the more diverse and sustainable lower levels of our three-tier government structure. It's not perfect and I welcome open, informed debate on any of the topics in my book. But just getting people engaged and talking about solutions and electing politicians who support a vision of a more locally grown world is my goal.

Q: Some of your critics argue that this would revert America back to tribalism. Do you identify as an American or Floridian?

A: Both. In fact, each of us has many faces. Father, wife, child, employee, Christian, Muslim, atheist, conservative, gay, African American, musician. Isn't true liberty the ability to freely wear all these hats and to associate with other like-minded people? So, I am an American who is also many other things. But what binds our diversity has to be the belief that freedom is the natural state of man and it is the primary role of government to protect that freedom. For what is diversity but the peaceful expression of and embrace of difference? Our Constitution was built with this in mind. To me, that is the beauty and genius of our republic.

Q: Michael Lewis in his new book The Fifth Risk asks the question, "What are the consequences if the people given control over our government have no idea how it works?" Lewis says people would soon figure out what the federal government does when it shuts down. But how would we manage with less of the federal government we currently depend upon?

A: My plan doesn't eliminate most federal government functions. It merely shifts the execution to a more local and accountable level. With my plan, federal tax rates actually increase as the wealthy pay more in our already progressive tax structure. At the same time, government at all levels takes a 10 percent haircut. Shared burden for all, but government will function better than it does now. What most citizens don't understand is that entitlements are crowding out all the other good things the Feds should be doing and that I mostly support. They don't understand that, left unchecked, these programs will collapse and those that have grown dependent on them with get much less, or nothing. I'm guessing Michael Lewis and I would disagree on the scope of some of what the Feds do now, but we'd might also agree on a lot. However, none of it matters if we cannot afford the level of government we have already.

Q: The critics of this book say your vision would be impossible to implement because there isn't the infrastructure to handle it and, if there was, you wouldn't get the consistent implementation of programs.

A: Well, exactly what federal infrastructure are we talking about? Let's take Social Security, about 18 percent of our federal budget. Locally Grown Government leaves this alone. Still checks coming from Uncle Sam. Medicare? Old folks don't drive to Washington to get their Medicare. They get it locally. All healthcare is delivered locally. The problem is that the funding and accountability mechanisms are completely broken and unsustainable. We already do transfers to the states for seven of the 10 major federal government budget categories. I am simply proposing to increase the transfers and let our 50 states and their 20,000 cities and towns work on sustainable solutions that fit their demographics. The federal government would have a primary role in collecting and sharing results and best practices. It would be a better version of what is done now by the organizations like the Census Bureau, Bureau of Labor Statistics, and Center for Disease Control.

Q: But that's the point, isn't it? You cannot have 50 states doing 50 different things for Medicaid.

A: Why not? The Feds already share expenses with the states. I propose capping the federal contribution because not doing so is unsustainable. I am confident sustainable, better-quality solutions will emerge that other states will copy. You may end up with five or six delivery models that, combined, fit the states' demographics and meet the mission of providing a safety net for citizens without creating a moral hazard that encourages fraud and abuse. People who make this criticism miss the point that the Founders wanted the states to do things differently to suit the specific needs of their citizens. Some things need to be the same, like not discriminating based on religion or race or gender, etc., and using a common currency. All of this is defined in the Constitution. Anything not specifically defined as a federal function inures to the states. That's the theory, but we've done a pretty good job ignoring much of it over the last two centuries.

Q: But what if a state doesn't do as good a job as the federal government?

A: If we consider 15-20 percent of spending falling to waste, fraud, and abuse being "a good job," as is the case with several of the largest federal programs, that won't be hard to beat. Keep in mind, the money being transferred to the states is a block grant, not an open checkbook. States and municipalities would have a lot of incentive to spend the money wisely in a given year, considering they would have to wait for the next budget cycle to receive the next transfer. If they still aren't running things efficiently after the sharing of best practices between government entities, then there is the discipline of elections to replace those who cannot get the job done with those that can. In my book, I point to the evidence that distributed digital networks perform better and scale much better than centralized networks as one form of evidence that distributed local will perform better than centralized federal in many areas.

Q: Your Locally Grown Government program calls for some draconian budget cuts: A 10 percent across-the-board federal cut is pretty big.

A: I wouldn't call that draconian. I think nearly all Americans given a choice of going personally bankrupt or cutting their household expenses by 10 percent wouldn't have too much trouble finding the savings. And remember, we are also increasing federal tax revenue by seven percent, state five percent, and local one percent. We are also transferring large chunks of the federal budget downstream to states and local so tax dollars can be spent more wisely by people who live much closer to where the money is being spent. There is no way to solve this massive fiscal problem without both cutting expenses and raising revenue. This burden will be shared fairly by all Americans. Rich people will pay a lot more and those dependent on the government still will be getting about the same level of support as we eliminate waste, fraud, and abuse in government across all three levels.

Q: As you know, we recently endured the longest government shutdown in our history. Over 800,000 federal workers waited over a month for their paychecks. Critical functions weren't being performed. Isn't that kind of a dress rehearsal for what happens with your plan?

A: Well, I think it was Warren Buffet who said, "You find out who is swimming naked when the tide goes out." The polls I read as to whether the shutdown affected them suggested that 66 percent said no affect at all, 20 percent felt a moderate impact, 10 percent severe impact. So, two-thirds of our citizens didn't feel the shutdown and less than one-third felt it. I don't like the fact that any of our citizens endure any pain, but we should have never outsourced so much power to the federal government in the first place. In a Locally Grown Government world, a federal government shutdown would have far less impact since many of the services being shut down now would be provided by state and local government partially financed by fixed federal block grants that are paid in advance each year. That means a spat between say the governor of Illinois and the Illinois Speaker of the House won't affect the other 49 states. It's better math and a more rational way to insulate the country from the effects of the personal interests of a few.

Q: There are people who believe illegal immigration is a fake crisis manufactured by a racist president. Some of these folks believe illegal

immigration should be de-criminalized and illegal immigrants should be given healthcare and other benefits for free. What say you?

A: Let's look at the facts. Immigration is an enumerated federal power in our Constitution. The federal government alone has jurisdiction in this area. Border security, making rules about who we let in, and enforcing the related laws are all exclusive powers of the federal government. We expect them to perform this role competently. Here are more facts about immigration:

- Our laws provide that anyone crossing our borders claiming political asylum can be detained for a maximum of 20 days, after which they are released into our country to await an immigration hearing.
- Undocumented immigrants who are waiting for their court hearings are free to work and entitled to many public benefits including education.
- According to a report by the Executive Office for Immigration Review, 28 percent of undocumented immigrants didn't show up for their court dates in 2017. [1]
- There is now a backlog of 869,000 immigration cases in our courts with new hearings needing to wait until at least 2022. [2]
- According the federal Customs and Border Patrol agency, as of 2015, approximately 12 million illegal immigrants live in the United States. That number increased dramatically with over 700,000 illegal crossings at our southwest border through July 2019. [3]

I believe immigration has historically been a source of strength for the United States. But the immigration must be legal. My Italian grandparents came here legally through Ellis Island at the turn of the 20th century. Although they faced significant prejudice for both their nationality and Catholic religion, America legally welcomed them into its melting pot. At the turn of the century, America contained only 80 million people but now we are four times that number. In fact, the population of foreign-born residents of the US is currently 13.7 percent, near the historic levels driven by the immigrant waves around the turn of the 20th century.

At the current rate of illegal immigration (144,000 as of May 2019 at southwest border alone) and our steadily decreasing fertility rate, my math shows America will go from a population comprised of 96 percent citizens today to a population of 84 percent citizens 30 years from now. The percentage of foreign-born residents (33 percent) will be more than double the 14.8 percent that existed in the previous high in 1890. This level of immigration will have profound impact on our nation as an increasing number of non-citizen residents expect public benefits. Economic opportunities will dwindle as the cost of providing benefits crowds out the private economy. As a sovereign nation, the United States has a duty to its citizens to control its borders. There are billions of people from other nations who would gladly immigrate to America if we let them. That would simply not be sustainable.

So given these facts, why are there so many elected federal representatives that consistently block any attempts to reform our broken immigration laws? If you listen to their rhetoric, they claim open borders and sanctuary cities that subvert federal authority are more moral than controlled borders and abiding by our established laws. I guess they translate America being historically a land of immigrants means that all immigration is desirable, legal or not. To disagree with their position on the grounds that uncontrolled immigration dilutes the rights and opportunities of existing citizens risks being labeled a racist. Tough to have a civil conversation with folks who react like that.

When you dig a little deeper, and start to connect the dots, you see another reason these politicians fight to keep open borders and expand public benefits for illegal immigrants. It all has to do with political power. Congressional seats, delegates to the US Electoral College, and many federal benefits are apportioned according the latest decennial Census, which counts ALL people in the United States including ALL non-citizens, legal or illegal. In a March 2018 report, "COUNTING FOR DOLLARS 2020:

The Role of the Decennial Census in the Geographic Distribution of Federal Funds", Andrew Reamer, a professor of public policy at George Washington University, identified more than $800 billion in federal funding based on the census count. The money is paid though 300 federal programs including Medicaid, Medicare, Head Start, and SNAP. [4] According to 2005 congressional testimony by the Center for Immigration Studies, the 2000 Census contained 18 million non-citizens, which accounted for 29 congressional seats. Furthermore, 70 percent of these non-citizens lived in just six states, which means those states gain at the expense of states comprised mostly of citizens. [5] It's no surprise that most of these states contain the majority of sanctuary cities in America. So, after all the moral grandstanding, it might all come down to a power grab by those using immigration policy as a weapon.

While our immigration problems cannot be solved by Locally Grown Government, I think it's important Americans understand what's at stake. The issue is so divisive that neither side of the aisle sees any common ground from which to engage. My view is that we need to find a way to bring both sides together to achieve common-sense immigration law reforms including a path to citizenship for people brought here illegally as children (the so called DACA kids), stronger border control, elimination of asylum law loopholes, and increasing work permits and legal immigration for people with skills we need. I think we need a constitutional amendment to reform how we apportion federal election districts, presidential delegates, and federal benefits to prevent the rigging of our system of government. I'd like to see our Locally Grown Government principle of "negotiating bundles of issues" used to get the comprehensive immigration reform we desperately need. Not rocket science here.

Q: You seem to make the argument that citizens will pay more attention and want to become more involved with government at the local level. About 56 percent of eligible voters cast ballots in the 2016 election, which means that 44 percent didn't care enough to vote. That's a big

number. How do you expect to get people to care about making government work more efficiently when they don't even bother to vote?

A: People naturally do what they think is in their best interest. Collectively across millions of people we call this behavior "the market." It's the basis of economics. I think if you make it worth their while economically, people will raise their interest level appropriately. Imagine if there wasn't a federal or state government, just local cities and towns. That's where all the tax money is spent, and services are delivered. Don't you think people will be more interested in decisions that affect them directly that are made in the city hall down the street? You certainly have a better chance of influencing those local elected politicians when you see them shopping at the same stores and kids going to the same schools as you. You have access. When most decisions about taxes and spending are made hundreds of miles away in insulated Washington, DC, the average Joe just doesn't have influence except every few years at the ballot box. Government becomes an abstract concept for many. By expanding local budgets by a factor of 2-4 times and delivering healthcare, education, and welfare locally, people will stand up and be counted because those decisions affect their personal interests. Of course, there is always the feature of our Locally Grown Government voting platform that can compensate people for certain participation.

I just look at millennials and other young people and how politically active they are nowadays. I am glad they are engaged, and as long as they've learned how to be tolerant of different views and debate civilly, I applaud the engagement. That's what we need in this country.

Q: Speaking of millennials, your book spends almost no time addressing one of the biggest issues for this demographic, which is climate change. The time you do spend is excoriating The Green New Deal rather than offering solutions. How do you expect to appeal to millennials and

millions of others who believe human-induced climate change represents a clear and present danger, when you seem to deny it's a problem?

A: Well, let me be clear. I don't deny climate change is a problem. I'm just not sure it's THE problem like the Green New Dealers believe. I do know that if the Green New Deal were implemented that would be THE problem because the economy would grind to a crawl and violent civil war would be a real possibility. Climate would be the last thing on most people's minds.

This is because the Green New Deal isn't only about climate. There's free college, free healthcare, universal basic income even for those who choose not to work, banning cows and other ideas that are simply unaffordable and would threaten our way of life. But let me focus only on the climate change part of the Green New Deal because it is a complex, important topic that would take another book to do it justice. In that regard, it's important to recognize progress has already been made with increasing the share of renewables in our energy production. Non-fossil fuels now represent 22 percent of total energy production, which is double from 20 years ago. [6] This has resulted in a combination of government regulation and free market innovation. What's needed are better incentives.

I believe the "cap and trade" or carbon tax model is an important part of the solution to reverse human greenhouse gas production. In 2013, the UK instituted a tax on carbon dioxide releases from electricity production and, in four years, their CO^2 decreased by 20 percent. Last year, coal (and the UK has a lot of cheap coal) accounted for only six percent of UK electricity production, down from 44 percent in 2012. Their carbon tax was just high enough to give natural gas and other renewables a cost advantage over coal with very little economic impact. The UK actually grew faster than the overall EU during this period and the carbon tax added just five percent to the average British household's electricity bill.

The success of this approach was mostly due to creating a price advantage for liquid natural gas over coal, something the Green New Dealers would reject because LNG is still a fossil fuel. However, it is a much cleaner fossil fuel and the UK has easy access to lots of it. The ultimate goal of reducing carbon emissions is achieved without grinding the economy to a halt like the Green New Deal would do.

We also need to reinvest in nuclear technology because it is the only zero-carbon technology that can scale to the needs of the global economy. We need to learn from the lessons of Three Mile Island, Chernobyl, and Fukashima but not let their failures deter us from investing in better nuclear solutions. Some easy lessons from these disasters are to replace old equipment and don't build nuclear plants in active seismic areas on the ocean. Basic stuff. France derives 75 percent of its electricity from nuclear power and is a leader in new reactor technology. If the United States invested in nuclear tech at half the rate we've done with solar and wind, we would have made even more progress on carbon emissions. The key is changing incentives with modest government regulation so that the market can do its work.

A big argument against nuclear has been that there are no good solutions of what to do with the waste. How about contracting the emerging commercial space companies like SpaceX and Blue Origin to blast the waste beyond Earth's gravitational field into deep space? Waste from all the nuclear power the US has ever generated amounts to the size of a football field at the depth of 10 yards. In comparison, a coal plant generates that volume of waste every hour. [7]

Q: Your book talks about organizing a new Constitutional Convention of States to make some amendments to the Constitution. The Constitution makes provision for this mechanism, but all 27 amendments that were ratified originated in Congress. Given the sharp divisions of our federal reps, it seems unlikely there would be enough consensus to muster the two-thirds majority to pass an amendment that could be sent to the states for ratification. The last time a convention was convened outside of Congress was in 1787. That's a long time. What makes you confident this can actually happen?

A: Support for new amendments has been gaining in recent years including term limits, mandatory balanced budgets, and clarifying the definition of citizenship. Organizations like the *Convention of States in Action* are working with state legislatures to convene a Constitutional Convention to propose new amendments. As of this writing, a resolution to convene has passed 15 state legislatures with significant support in 10 more states. Thirty-four states are the magic number so it's an uphill battle, but they are well organized and growing. As citizens' trust for their federal institutions continues to diminish, and political gridlock causes us to lurch from crisis to crisis, I think citizens will have had enough and a new Convention will be a reality. I can imagine what a raucous affair that might be!

Q: Your book makes you sound like a Republican. Are you?

A: I'm an independent and didn't vote for either Donald Trump or Hillary Clinton in 2016. I find them both to be self-serving big egos who play fast and loose with the truth. I embrace ideas that promote long-run sustainability of our nation. The best way to describe my political views is a "Liberal Libertarian." Freedom trumps equality in most situations but not all. Pure Libertarians would never tolerate the scope of government that the Locally Grown model still leaves in place. Some liberal folks might be comfortable with the diminishment and new limits on federal power from Locally Grown. That puts me somewhere in the middle, just where I should be.

Q: To many, a strong federal government seems the only logical choice to balance the common good with personal freedom, keep the economic engine humming, address climate change, and guarantee world peace. America is a big idea that needs a big government. How would you answer your critics who point to the economies of scale as the justification for a strong central government?

A: I'd say yes to all of this if it were sustainable. The business world has long exploited the economies of scale to ensure sustainability and growth. However, government with debt and other liabilities at nearly double the annual GDP is anything but sustainable. Still, there are in increasing number of politicianscalling for 70 percent federal income tax rates and wealth taxes to fund further redistribution. They claim a moral high ground and perpetuate the myth that there is enough money to fund their utopian visions by simply raising taxes on the wealthy. This is a devastating lie. As I explain in my book, taxing the "one percent," 100% of their income and irrationally assuming they will continue to work at the same level, doesn't come close to closing the gap on the funding promises we have already made. Look no further than the most recent example of Venezuela to see how this all ends. We see the early stages of this in our own country where several large states have accrued massive debt driven by public pension costs that has them teetering on bankruptcy. While this is happening in plain view, politicians in these states whistle past the graveyard as they steadily raise taxes and drive businesses and citizens to more economically sustainable states. So here we are. If we keep doing the same thing, it will not end well.

CHAPTER 17

Final Thoughts

The late Tip O'Neill famously declared that "all politics is local." A career politician, he knew the secret to being reelected was directing federal tax dollars to his congressional district. In the Boston area where I'm from, the evidence is everywhere of how successful Tip was. From tens of billions of dollars of infrastructure projects to the buildings that bear his name, he delivered for the citizens in the 12th US Congressional District. Tip also knew that negotiation was essential to getting things done in our republic. His ability to put aside differences and negotiate with his ideological adversaries, like President Reagan, was fundamental to making government work for the people. They were two Irishmen who could have a beer together and focus on things they agreed on and then horse trade the differences.

Today, it seems we are far away from that time. Negotiation looks like a lost art, replaced by brinksmanship that has broken the American political user experience. Today, government seems to willfully violate all the rules of what we know to be best practice design principles like transparency and simplification. It's as if opacity and complexity is a feature and not a bug. Hopefully, I've said this enough that you get my point.

I think human existence mostly obeys Pareto's Law, where 80 percent of effects come from 20 percent of causes. The 80 percent is behavior rooted in natural law and informed by millions of years of evolutionary experience. Pain is the body's mechanism for telling us something is physically wrong. Fear is a survival instinct telling us to beware of danger. Likewise, the notion of sharing enabled the growth of larger social groups. This behavior built up trust and made competing tribes less likely to fight with one another. Thus, the early social contract was born. Other basic rules for maintaining social order were added like "thou shall not kill, lie, bear false witness, honor your parents," and these became the foundation of western culture through Judeo-Christian religious doctrines. Other cultures have similar governing virtues. These religious and cultural practices were a common operating system for large groups of people that created affinity and identity that could be recognized from afar. These positive behaviors were passed down orally to each generation by elders using mythology and eventually became institutionalized as religion. So regardless of their flavor, all religions share a common process of trial and error to discover the behaviors that were most likely to improve the chances of survival and prosperity. The sacred texts underpinning these ancient religions were formed by rational processes of trial and error. They were common-sense rules for maintaining social order.

On the other side of Pareto's equation, the 20 percent of outcomes not explained by self-evident natural law is discovered by science and mathematics. Like religion was an ancient form of truth discovery, so is science a discovery mechanism for truth. Core to the scientific method is that a theory proven by experimentation must have results that can be duplicated by others who follow the recipe. Religion also contains recipes for human behavior, that if followed, result in consistent outcomes. Science presents evidence to help explain how our universe works and why certain behaviors are bad or good. Science improves our health and our lifestyle. Philosophy and ancient religions track the evolution of successful social behaviors to make them available for future generations. This is a vision of law that is deeply embedded in western civilization, through the ideas of the ancient Greek and Roman philosophers and statesman. Natural law is universal and timeless. Like the theory of conservation of matter, it can neither be created nor destroyed. It just is. Natural law underpins civilization, especially in the US where the Founders explicitly enshrined its concepts into our Constitution when forming our republic. The familiar ideas of "all people are created equal" and "freedom of speech" were embraced thereafter by many countries, who also enjoyed the prosperity that recognition of these basic human rights provided. I think that our Constitution reasonably balances the competing interests of individual freedom and the common good. However, things have become unbalanced and the rhythmic sine wave of the pendulum must swing again. Our government is a machine that is in constant battle with itself over the end of one man's liberty and the beginning of another's. But whatever choices are made must be sustainable, or we all suffer.

Human evolution continues through the growth of our technology. It seems we also possess the tools to bring about our own extinction. Nuclear war would confirm a fatal defect in our DNA that is contrary to the species' survival instinct. Artificial intelligence and tinkering with biology through genetic engineering promise great evolutionary strides but also contain the seeds of our demise. Once Pandora is out of her box, bad events could become exponential and maybe our species goes the way of the dinosaurs; or maybe a remnant survives with a newly clean slate from which to continue human evolution. The cockroach has survived 320 million years through all measure of calamities we cannot imagine. Maybe humans will be a footnote like the dinosaurs. Top of the food chain when they walked the earth, but extinct now because they ultimately couldn't hit the curveballs nature threw at them. One thing I am confident in is that, if we are to survive, Locally Grown must be a big part of the mechanism for government all the time, not just in between societal upheavals. Individuals acting on their inherent power without the constraints of heavy-handed nation-states will always find a way to survive.

I hope this book doesn't give the impression that good government is easy and simple and that if we reduce the size and influence of the federal government, all will be well. That's not the message. Our Founders gave us three levels of government to work with and we need to restore the proper balance between them. Good government is complicated and hard work, which seems to be getting harder by the day. Trying to bias toward inherent power in a nation of 327 million diverse people is a tough problem to solve. Hopefully, I have made the case that when it comes to solving difficult problems, many heads are better than a few. I believe the process of pushing back down to state and local levels, functions that should have never been ceded to the federal government in the first place, will re-energize and re-civilize our politics and our economy. I have laid out a plan that pushes some big federal functions down to the state and local level along with the money to implement those functions. All that money moving from Washington, DC, to states and cities and towns will be the largest social and physical infrastructure spending stimulus in history. I think it will create tons of new jobs and new companies and unlock incredible innovation. My plan is realistic in that it raises tax revenues while cutting expenses and eliminating waste fraud and abuse. It's clear this bottom-up bias was explicitly the point of our Founders. The rebalancing process will also not be without pain as politicians, constituencies, and industries feeding from the federal trough must adapt to a new order.

Changing country fundamentally from its roots is not the answer. While I understand the perspective that our history has included some bad things like racial and gender discrimination, it ignores the tremendous progress the country has made. Installing more top-down solutions that are completely unsustainable and would result in economic calamity. Even if this power consolidation was successful, we would still end up in a Locally Grown Government scenario because that is always what emerges after calamities. Doesn't it seem rational to convert to Locally Grown Government as a plan rather than as a post-catastrophe last resort? I think that by embracing the eternal creative destruction process in a planned way, America will emerge from the other side a stronger, healthier, and sustainable nation.

Good government involves a lot of details, most of which the average person cannot and doesn't want to manage. Our republic provides for citizens to choose other citizens to represent their interests in these matters. Politicians need accountability, but how does the average citizen deal that with all that detail? They may be happy to outsource it. But how can we outsource our government when we *are* the government? The answer is that all citizens must become more involved in their local government where more is at stake for them personally. So how do you distill and simply present the key points people need to make an informed political decision without overwhelming them? Locally Grown Government offers a solution that starts with a private, secure, election system that permits fluid delegation of voting power, a primary expression of our inherent power in support of the common good. Locally Grown Government would permit citizens to delegate political decisions to other citizens based on their subject matter expertise and interest rather than voting for a single politician belonging to one of two political parties to handle everything. The system would even provide incentives for participation similar to what has proven to be effective in our digital world. Locally Grown Government can become an informed, active, and viral voting community. This is like social media, and we know how much consumers enjoy that.

Another important phenomenon we expect to occur if Locally Grown Government takes root is an economic revitalization for our middle class. In large organizations, the economies of scale inure to the relative few. When you break large organizations into components, as was done with business monopolies over our history, you unlock more human potential. When Standard Oil and American

Tobacco were broken up in the early 20th century using the Sherman Anti-Trust Act, the process created several new smaller but still large competitors with their own human resources, finance, production, and marketing departments, all of which needed to be staffed with humans. In 1982 when AT&T was broken up into the regional "Baby Bells," we created seven new companies. Sure, some economies of scale were lost, but we created new jobs and the prices of these critical services were reduced because of the new competition. It's like the natural process of cell mitosis or splitting atoms. Massive new energy is released from the decomposition.

You may now be thinking that Locally Grown Government is about everything at the local level. Not at all. The Constitution clearly lays out those powers given to the federal government and they are substantial. But nowhere in the Constitution does it explicitly give the federal government the power to run our entire national healthcare system or the power to invade your privacy on an industrialized scale based on the notion that some of it will be useful in crime solving and national defense. These powers have been slowly usurped by a federal political establishment that has deferred to Hamiltonian interpretations of the Constitution. The federal government needs to stick to its fundamental job of protecting our civil liberties. If we keep the federal side within its natural scope, the result will be sustainable. If Locally Grown Government is about one thing, it's sustainability.

I'm sure there will be critics who will say that Locally Grown Government is just a return to tribalism and factionalism and America will lose one of its most important assets: its national identity. To that I say, "Take a good look around you now." America, and a good chunk of the world, is already devolving into factions and tribes because of the failure of central governments. Britain is in the midst of a messy Brexit where the country still cannot seem to make up its mind. Venezuela's experiment with authoritarian socialism has had a predictable catastrophic result. The Five Star movement has turned Italian politics on its head, refusing to bend to the will of the EU while the country's debt has it teetering on the brink of insolvency. Other populist movements in Europe raise the question of whether the EU can even survive. In this country, an increasing number of people identify more with a myriad of racial, gender, and cultural factions than with being an American. Compounding this problem, the Hero Generation that fought WWII is all but gone, taking with it the institutional memory of the patriotic strength required to overcome calamity. There seems to be nothing comparable to take its place, which should make us all worry whether America has the tools to address the next set of calamities that are on their way.

Locally Grown Government recognizes that the creative destruction process is part of natural law and there is only so much we can do to forestall the inevitable. Planning was a critical behavior in human evolution, and we need to engage with our better angels on this front sooner rather than later. Locally Grown Government delivers a starting point to mitigate the pain and provide strength when the calamities occur. With much of our domestic governance being provided by state and local, there would be less to blame the federal level for. This can be a starting point to rebuilding the trust and patriotism at the federal level so it can act effectively when it is needed most. *E Pluribus Unum*: Out of the many, One.

Despite lots of eloquent descriptions of the problems our country faces by other authors and thinkers, I see few solutions proposed outside of more federal government control from the left or tear down the federal government from the right. As always, the solutions lie somewhere in the middle, and Locally Grown Government is attempting to find that middle and offer starting points for solutions. I'll be the first to admit there are probably many flaws in this book and there is much that can be done to improve my ideas. I look forward to continuing the dialog and evangelizing Locally Grown principles around this country. Raise your hand if you'd like to engage with me. Modernizing and rebalancing our government will be hard but important work, and the more, smart, committed minds involved, the better. Let's get started.

NOTES

Chapter 1

1. https://en.wikipedia.org/wiki/Exorbitant_privilege
2. https://fred.stlouisfed.org/series/GFDEGDQ188S
3. https://www.pewresearch.org/fact-tank/2010/12/29/baby-boomers-retire
4. https://www.cdc.gov/nchs/data/hus/2010/022.pdf
5. https://fiscal.treasury.gov/reports-statements/financial-report/
   long-term-fiscal-outlook.html%22%20/l%20%22_ftn21
6. https://www.cbo.gov/publication/52142
7. http://gabriel-zucman.eu/files/PSZ2017.pdf
8. https://www.nber.org/papers/w13264
9. https://news.gallup.com/poll/149678/americans-express-
   historic-negativity-toward-government.aspx

Chapter 2

1. https://evolution-institute.org/the-seven-moral-rules-found-all-around-the-world

Chapter 3

1. https://medium.com/office-for-the-future/
   six-core-strands-new-world-spirituality-dharma-marc-gafni-2215619c7a00
2. https://www.wsj.com/articles/how-hinduism-has-persisted-for-4-000-years-11547770953
3. https://amiracarluccio.com/2018/02/27/
   ancient-indian-legend-the-rice-and-the-chessboard-storylearning-about-mathematics
4. https://en.wikipedia.org/wiki/Albert_Allen_Bartlett
5. http://cmore.soest.hawaii.edu/summercourse/2014/
   documents/Karl_05-27/Moore_1965.pdf
6. https://en.wikipedia.org/wiki/Maslow%27s_hierarchy_of_needs
7. https://us.macmillan.com/books/9780312611699

Chapter 4

1. http://www.commonsenserevisited.com
2. https://www.psychologicalscience.org/observer/
   who-is-that-the-study-of-anonymity-and-behavior
3. https://www.amazon.com/State-Collected-Papers-Anthony-Jasay/dp/0865971714
4. https://www.econlib.org/library/Buchanan/buchCv3.html
5. https://news.gallup.com/poll/240725/democrats-positive-socialism-capitalism.aspx

6. https://www.npr.org/2019/02/07/691997301/
   rep-alexandria-ocasio-cortez-releases-green-new-deal-outline
7. https://www.americanactionforum.org/research/
   the-green-new-deal-scope-scale-and-implications
8. *https://pjmedia.com/trending/*
   ocasio-cortezs-green-new-deal-would-cost-more-than-the-gdp-of-most-countries
9. https://www.washingtonpost.com/news/magazine/wp/2019/07/10/
   feature/how-saikat-chakrabarti-became-aocs-chief-of-change/?mod=article_
   inline&noredirect=on&utm_term=.46dba6cb2d5d
10. https://www.imf.org/en/Publications/WP/Issues/2019/05/02/Global-Fossil-Fuel-
    Subsidies-Remain-Large-An-Update-Based-on-Country-Level-Estimates-46509
11. https://www.atr.org/
    here-s-every-democrat-who-supports-ocasio-cortez-s-crazy-green-new-deal?amp

Chapter 5

1. https://en.wikipedia.org/wiki/John_Forrest_Dillon
2. "https://en.wikipedia.org/wiki/Home_rule_in_the_United_States" \l "cite_note-Lang-1
3. https://www.amazon.com/Cities-without-Suburbs-Census-Perspective/dp/1938027043
4. https://www.economist.com/united-states/2018/12/22/
   why-american-cities-are-so-weirdly-shaped?frsc=dg%7Ce
5. https://www.economist.com/united-states/2008/06/19/the-big-sort
6. https://en.wikipedia.org/wiki/Big_Seven_(United_States)

Chapter 6

1. https://www.economist.com/leaders/2018/09/13/a-manifesto-for-renewing-liberalism
2. http://web.stanford.edu/~ldiamond/iraq/Decentralize_Power021204.htm
3. https://www.cdc.gov/drugresistance/threat-report-2013/index.html
4. https://www.amazon.com/One-Many-VISA-Chaordic-Organization/dp/1576753328
5. https://www.amazon.com/Birth-Chaordic-Age-Dee-Hock/dp/1576750744
6. https://www.sparknotes.com/us-government-and-politics/
   american-government/the-media/section3
7. http://gs.statcounter.com/search-engine-market-share
8. https://www.pewresearch.org/fact-tank/2018/12/10/
   social-media-outpaces-print-newspapers-in-the-u-s-as-a-news-source
9. https://www.wsj.com/articles/kill-section-230-you-kill-the-internet-11561924578
10. https://www.cosaction.com
11. https://catalogdna.com
12. https://www.census.gov/content/dam/Census/library/
    visualizations/2018/demo/p60-263/figure4.pdf
13. https://www.plasticbank.com/what-we-do/" \l ".W9j1_JNKhPY
14. https://iwilife.com/
15. http://www.safetraces.com
16. https://en.wikiquote.org/wiki/Meet_the_Parents
17. https://www.wsj.com/articles/
    college-kids-not-endorsing-socialism-but-theyre-open-to-it-1540848218
18. https://www.washingtontimes.com/news/2018/apr/26/
    democratic-professors-outnumber-republicans-10-to-/
19. https://en.wikipedia.org/wiki/Okun%27s_law
20. https://www.freedoniagroup.com/industry-study/elder-care-services-3214.htm

21. http://www.firstresearch.com/Industry-Research/Child-Care-Services.html
22. https://en.wikipedia.org/wiki/William_J._H._Boetcker
23. https://www.census.gov/newsroom/press-releases/2018/cb18-41-population-projections.html
24. https://www.csc.gov.sg/articles/successful-ageing-progressive-governance-and-collaborative-communities
25. https://www.gorhamhouse.com
26. https://www.nesterly.io
27. http://www.simonandschuster.com/books/Lean-Thinking/James-P-Womack/9780743249270
28. https://www.fns.usda.gov/pd/supplemental-nutrition-assistance-program-snap
29. https://www.cbpp.org/research/federal-budget/policy-basics-where-do-our-federal-tax-dollars-go

Chapter 7

1. https://en.wikipedia.org/wiki/Sapiens:_A_Brief_History_of_Humankind
2. https://www.wsj.com/articles/the-human-promise-of-the-ai-revolution-1536935115
3. https://www.yang2020.com/what-is-freedom-dividend-faq
4. https://www.amazon.com/Aristotle-Politics-Loeb-Classical-Library/dp/0674992911
5. https://en.wikipedia.org/wiki/Wisdom_of_the_crowd" \l "cite_note-8
6. https://bitcoin.org/bitcoin.pdf
7. https://e-resident.gov.ee/digitalnomad/
8. https://uidai.gov.in/about-uidai/unique-identification-authority-of-india/vision-mission.html
9. http://fortune.com/2018/02/10/arizona-bitcoin-taxes/
10. https://givingusa.org/giving-usa-2018-americans-gave-410-02-billion-to-charity-in-2017-crossing-the-400-billion-mark-for-the-first-time/

Chapter 8

1. https://en.wikipedia.org/wiki/Bretton_Woods_system
2. https://fiscal.treasury.gov/reports-statements/financial-report/nation-by-the-numbers.html

Chapter 9

1. http://www.cbpp.org
2. https://www.techemergence.com/ai-in-law-legal-practice-current-applications/
3. https://www.census.gov/library/publications/2015/demo/p20-577.html
4. https://www.pewtrusts.org/en/research-and-analysis/issue-briefs/2017/06/why-are-millions-of-citizens-not-registered-to-vote
5. https://www.cbo.gov/publication/55384
6. https://www.usgovernmentspending.com/year_spending_2018USbn_18bs2n_H0J0" \l "usgs302
7. https://finance.yahoo.com/video/carlyle-groups-david-rubenstein-market-183836563.html
8. https://www.gao.gov/assets/700/696516.pdf
9. https://spectator.org/42174_unemployment-and-stimulus/
10. https://www.amazon.com/Atlas-Shrugged-Ayn-Rand/dp/0451191145
11. https://www.usgovernmentspending.com/

Chapter 10

1. https://www.congress.gov/resources/display/content/
   The+Federalist+Papers" \l "TheFederalistPapers-41
2. https://en.wikipedia.org/wiki/Helvering_v._Davis
3. https://www.wsj.com/articles/why-bernie-sanders-is-wrong-about-sweden-11566596536
4. https://www.cbo.gov/publication/51443
5. https://www.investopedia.com/articles/retirement/120516/
   social-security-fraud-what-it-costing-taxpayers.asp
6. https://www.cbo.gov/publication/51443
7. https://data.oecd.org/gga/general-government-debt.htm
8. https://www.usgovernmentspending.com/year_spending_2018USbn_18bs2n
9. https://www.ais-cpa.com/average-cpa-salary-and-compensation/
10. https://www.usgovernmentspending.com/defense_spending
11. https://fas.org/sgp/crs/misc/R43590.pdf
12. https://www.opm.gov/policy-data-oversight/data-analysis-documentation/
    federal-employment-reports/reports-publications/federal-civilian-employment/
13. https://laedc.org/wtc/chooselacounty/regions-of-la-county/
14. https://www.justice.gov/opa/pr/
    justice-department-recovers-over-28-billion-false-claims-act-cases-fiscal-year-2018
15. https://jamanetwork.com/journals/jama/article-abstract/1148376
16. https://www.federalreserve.gov/paymentsystems/2017-
    December-The-Federal-Reserve-Payments-Study.htm
17. https://www.kansascityfed.org/PUBLICAT/ECONREV/PDF/10q2Sullivan.pdf
18. https://www.governing.com/gov-data/public-workforce-salaries/state-
    government-employment-by-agency-job-type-current-historical-data.html
19. https://itep.org/who-pays-taxes-in-america-in-2018/
20. https://www.businessinsider.com/
    the-national-debt-is-rising-much-faster-than-the-economy-2018-3

Chapter 11

1. https://nces.ed.gov/programs/coe/indicator_cmd.asp
2. http://www.pewresearch.org/
   fact-tank/2017/02/15/u-s-students-internationally-math-science/
3. https://nces.ed.gov/fastfacts/display.asp?id=372
4. https://www.heritage.org/education/report/
   assessing-the-compensation-public-school-teachers
5. https://www.census.gov/data/tables/2016/econ/school-
   finances/secondary-education-finance.html
6. https://cis.org/Report/Mapping-Impact-Immigration-Public-Schools
7. https://www.huffingtonpost.com/jack-jennings/
   proportion-of-us-students_b_2950948.html
8. https://www.edreform.com/wp-content/uploads/2014
   /02/2014CharterSchoolSurveyFINAL.pdf
9. https://credo.stanford.edu/pdfs/CMO%20FINAL.pdf
10. https://www.migrationpolicy.org/article/international-students-united-states
11. https://nces.ed.gov/fastfacts/display.asp?id=51
12. https://www.nbcnews.com/news/us-news/
    college-admissions-scandal-department-education-opens-probe-yale-usc-other-n987666
13. https://trends.collegeboard.org/sites/default/files/2017-trends-in-college-pricing_0.pdf

14. https://www.forbes.com/sites/zackfriedman/2018/06/13/
student-loan-debt-statistics-2018/" \l "3a34a0937310
15. https://www.purdue.edu/newsroom/releases/2019/Q1/purdue-announces-ongoing-
tuition-freeze,-staff-appreciation-payment-for-west-lafayette-campus.html
16. https://www.forbes.com/sites/susanadams/2018/09/11/mitch-daniels-is-making-
purdue-more-affordable-and-upping-enrollment-higher-ed-purists-are-aghast/
17. https://www.bbc.com/news/business-48145563
18. https://tradingeconomics.com/united-states/wages-in-manufacturing
19. https://nces.ed.gov/programs/coe/pdf/Indicator_CBA/coe_cba_2014_05.pdf
20. http://graphics.wsj.com/international-students/
21. https://thebestschools.org/features/richest-universities-endowments-generosity-research/
22. https://nces.ed.gov/fastfacts/display.asp?id=73
23. https://www.usnews.com/education/best-colleges/the-short-list-college/
articles/2018-02-06/10-national-universities-with-the-most-international-students
24. https://www.benefits.va.gov/GIBILL/resources/benefits_
resources/rates/ch33/ch33rates080117.asp
25. https://download.militaryonesource.mil/12038/MOS/
Reports/2013-Demographics-Report.pdf
26. https://static1.squarespace.com/static/556718b2e4b02e470eb1b186/t/5bfd81c1cd
8366780d4c1a6c/1543340482077/Final+NCLC+paper+v.+2.0+%283%29.pdf

Chapter 12

1. http://davidsplinter.com/AutenSplinter-Tax_Data_and_Inequality.pdf
2. http://davidsplinter.com/AutenSplinter-Tax_Data_and_Inequality.pdf
3. https://www.usgovernmentspending.com/year_spending_201
8USbn_18bs2n_4041424346_605_609" \l "usgs302
4. https://www.census.gov/data/tables/time-series/demo/
income-poverty/cps-pov/pov-26.html
5. https://www.nber.org/papers/w19237
6. https://www.manhattan-institute.org/html/poverty-after-welfare-reform.html
7. http://app.lla.state.la.us/PublicReports.nsf/0/4C858DCBA6
E2F5D18625821F00667334/$FILE/00017514.pdf
8. https://www.usgovernmentspending.com/year_spending
_2018USbn_20bs2n_4041_605" \l "usgs302
9. https://www.census.gov/quickfacts/fact/table/indianrivercountyflorida/PST045217
10. https://www1.nyc.gov/assets/nycha/downloads/pdf/PNA%202017.pdf
11. https://www1.nyc.gov/assets/nycha/downloads/pdf/PNA%202017.pdf
12. https://www1.nyc.gov/assets/nycha/downloads/pdf/NYCHA-Fact-Sheet_2019.pdf
13. https://www.wsj.com/articles/
counter-inequality-with-private-social-security-accounts-11564094326

Chapter 13

1. https://www.ibisworld.com/industry-trends/market-research-reports/finance-
insurance/carriers-related-activities/health-medical-insurance.html
2. https://csimarket.com/Industry/industry_Profitability_Ratios.php?s=800
3. https://www.cms.gov/Research-Statistics-Data-and-Systems/Statistics-Trends-
and-Reports/NationalHealthExpendData/Downloads/highlights.pdf
4. https://www.sanders.senate.gov/download/options-to-finance-medicare-for-all?inline=file

5. https://www.cms.gov/Research-Statistics-Data-and-Systems/Statistics-Trends-and-Reports/NationalHealthExpendData/Downloads/PieChartSourcesExpenditures.pdf
6. https://www.rand.org/pubs/research_reports/RR3033.html
7. https://www.washingtonexaminer.com/opinion/editorials/bernie-sanders-own-state-showed-medicare-for-all-wont-work
8. https://www.dailysignal.com/2018/08/29/single-payer-health-care-the-more-coloradans-knew-the-less-they-liked-it/
9. https://www.governing.com/topics/health-human-services/tns-california-single-payer-price.html
10. http://www.worldstopexports.com/drugs-medicine-exports-country/
11. https://www.brookings.edu/research/the-global-burden-of-medical-innovation/
12. https://www.rcseng.ac.uk/news-and-events/media-centre/press-releases/nhs-stats-march-2019/
13. https://www.usnews.com/news/best-countries/slideshows/countries-with-the-most-well-developed-public-health-care-system
14. https://www.wsj.com/articles/banishing-profit-is-bad-for-your-health-11552949981
15. https://www.cdc.gov/obesity/data/adult.html
16. https://fosterfriess.com/2017/02/28/when-hospitals-resist-change/
17. http://blr.healthleadersmedia.com/content/241965.pdf
18. https://www.icsi.org/_asset/y74drr/eliminating-waste-in-the-us-healthcare-2012.pdf
19. https://fosterfriess.com/2017/02/28/when-hospitals-resist-change/
20. https://www.usgovernmentspending.com/federal_budget_detail_fy19bs22019n_10163033_703" \l "usgs302
21. https://www.militarytimes.com/news/your-military/2018/12/08/why-the-va-may-be-getting-too-much-money/
22. https://www.economist.com/united-states/2019/01/12/hospital-prices-are-now-public?frsc=dg%7Ce
23. https://healthcare.mckinsey.com/next-imperatives-us-healthcare
24. https://www.bestmedicaldegrees.com/is-medical-school-worth-it-financially/
25. https://aamc-black.global.ssl.fastly.net/production/media/filer_public/85/d7/85d7b689-f417-4ef0-97fb-ecc129836829/aamc_2018_workforce_projections_update_april_11_2018.pdf
26. http://www.medscape.com/features/slideshow/compensation/2015/public/overview
27. https://www.wsj.com/articles/health-cares-killer-app-life-insurance-11553122054
28. https://www.medicalbillingandcoding.org/qnas/what-are-the-different-types-of-medical-coding-classification-systems/
29. https://www.pregnancyandchildren.com/pregnancy/pregnancy_midwives.htm
30. http://www.midwife.org/CNM/CM-attended-Birth-Statistics
31. https://www.ncbi.nlm.nih.gov/pmc/articles/PMC3934668/
32. https://www.ncbi.nlm.nih.gov/pubmed/8658331
33. https://www.qualityforum.org/Publications/2017/04/Surgery_2015-2017_Final_Report.aspx
34. https://thejns.org/view/journals/j-neurosurg/126/2/article-p620.xml

Chapter 14

1. http://www.ncsl.org/research/elections-and-campaigns/voter-id.aspx
2. https://www.pewtrusts.org/~/media/legacy/uploadedfiles/pcs_assets/2012/pewupgradingvoterregistrationpdf.pdf
3. https://www.sun-sentinel.com/local/broward/fl-ne-brenda-snipes-ends-court-case-20190124-story.html
4. http://www.brynosaurus.com/deleg/deleg.pdf

5. https://www.census.gov/data/tables/1995/econ/gus/gc9-1-2.html
6. https://www.bls.gov/webapps/legacy/cesbtab1.htm

Chapter 15

1. https://en.wikipedia.org/wiki/Nash_equilibrium

Chapter 16

1. https://www.justice.gov/eoir/page/file/1107056/download
2. https://usafacts.us14.list-manage.com/track/click?u=ff1bc9abb
    222ec965ded81e5e&id=af89047bab&e=989038cf02
3. https://www.cbp.gov/newsroom/stats/sw-border-migration
4. https://gwipp.gwu.edu/sites/g/files/zaxdzs2181/f/downloads/
    GWIPP%20Reamer%20Fiscal%20Impacts%20of%20Census%20
    Undercount%20on%20FMAP-based%20Programs%2003-19-18.pdf
5. https://cis.org/Testimony/Impact-NonCitizens-Congressional-Apportionment
6. https://www.instituteforenergyresearch.org/renewable/fossil-fuels-dominate-u-
    s-energy-production-but-receive-a-small-percentage-of-federal-fuel-subsidies/
7. https://www.nei.org/fundamentals/nuclear-waste

Table Credits

Table 3–https://www.usgovernmentspending.com/us_debt_to_gdp
Table 4–https://www.cbo.gov/topics/budget
Table 5–https://www.bls.gov/charts/employment-situation/
civilian-labor-force-participation-rate.htm
Table 7–https://www.historyonthenet.com/the-egyptians-society
Table 12–https://books.google.com/books?id=bMi1XVXAl48C&printsec=f
rontcover&source=gbs_ge_summary_r&cad=0#v=onepage&q&f=false
Table 14–https://www2.census.gov/geo/maps/metroarea/us_wall/Aug2017/cbsa_us_0817.pdf
Table 16–https://www.coinbase.com/price/bitcoin
Table 17–https://fiscal.treasury.gov/reports-statements/
financial-report/nation-by-the-numbers.html
Table 18–https://images.fineartamerica.com/images-medium-large-5/
night-time-satellite-view-of-paris-panoramic-images.jpg
Table 24–https://www.usgovernmentspending.com/breakdown_2014USpt_20ps5n
Table 25–OECD
Table 29 & 30–https://www.niche.com/blog/charter-school-statistics/
Table 31–Compiled using data from Council for American Private Education,
US GovernmentSpending.com, National Center for Education Statistics
Table 32–Compiled using data from USGovernmentSpending.com, Habitat for Humanity
Table 33–https://www.sanders.senate.gov/download/
options-to-finance-medicare-for-all?inline=file

ABOUT THE AUTHOR

After attending Syracuse University, Jim Fini began his career at JP Morgan, where he developed an allergy to the inertia and politics that typically plague large organizations.

After four years on Wall Street, he took an entrepreneurial track, working at, founding, and investing in technology companies from Silicon Valley to Boston. One company he founded, Enservio, is a leading insurance technology provider and was recently acquired by a large public company.

His success is rooted in learning from failure, a passion for solving problems and translating complexity into simplicity. Jim lives in Vero Beach, FL with his wife, Kati, and their teenage children, Marcus and Emma.

Learn more at JimFini.com
Facebook and Twitter @ Locally Grown Government